A WAR for GOD

A CHRISTIAN VIEW OF ISLAM

DAN WOLF

A War for God

Cover designed by Exodus Design Studios

Printed by CreateSpace

Other books by the author:
Do You Want To Be Free
Collectivism and Charity

Visit the author website:
http://www.livingrightly.net

Other articles by the author can be found at:
http://www.vachristian.org

ISBN: 978-0-998756-70-7 (eBook)
ISBN: 978-0-998756-71-4 (Paperback)

Version: 2017.01.20

Table of Contents

A War for God

A Christian View of Islam

Acknowledgements

I would like to thank all of those who helped in putting together this book. For Jeff, Keith, and Felix on their input and feedback. For Kris, on her ideas for the cover design. For Don, at the Virginia Christian Alliance, who's idea it was to take the articles written there and turn them into a book. Without his suggestions, this project would likely not have happened. Anything of benefit from this work comes from their support. Any errors or omissions are mine.

I would also like to especially thank my wife and companion, Barb, for her dedication and support through all of the ups and downs that come with writing. Without her presence, I could not do all that I have. Finally, I thank God through whom all things are truly possible. I pray that this work will serve to educate all who read it in ways that will help to bring us together.

As are men's wishes, so are their words; As are their words, so are their deeds; And as their works, such is their life.

— Clement of Alexandria, 2nd century.

Introduction

This is the third book arising from some conversations I had with Muslim friends about politics and freedom several years ago, but it is the one that I originally planned to write. Looking back, I wasn't yet prepared to write such a work. All of the relevant pieces were not yet in place. That has changed with the last several years of further exploring our own history.

During my fifteen years of research and teaching about the differences between Islam and Christianity, I have found many good sources on the subject. However, each source focused on only a specific aspect of the overall topic. I could find no comprehensive source enabling someone to learn about Islam's basic tenets or history and compare those to relevant Christian principles, especially those that our society is founded upon.

That situation was the driving force for writing this book, as its content is needed more in today's world than ever. It is not my wish to offend or judge, but we cannot communicate effectively unless we are open and honest. What I have tried to do is present the facts and where those facts lead.

The Obama administration's policies have left the world much less secure. One consequence of those policies is increased instability in the Middle East and massive surges of people fleeing this region to relative safety in other areas. There is risk in accepting immigrants if they do not share the same values as the society accepting them, and history has shown Islam exhibits little intent to change its values. While accepting immigrants is compassionate and good, it must be done in the full light of understanding.

That is not happening today. Our previous administration has actively taken steps to prevent such a national discussion, and the media has presented incomplete or false information on the subject of Islam. All that is needed is truth. No one should fear it. If fear is present then something is wrong. We are off-track, and many people in America think that has been the case for some time. We see it and feel it. It is one reason for this year's election results and the earlier Brexit vote in Great Britain. People recognize that we've largely abandoned the principles that brought us success.

We are called to live in the truth and become good and by that process to know our Creator. It is our purpose, and the charity exhibited by helping others in need is the way in which that purpose is fulfilled. However, we are called *both* as individuals and collectively to be the people of God. That means living according to biblical principles that have their basis in divine law, and these are what America's society was founded upon. These principles have their basis in two simple ideas: first, loving God; second, loving your fellow man. While we have not always been successful in achieving it, what matters is that our effort is expended toward reaching those objectives.

So how consistent or different is Islam from the Judeo-Christian roots of our society? Some of the basic questions which need to be answered about Islam's tenets and how those differ from our founding principles include the following:

1. What is Islam? Is it just a religion or something more?

2. What are its basic beliefs?

3. Who is Allah? Is he the same as Christianity's God?

4. What is Islam's history and culture? What do these say about its principles and beliefs?

5. How do Islam's followers view the non-Muslim world?

6. Given all of the above, is there a threat? If so, what is its extent, and what are some options to address it?

As a people we should be having such a discussion and then make decisions and commitments based upon our understanding. Our leaders have failed us, but it is not their fault. It is ours for not being engaged, taking the time to learn, and holding our leaders accountable. In any republic, the power truly rests with the people. That requires the people to not only be engaged, but they are also called to meet a higher bar. They must also be a moral people, for the protection of our rights requires virtue—in both a society's people and its government as that government's basic purpose is the protection of our rights. Government is not to be in the business of creating new rights.

Islam added nothing new to man's understanding of our Creator. Instead, it borrowed from every culture and ideology around it. This borrowing was not limited to theology alone, but included civics, law, politics, the military—in short, every significant aspect of society. What was new was the marrying of the Bedouin culture with monotheism. With all of this in mind, the present book is laid out as follows.

> The first four chapters deal with Islam's tenets and their development. Chapter 1 considers the world as it existed at Muhammad's birth. It looks at some of the religious ideas it borrowed and some of the cultural norms that were carried over into Islam. It presents the case for Islam being much more than a simple religion. Finally, it compares what I call the two threads of individual and collective approaches to governance. We will see in subsequent chapters that Islam is a variant form of collectivism, or statism if you prefer, and all forms of collectivism are antithetical to our form of governance.

> The next three chapters provide some basic information about Islam. Chapter 2 introduces you to Islam's texts and their development, which took place over about three centuries. It also reviews the relationship that exists between these sources, how they fit together into a comprehensive whole. Chapter 3

reviews Muhammad's life, the tenets that came from his actions and decisions, and their modification over time. Chapter 4, the final chapter in this group, examines the concepts that arose from these teachings, focusing on the concepts concerning Allah, creation, man, and some implications based upon those ideas.

Chapter 5 examines some of the differences between Christianity and Islam. It briefly reviews the concepts related to Allah from the previous chapter and then reviews the development of their counterparts supporting the Christian notion of God. It identifies some inconsistencies within the Islamic concept of Allah and concludes with some implications in areas such as man's relationship with his Creator, morality, freedom, governance, man's nature, truth, and knowledge.

The next two chapters look at some of the implications from the previous chapter's contents. Chapter 6 reviews Islam's history, particularly related to issues of governance using jihad and dhimmitude. Contrary to a common portrait of the caliphate, it was not a peaceful period where a single group ruled. There were several kingdoms and dynasties that rose and fell, controlling different parts of the Islamic world at the same point in time. At times these were based on religious differences, and at times upon simpler ideas such as race or power. The development and implications for governance, jihad, and dhimmitude are discussed in relation to the concepts identified in previous chapters. This chapter ends with some comments our sixth president, John Quincy Adams, made in 1830. Adams was very familiar with Islam, served extensively as a diplomat throughout Europe and was America's first representative to Russia. He saw the rise of European nationalism within the Ottoman Empire and the Turkish response.

Chapter 7 considers some relevant attitudes in the areas of religion, politics, law, and culture. Some discussion within this chapter reinforces earlier assertions that we may use the same words, but that they often have a very different meaning. In order to effectively communicate, we must understand these differences. Some examples include what are extremism and freedom, and what is religious freedom. Words and their definitions matter.

The final chapter consolidates and summarizes the previous chapters. It presents additional information about jihad, slavery, and refugees that needs to be considered in any response that may be expressed. The differences between the individualism, Islamic, and collectivism (statism) models are also compared. These differences are taken into consideration and used to formulate a series of responses to Islam's ideology.

These responses are split between individual and policy actions, and the spiritual and temporal. Most writing I have seen focuses on the temporal aspects alone. That may halt the ideology, but it is unlikely to defeat it. Unlike previous forms of collectivism that had either no religion or a state controlled one, Islam has a religious facet that is integrated into its ideology. Without considering both the spiritual and temporal aspects, the best that can be expected is simply a stalemate. This conflict has existed for almost fourteen hundred years already. A continued stalemate is simply not acceptable.

This book is intended to provide—within a single resource—a starting point for understanding Islam and its compatibility with our underlying governing principles. It is my hope that your search will not end here, but that you will continue to grow, learn, and understand. It is through that search, and the effort it takes, that we begin to fulfill our purpose. We must search for the truth; when we find it, we must allow ourselves to be transformed by it. As always, when we find truth it must be presented directly and honestly, and also be presented with love.

January, 2017

Chapter 1

The World Before Muhammad

Before we can evaluate something, we must first understand it. Much of what we read in the media or see on television about Islam is either very selective in its presentation or simply wrong. This book's primary goal is to help you understand some of Islam's basic tenets, their development, and some of the attributes present today that arise from those beliefs. Along the way we will examine some of the significant differences between Islam and Christianity and their implications. My goal is not to tell you what to think, but instead to provide you with information you can use to make up your own mind. I am simply going to present the facts and places where you can find more information if you want it. Where possible the information in this book will come directly from original sources. They are the best places to look if you truly want to learn about something.

Islam is usually presented merely as a religion, but is it that simple? Before we go further, let's first define a couple of terms we are going to use: *religion* and *ideology*. Religion is a particular system of beliefs, attitudes, emotions, behaviors, etc. that constitute man's relationship with some universal principle, power, or being. This provides a flexible structure as to what is worshipped and how it is worshipped. An ideology, on the other hand, is a set of ideas or objectives that influence a whole society or culture, especially their political and social structures. So religion is related to man's relationship with some deity or power, while an ideology relates to how man governs himself and interacts socially.

We will see that Islam has a religious facet, but that it is also much more. Islam is a religion that informs politics and governance. In addition, it is law. The military aspects of society are also included within its tenets, as are civics and culture. In short, all within society is Islam—it is an ideology. Everything from when and how you worship to the way you should get dressed are all prescribed for you within Islam. These differences often make it difficult for Muslims to understand Jews or Christians and vice versa as our frames of reference are often not only entirely different but contradictory.

In this chapter, we'll start with some relevant history leading up to the time of Muhammad's birth. But before we start that discussion, there is something very important that you need to hear and understand. The subject of this book is Islam and not Muslims. Muslims are people, and we all share the same nature that God has given to each one of us. Yes, you will find bad Muslims and good Muslims, just like you will find bad Christians and good Christians.

We have each been given the gift of free will to make our own choices, and it is our choices—and the way those choices are implemented—that define who we are. When we talk about Islam we must remember that we are talking about its tenets and ideology not people. As we are called to do, we will present the truth and present it in love.

The Time Leading Up to Muhammad's Birth

Muhammad was born about 570 AD, over five hundred years after Christ's crucifixion. Some significant events occurring in the five centuries between these two points in time include the following:

1. It has been almost two hundred and fifty years since Constantine's conversion, making Christianity the Roman Empire's official religion. Christianity has assumed an imperial role as well as a religious one.

2. The Roman Empire has split into East and West. The western empire originating from Rome is gone. Only the Byzantine portion in the east remains. There is a schism, too, within Christianity between east and west, although the rift has temporarily been healed after the fifth ecumenical council of 553. There is a Pope in Rome and a Bishop in Constantinople.

3. It has been almost one hundred and fifty years since Attila and the Huns sacked Rome.

4. It has been about one hundred and forty years since Augustine of Hippo's death, as the invading Vandal fleet lay off-shore.

5. The monastic movement is well underway, a development that will be critical to later history.

6. Few people speak Greek in the west any longer, and many documents are being translated into Latin.

7. The Roman and Persian Empires have been fighting each other for five hundred years, with most of the conflict occurring within the area we know today as the Middle East.

A Map of the World

If one were to look at a map of the known world at the beginning of the seventh century, with its epicenter in Jerusalem, it could be divided into four quadrants as shown below.

Figure 1-1: The World About 600[1]

To the northwest and portions of the southwest lie the remains of the Roman Empire, along with the Lombard, Frankish, Visigoth, Saxon and other kingdoms in Europe and around the Mediterranean Sea. Albion is King of Italy at the birth of Muhammad, and Justin II is the Emperor in the East. This quadrant is primarily Christian.

To the northeast is the Persian Empire which stretches from modern Syria through Iraq and Iran toward modern India. Chosroes I is King of Persia. The Silk Road connecting China and India with Europe runs through Persia. The teachings of Zoroaster are prevalent among the ruling and military classes within Persia, but its society was very accepting of other religions. Significant populations of Nestorian Christians, Jews, Monophysite Christians (Jacobite), and gnostics are also present. Many wars have been fought between Persia and Byzantine. Beyond Persia is the Kushan Empire in what is now Afghanistan. They were primarily Buddhist.

Persia conquered the Holy Land in 614 under Chosroes II, including Jerusalem, and removed the "True Cross" to Ctesiphon during Muhammad's life. Heraclius (Byzantine) reconquered Jerusalem in 628 and took back lands in Egypt, Syria, and Armenia. Both sides employed Arab tribes to defend their frontiers. The Ghassanids were paid by the

Byzantines and were largely Monophysite Christians. The Lakhmids were employed by the Persians and were primarily Nestorian Christians. Based on religion, these tribes would have viewed each other as heretics.

To the southwest on the African continent is the Kingdom of Abyssinia (Axum) that corresponds to portions of modern Ethiopia, Eritrea, and Somalia. It had held parts of modern Yemen and southern Saudi Arabia, but these were taken by the Persians late in the sixth century. Abyssinia was the greatest market in northeastern Africa. Yemen also contained important seaports on the trade routes between India and Europe and possessed its own architecture, culture, and legal system. Abyssinia is ruled by the Negus, and is primarily Monophysite Christian.

The last quarter in the southeast is often labeled the "Empty Quarter" on maps from this time and consists of the Arabian Peninsula. It is very unlike the other parts of the known world described above. There is no central source of authority. Instead this part of the world is subject to tribal rule. We'll talk more about the people of this peninsula later in the chapter. The Arab tribes do not possess the wealth of Byzantine, the power of Persia, or the commerce and architecture of Yemen. Rome, Persia, and Abyssinia had each in turn attempted to conquer the Arabian Peninsula, and each in turn had failed.

While the lands in the other three quarters were largely monotheistic, this quadrant was primarily pagan. There were Christian and Jewish Arab tribes, and these lived together with the pagan ones at this time. The pagan tribes built shrines to worship their gods. Each shrine was controlled by a devout family. Some of these sites became significant enough to be established as a haram. A haram was a sacred place where overt conflict was forbidden. It was a sanctuary. These places served as a neutral ground for negotiations between feuding tribes, and a site for conducting trade fairs. This arrangement worked because the tribes believed that violating the sanctuary would bring about divine punishment.

The family in charge of a haram acquired substantial political power. The head of the family that controlled the haram was called a mansib and often served as a mediator in tribal disputes. They could also deny tribes access to a haram. Even more powerful were the kahins. These were shamans. They often presented their sacred formulas as poetry, which was a major art form in Arabia at this time.

Muhammad was a member of the Quraysh tribe, and his family was in charge of the haram of Mecca. This haram (the Kaaba) was perhaps the most significant sacred site in all of Arabia. It is said that the Kaaba contained about 360 idols; these included all of the gods of all of the tribes in Arabia. One of Muhammad's uncles was the mansib of this haram. There was an annual trade fair in Mecca that was attended by all parts of Arabia. Poetry contests were often held and the highest honor was to have a poem inscribed and placed within the Kaaba.

Most people on the Arabian Peninsula lived in a narrow strip of land no wider than 200 miles along the Red Sea called the Hijaz. Mecca was not located along any major trade routes. The trade routes through the Hijaz connected Syria and Egypt in the north with Abyssinia and Yemen in the south. There had been a large Jewish kingdom in southern Arabia in what is now Yemen that was called Himyar. It contained the city of Najran, which fell to Abyssinia in about 500 AD, and the area became primarily Christian. Recent findings in the area appear to connect the development of the modern Arabic language to Christian and Jewish roots in this area.[2]

The above is a brief overview of history leading up to the beginning of the seventh century. But what about the principles and beliefs supporting Islam's ideology? What were they? Were they new? That is where we will head next. We will start with a brief general comparison of Christian and pagan philosophy, and then look at the specific religious beliefs that Islam incorporated. We will see that much of Islam comes from either pagan or heretical ideas.

The Two Threads

According to Clement of Alexandria (Clement), there were two threads within Greek philosophy. Both were evident in the writings of Plato and

Aristotle, among many others. One thread was based upon the Hebrew Old Testament. The other thread was based upon pagan thought. America's Founders were grounded in the first thread through their study of the Bible and classical literature in their education and culture. They attempted to create a government structure in accordance with both divine and natural law. But what of the second thread? This thread existed before the Hebrew Old Testament and historically was the basis for rule by divine right found in the ancient state religion societies. This second thread is not grounded in the Creator, but instead in man himself.

Below is a diagram from *Collectivism and Charity*[3] that outlines some of the significant differences between these two threads. The Individualism model is derived from the writings of the early church fathers and was applied in creating our governance structures by our Founding Fathers. The second thread is represented by collectivism and comes from pagan thought. It is represented by rule of the elites, such as the Caesars of Imperial Rome and Pharaohs of ancient Egypt.

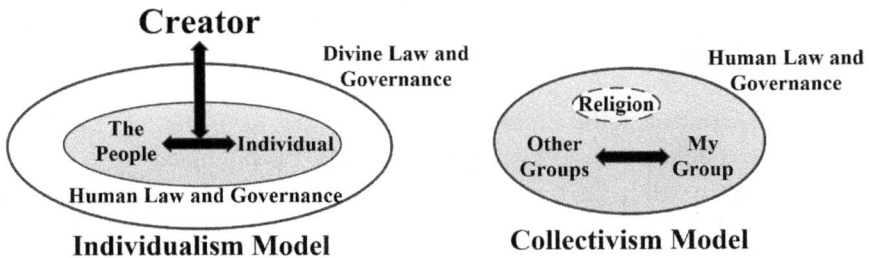

Creator

Divine Law and Governance

The People ⟷ Individual

Human Law and Governance

Individualism Model

Human Law and Governance

Religion

Other Groups ⟷ My Group

Collectivism Model

The development of these two threads can be traced through the individuals noted below. The individualism thread is developed above the timeline, and the collectivist notions below the line in relation to Islam. This diagram does not include all philosophers within each thread during this period, but those shown are recognized as being significant and their writings form a chain of thought as each builds on the work of those who came before them. Note that Plato was a pagan. Although he knew the Old Testament; he didn't understand it. The early church fathers largely wrote in response to Plato as his ideas were closer than

any other Greek philosopher to basic Christian ideas, but Plato's ideas
were still pagan.

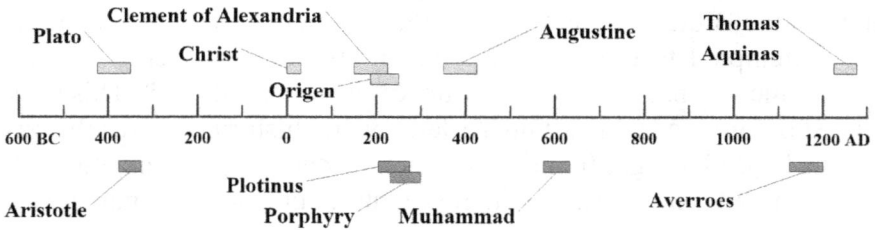

The First Thread: Grounded in the Hebrew Old Testament

From the first thread we get the following ideas:

1. Our rights come from our Creator. They were His gift to us.

2. We have an equality of nature which is innate. Because we are
    created with this same nature, we also all have the same rights
    from our Creator. This is true equality, an equal standing based
    upon who and what we are.

3. Our Creator is the embodiment of divine governance and divine
    law. These are supreme and can only be changed by Him. All
    things human lie below His directives and must be consistent
    with them.

4. We were created for the purpose of knowing our Creator.
    Happiness can only be found in the fulfillment of that purpose.

5. Knowledge, faith, and the creation of virtue within each of us
    serve to lead the way toward fulfilling our purpose. We are not
    born with any of these things, but instead have a nature which
    lends itself to acquiring them. We have each been given free
    choice as to whether we turn toward or away from our purpose.
    That is the gift of freedom.

6. Government is to be molded to fit the needs of its people in compliance with our Creator's divine and natural law.

7. Dispersion of power is to be used to reduce the potential for corruption as we are imperfect beings. The greatest prophets, such as Moses, realized the weight being a leader before our Creator carried, and asked for that weight to be shared among others. Checks and balances are needed in order to prevent some portions of human government from becoming dominant and reducing or eliminating the role of others.

The Second Thread: Grounded in Man

From the second thread within Greek philosophy we get the following ideas:

1. The state is supreme.

2. Our rights come from the state.

3. Gods are made by man.

4. It is only the collective society that matters. The individual matters only to the extent that he or she contributes to society.

5. As we matter in accordance with our ability to contribute, there is no innate equality of nature. We have instead a hierarchy based upon ability as some gifts of nature make others superior. According to Greek philosophy, this is both "expedient and right."

6. As all are not equal, the acquisition of knowledge and virtue is only for the elite. Only for those who have the ability to properly use them.

7. Citizens are to be molded to fit the needs of the state. As our rights come from the state, they can and should be changed by the state in order to fit its goals and needs.

8. Rule can be by the one, few, or many. However, the power is to be concentrated and absolute. It is only the elite who have the capabilities and gifts to lead.

9. Happiness is harmony within society and is achieved by either persuasion or compulsion.

10. Citizens are the herd of the state, to be bred and cultivated for its own ends.

Where Grounding in Man Leads

There are several implications made manifest by the differences between the two threads. We will discuss two of them. The first is one's beginning point: In one thread the beginning point is our Creator while in the other thread it is man himself. A second difference is the first thread focuses on our actions and how we are to live, both in relation to our Creator and each other. This same standard applies to each and every one of us. The second thread merely points to who we are. How we each live and behave is dependent upon who we are within a society.

Francis Schaeffer discusses these differences in several of his books. The following diagram appears in his book *Escape from Reason*.[4]

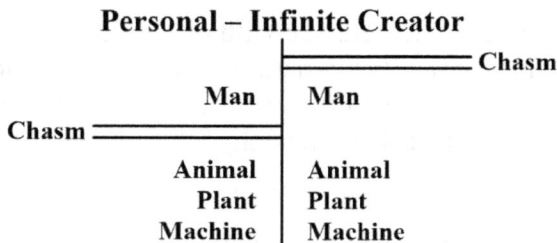

Personal – Infinite Creator

	Man	Man	Chasm
Chasm			
	Animal	Animal	
	Plant	Plant	
	Machine	Machine	

Schaeffer asserts that: (1) our Creator is not only infinite but he is also "personal," and (2) that man has a unique place in all of creation. Both notions are consistent with the writings of Clement, Augustine, and St. Thomas Aquinas (Thomas). Our Creator created everything, including us. He is infinite and all-powerful. He is the First Principal from which all other things are derived. He is beyond space and time. In this respect He is beyond our knowing as we, along with the rest of creation, are finite and complex unities. From this perspective, man is no different from the rest of creation. This is indicated by the chasm between Creator and His creation on the right side of the diagram.

On the other hand, man alone was given His image by our Creator, an internal image. This both sets man apart from the rest of creation and allows him to have a personal connection to his Creator. Indeed, this is necessary if we are to fulfill our purpose as part of His creation. From this perspective it is possible for man to have some knowledge of His Creator. It will not be full knowledge, but it will be true knowledge. It will not be direct knowledge of Him, but instead knowledge of Him based on His revelatory actions, what He has told us about Himself, and what we observe within His creation. This relationship between man and Creator is indicated by placing the chasm on the left side of the diagram between man and the rest of creation.

When man turns from His Creator, he is left with a dilemma. The top part of the above diagram disappears. Man's intellect becomes autonomous. What can man then use as a starting point for himself or creation? There is no longer a Creator. There is nothing in creation which provides a consistent logical starting point outside of our Creator which explains man's own existence, let alone how he should behave— his morality.

Plato asserted that philosophy is divided into the areas of being, morality, and knowing. The area of "being" is the problem of existence: "This includes the existence of man, but we must realize that the existence of man is no greater problem as such than is the fact that anything exists at all. No one has said it better than Jean-Paul Sartre, who has said that the basic philosophical question is that something is there rather than that nothing is there."[5] This first area then is metaphysics. The first thread provides an explanation for the existence of all creation, the second asserts that creation has always been—there is no starting point as creation has always been. The latter belief underlies much pagan philosophy.

The second area of thought is that of man's moral dilemma as mentioned above: "Man is personal and yet he is finite, and so he is not a sufficient integration point for himself. We might remember another profound statement from Sartre that no finite point has any meaning unless it has an infinite reference point."[6] Man is different from non-man, and our entire observation through history supports this notion. From these observations we see that man is noble. Look at the news: people willingly risk their own lives to save someone whom they do not even know, simply because the person is a fellow human being. However, man can also be cruel. Look at the actions of Genghis-Khan, Hitler, Stalin, Che, Mao and many others. No one can reasonably doubt the existence of both.

So we have a dual dilemma. The first is that man is an insufficient integration point for himself because he is both personal and finite. The second is man's contradictions between his nobility and his cruelty.

Those who support a position of behaviorism, or determinism, generally assert that man is not personal. He is not "intrinsically different from the impersonal."[7] This is nothing more than the notion that man is a mere machine. There are two problems with this position. First, it denies the evidence of historical reality. Second, there is not a single behaviorist or determinist capable of consistently living on the basis of his or her behaviorism or determinism. Even the writings of Francis Crick and B. F. Skinner show this tension.[8] The first thread provides an explanation for man's existence as it provides a sufficient integration point, and a basis for his morality. The second thread can espouse theories, but these are theories in search of evidence supporting them.

The third philosophical area is epistemology: the problem of knowing. Plato understood this area well. This area deals with the problem of particulars and universals, of the one and the many. Particulars are the things we see all around us in the world. It is the universals which provide meaning to particulars. He provides an example of the use of the word "apple." When we are discussing apples, we do not refer to all of the different kinds of apples that exist each and every time. Instead we put all of these together under the word "apple" to convey meaning. Greek philosophers looked for a universal which would provide meaning to their existence. They first looked at the *polis* as a possible universal. This word originally meant more than just a mere city-state. It referred to the society within the city-state. They realized that this was insufficient. They next turned to their gods to provide a universal, but while their gods were personal, they were not substantial enough to provide a universal.

The first thread, particularly the writings of Clement, provide an answer to knowing: *reason and faith*. These provide a basis for a relationship with our Creator. The second thread attempts to find a universal, the first principal, but is unable to do so in a consistent manner. We will return again to these thoughts in Chapter 5 when discussing Allah's nature.

Religion's Influence

Islam added nothing new to religion from a theological perspective; instead, it borrowed from all those it encountered. As we will see later, this also holds true for many other aspects of this ideology. Ignaz Goldziher was a prominent twentieth century Islamist who wrote extensively about Islam's development. His writings are considered classical studies of Islam today. He said the following:

> The dogmatic development of Islam took place under the sign of Hellenistic thought; in its legal system the influence of Roman law is unmistakable; the organization of the Islamic state as it took shape during the Abbasid caliphate shows the adaptation of Persian political ideas; Islamic mysticism made use of Neoplatonic and Hindu habits of thought. In each of these areas Islam demonstrates its ability to absorb and

assimilate foreign elements so thoroughly that their foreign character can be detected only by the exact analysis of critical research.

With this receptive character Islam was stamped at its birth. Its founder, Muhammad, did not proclaim new ideas. He did not enrich earlier conceptions of man's relation to the transcendental and infinite.... The Arab Prophet's message was an eclectic composite of religious ideas and regulations. The ideas were suggested to him by contacts, which had stirred him deeply, with Jewish, Christian, and other elements, and they seemed to him suited to awaken an earnest religious mood among his fellow Arabs. The regulations too were derived from foreign sources; he recognized them as needed to institute life according to the will of God.[9]

What was new within Islam was the marriage of monotheism with the Bedouin culture, which is why this chapter is included for it is almost impossible to understand Islam without some knowledge of the culture from whence it came.

We'll close this section by briefly looking at each of the religions mentioned so far. In the next section we'll look at some of the specific borrowings from each and then some relevant aspects of Bedouin culture.

The Roman Empire consisted of Roman Catholics in the west and Eastern Orthodox in the east. Christian tenets include, but are not limited to the following:

1. A triune God. Three persons in one essence. Another way to say this is that God is one and many at the same time, but in different senses.

2. Christ is one person with two natures, both divine and human.

3. Christ died on the cross and was resurrected for the remission of man's sins.

4. Six periods of creation.

5. Man descending from a single couple (Adam and Eve).

6. Man was created in God's image, an inward image, and was intended to have a personal relationship with his Creator. Man was given free will by his Creator which he has exercised in a manner that separates him from his Creator.

7. Man is regenerated by the Holy Spirit through baptism.

8. The Bible is the infallible, inspired Word of God.

9. There will be a final day of judgment, for all mankind, past and present.

As mentioned earlier, Persia was multi-religious and included each of the following groups. Most of these groups also existed outside of Persia:

1. Zoroastrian (Mazdaism). Zoroastrianism is monotheistic, but it does not believe in the God of Abraham. Instead its followers worship a deity called Ahura Mazda, who governs the universe through his holy spirit. There is an evil counterpart (Ahriman), who will in the end be overcome. Some parallels exist with Christian beliefs and include six periods of creation, man descending from a single couple (Mashya and Mashyana), rebirth of the world, the coming of a Messiah, the existence of a perfect kingdom, the resurrection of the dead, and everlasting life. Zoroaster was Ahura Mazda's prophet. Traditions suggest Zoroaster was a contemporary of Cyrus the Great, may have met and influenced Pythagoras, and that he was known to the Jews as Ezekiel (although this last is not supported).

There was a significant following of Zoroastrianism among Persia's aristocracy, military, and commoners. Christians and Jews were predominant among the peasant and urban populations. Zoroastrianism was referred to as Madjus in the Qur'an, and considered to be on a par with Christianity and Judaism as a People of the Book.

2. Nestorian. This sect asserted Christ's humanity through Jesus being two distinct persons, a complete man who through the Incarnation was assumed by the Word. Nestorius was a bishop in the Orthodox Church. His views resulted in calling the Third Ecumenical Counsel at Ephesus. Nestorius was deposed as a result of the Counsel. This Christian sect was forbidden in the Byzantine empire but welcomed in Persia. It was the largest non-Zoroastrian population in Persia. It was widespread in Babylonia, Khuzistan (Iran), the eastern Arabian coast, and reached as far east as Afghanistan and China.

3. Judaism. Judaism was the second largest non-Zoroastrian group in Persia. Jews lived primarily between the Tigris and Euphrates rivers and were the largest population in this area. There were also large populations in Syria and Iraq to the Zagros Mountains. Large populations also resided outside of Persia in Palestine, Egypt, and along the North African coasts.

4. Monophysite (Jacobite). This sect believed that Christ had only one nature: divine. The Chalcedon view was that Christ had two natures: human and divine. The Jacobite were considered to be heretics by the Byzantines and were the third largest non-Zoroastrian group within Persia. They had sizable communities in Mesopotamia from Armenia to Syria and along the Tigris River (Assyria). They also had sizable populations within Egypt and Abyssinia. The seat of the Eastern Monophysite Primate was Tagrit in what is now Iraq, along the Tigris River.

5. Gnostics. Gnosticism was a pagan response to monotheism. In general it expressed a dualistic mysticism claiming the need for

a special/secret knowledge. It found a refuge within Persia and also had a significant presence in both Syria and Egypt. The Persian gnostics generally did not believe in Moses, Jesus, or Muhammad. Instead, their beliefs focused on John the Baptist and the "Knowledge of Life." The Egyptian and Syrian gnostics combined paganism with Plato's philosophy. Their works include the Secret Book of John and the Gospels of Thomas and Judas.

Egyptian gnostic thought grew from writings emanating in Alexandria. References to gnosticism first appeared in the writings of Irenaeus in about 180 AD and Clement a short time later. The basic line of gnostic thought included (1) creation was made by an inferior godling, (2) creation was corrupt, (3) it was this malicious godling who prevented man from attaining his true perfection, and (4) Jesus was a teacher who revealed secret knowledge that would free us from the godling's constraints.

6. Pagan. While there were some Jewish and Christian Arabs, most were pagan. Many appear to have acknowledged a creator god called "Allah," but he does not appear to have been generally worshipped. The primary pagan gods of the Arabs in Mecca were the following:

    a. Hubal: God of the moon. Along with the sun goddess, they had three daughters.

        i.   Al-Lat: a solar divinity

        ii. Al-Huzza: the planet Venus

        iii. Manat: a goddess of fate, the Evening Star

Muhammad spoke against the three daughter goddesses, but stopped short of saying anything negative about Hubal. Hubal's idol in Mecca was located within the Kaaba, next to the Black Stone, and it is believed that the two were connected.

Religious Borrowings

The last section provided an overview of the religions from which Islam borrowed. This section reviews some of the specific ideas that were borrowed from those religions and the next section some relevant cultural aspects of the Arabic people.

This list of Islamic borrowings is not complete, but does show how extensive they were. This view is reinforced by the words of Ignaz Goldziher noted earlier.

From Zoroastrianism:

1. The Mizan: a balance weighing the actions of men to determine whether they go to Paradise or Hell.

2. Merit is earned by reciting verses from the Avasta (holy text) to relieve demerits earned in life, a form of salvation by works.

3. The recitation of daily prayers. Islam initially had two sets of daily prayers, then went to three (based on the Jewish schedule), and then to five (based upon the Zoroastrian schedule).

4. The story in the Qur'an about Muhammad's night time ascent from Jerusalem is very similar to the Pahlavi Artay, written sometime in the fourth century.

5. Zoroastrianism was Persia's official religion, and prevalent among the aristocrats and military. A Caliph headed this religion. The church and state were one.

6. The concept of the Road or Path (sirat), the right way of religion. This also refers to the razor-thin bridge between heaven and hell that the unrighteous cannot pass on the final day of accounting.

7. Descriptions of what Paradise is like, which is full of physical pleasures.

8. Some Persian words are included within the Qur'an as there were no Arabic language equivalents. Research puts between 107 and 275 foreign words within the Qur'an that come from Aramaic, Ethiopic, Greek, Hebrew, and Syriac in addition to Persian.

From Judaism:

1. Concept of monotheism.

2. Muhammad claimed he was the last of the Old Testament line of prophets that began with Moses.

3. Facing the Holy City for prayers (initially Jerusalem and later Mecca).

4. Rabbinical words contained within the Qur'an where no Arabic equivalents existed.

5. Rabbinical writings from the Talmud (written about 200 AD) form the basis for many of the Qur'an's stories such as

   a. A raven is sent to Cain after killing Abel in Genesis.

   b. Murdering an individual being equivalent to killing a whole race.

6. Religious doctrines.

   a. The unity of God, although as we'll see later the Islamic concept of Allah was heavily influenced by Plotinus and neoplatonic thought.

   b. Written revelation.

   c. Six days for creation, although the Qur'an is inconsistent in the number of days taken for creation.

      d. The existence of seven heavens and seven hells (this also appears within Zoroastrianism).

7. Mount Caf being the highest point on the Earth, a misunderstanding of the translation of the word "thohu" from the Hagigah.

8. One story of Adam's creation comes from the Midrash Rabbah.

9. The angels being ordered to worship Adam.

10. The story of Cain and Abel.

11. Gog and Magog.

12. Noah's character and conversations within sura 7 come from the rabbinical writings in Sanhedrin 108.

13. Sura 11 and 33 mention boiling water occurring in the Flood as punishment and come from Rosh Hashanah 16.2 and Sanhedrin 108.

14. From sura 34, Solomon commanding demons and tricking them into building the Temple in Jerusalem appears in Gittin 68. There are many more examples that could be cited.

From Nestorian (heretical) Christianity:

1. Jesus was only a man inspired by God.

From Gnosticism (heretical):

2. Jesus being born under a palm tree and asking the tree to provide Mary its fruit is contained in the Coptic History of Mary and Protevangelium of James the Less.

3. Making clay birds and breathing life into them and speaking at birth to defend Mary's honor are in the Gospel of Thomas.

4. Christ was only a prophet.

5. The Trinity consists of God, Christ, and Mary.

6. From the Basilidians, Jesus was not crucified. God would not let a prophet die such a humiliating death. Instead, God substituted someone who looked like Jesus, and took Jesus directly up into heaven.

7. The story of the Seven Sleepers of Ephesus comes from James of Sarug (Syrian bishop).

From Paganism:

1. Pagan practices kept by Islam include slavery, polygamy, easy divorce (for the man), demonic pollution, and ritual cleansing.

2. Existence of Jinns.

3. The folk tales of Ad and Thamud.

4. The Hajj came from pre-Islamic pagan rituals that were familiar to Arabs and centered on the Kaaba in Mecca. These include the following:

   a. The pilgrimage occurring during Ramadan.

   b. Kissing the Black Stone in the Kaaba. Arab pagan gods often resided in stones, and there are references to Arabs worshipping and kissing stones in the second and third centuries (Clement and Tacitus).

   c. Circumambulating the Kaaba seven times, three times fast and four times slow, representing the seven known planets. Each time kissing another stone in the Yamani corner of the Kaaba (this is the side of the Kaaba facing Yemen).

    d. Running from the Kaaba to the top of As Safa and then to and from Al-Marwah (another hill) seven times. The purpose of this run in pagan times was to kiss the stones Isaf and Naila located on the top of each hill.

    e. Casting of seven stones at each of three pillars in the village of Mina, just east of Mecca, to drive away evil.

From Christianity:

   1. All people will experience death and an intermediate state.

   2. The return of Jesus.

   3. A resurrection prior to the final day of judgment.

   4. A final day of judgment for all people.

The Arabic People

At the beginning of the sixth century, the Arabian Peninsula was peopled by two groups: the Saracens in the north and in the Hijaz, and the Sabeans in the south. The Saracens consisted of two sub-groups. One was both nomadic and semi-nomadic (Bedouins), and the second sub-group was settled. The Bedouins generally raised animals such as goats, sheep, or camels. They migrated based upon the availability of grazing land as their ancestors had done. They relied on trade with the settled communities for food and metal items such as weapons, and they excelled in fighting. Bedouins supplemented their own wealth with raids on settlements and caravans, and also extorted protection fees from some communities. Fighting was also considered to be a form of entertainment, a game that reduced the monotony of dessert life. The nomadic groups were usually family members of not more than two dozen people or so. Clans and tribes rarely gathered together in large groups, and then not for very long.

The settled sub-group of Saracens generally farmed, mostly growing crops such as figs and dates. Farming required irrigation in all parts of Arabia except the southwestern parts of the peninsula in what is now Yemen. Most of the settled communities in the Hijaz and north were around oases. They traded both with the Bedouins and the outside world through caravans to obtain what they could not produce for themselves. The caravans contributed to the wealth of these communities not only through the trade that was conducted, but also through hiring on as drivers and workers in the caravans, supplying the caravans, and selling safe passage. Jewish tribes also had land holdings in many of the most prosperous locations, such as Khaybar, Mecca, Yathrib (Medina), Taima, and Fadak. The Jewish and pagan tribes lived together in these communities.

The two sub-groups of Saracens were in conflict. The settled tribes often paid protection to a particular Bedouin clan to keep them safe from other tribes. These alliances changed, shifting based upon the current needs of each particular tribe. Life was very difficult as often not enough goods could be produced to maintain living conditions. Society itself was organized around the tribe and, to the extent it existed in Arabia at this time, the tribes were the ruling authority. Although the ties of tribal blood had held society together, this was slowly changing and being replaced by common self-interest through trade associated with merchants and agriculture.

The quality known as muruwa (virility or manliness) was paramount within Arabic society. This trait was reflected by honor, courage, endurance, loyalty to one's group (tribe or clan), and one's social obligations. Muruwa could be increased by creating alliances beneficial to one's tribe or performing heroic acts. Infringements of this moral code rendered the individual liable to insults and the loss of honor. Blood feuds were frequent and required if one's muruwa was impugned. The killing outside of one's clan wasn't viewed as necessarily bad. It depended upon whether the results were judged to achieve a good end for the tribe. Relations between tribes had generally been held together by blood and mutual self-interest.

Here are two quick examples that highlight some of the cultural differences between the Arabic peoples and the West. The first example is the making of a vow. In the West this is normally a solemn promise, sometimes one made to God. The intent of the person making the vow is to keep it, no matter what happens. Within the Arabic culture, we have the following sentiment from a 13th century poet: "What good is a vow if there is no way out." This isn't good or bad in itself, but is simply a reflection of their environment, where needs could change rather abruptly so commitments needed to be flexible as well. The survival of one's clan could depend on it.

The second example relates to what one should do if they get into an argument with a friend and later find out they were in the wrong. In the West, the person who was wrong would normally apologize. However, the following adage comes from Eastern culture: "To have a fault is one fault, to admit a fault is two faults." Again, a very different cultural standard, neither right nor wrong but simply different.

The Sabeans had a well-developed culture with their own architecture, written language, and legal system. They had significant seaports that traded with India and eastern Africa. In addition to trade, they also raised crops, cattle, and grew trees for perfumes and spices. They were primarily pagan, but the area around Najran was formerly a Jewish kingdom that by the early sixth century was peopled primarily by Christians. In comparison with most of the Saracens, they lived fairly wealthy and peaceful lives.

Summary

To summarize, the following are this chapter's main points so far. First, Islam is not just a religion, but an ideology with a religious component. Second, it borrowed heavily not only within the religious sphere, but also within other aspects such as law and governance. Third, conflict was prevalent within the Arabic culture, and this conflict was often driven by the scarcity of goods and the speed at which wealth could disappear. Alliances had to shift with changing needs in order to survive. This played itself out in other significant cultural differences that must be understood in order understand Islam. Fourth, the ties of kinship were paramount in Arabia early in the sixth century. However, this was changing and being replaced by economic ties and mutual self-interest by the latter part of the century when Muhammad was born.

Arab Ancestry and Language

This final section provides some additional material for understanding Islam. We will take a quick look at the ancestry of the Arab peoples, the Arab language, and some common cultural practices that carried over from pre-Islamic times. These will become relevant later as we look at Islam's growth, and the development of its tenets and sources.

Arab Ancestry

Arab Muslims often claim to be descended from Ishmael. However, the Arab peoples are far older than Ishmael and trace their roots to other individuals. The word *Arab* does not appear until the 9th century BC in Assyria. From the book of Genesis we have the following peoples identified:

1. The descendants of Noah's son Japheth include Gomer, Magog, Madai, Javan, Tubal, Meshech and Tiras. From these the coastlands of the nations were separated into their lands, every one according to his language, according to their families, into their nations. (Gen. 10:2-5)

2. The descendants of Noah's son Ham include Cush, Mizraim, Put, and Canaan. From Cush came Nimrod who went into Assyria and founded the city of Nineveh. Mizraim's descendants included the Philistines. The descendants of Canaan settled in the land from Sidon to Gaza. (Gen. 10:6-20)

3. The descendants of Noah's son Shem include Peleg, "for in his days the earth was divided; and his brother's name was Joktan." Joktan's descendants included Almodad, Sheleph, Hazarmaveth, Jerah, Hadoram, Uzal, Diklah, Obal, Abimael, Sheba, Ophir, Havilah, and Jobab. They settled in the hill country of the east. (Gen. 10:21-32)

4. Lot's daughters from whom the Moabites and Ammonites descended. (Gen. 19:37-38)

5. The descendants of Abraham through his second wife Keturah, after the death of Sarah. These descendants included Zimran, Jokshan, Medan, Midian, Ishbak, and Shuah. These and the sons of his concubines he sent to the east away from his son Isaac. (Gen. 25:1-6)

6. The descendants of Jacob's brother Esau. Esau was the father of the Edomites. (Gen. 36:9-43)

7. The descendants of Ishmael included Nebaioth, Kedar, Adbeel, Mibsam, Mishma, Dumah, Massa, Hada, Tema, Jetur, Maphish, and Kedemah. Ishmael settled in the lands to the east of Egypt toward Assyria in defiance of all his relatives. (Gen. 25:12-18) Additional information about Ishmael in Genesis says that "his hand will be against everyone, and everyone's hand will be against him; and he will live to the east of all his brothers." (Gen. 16:12) Kedar is the father of the Bedouins.

From the above, it is the Bedouins alone who can make a clear claim as being a descendent of Ishmael.

Arab Language

The Arab language is Semitic. Words were formed from three characters in one of three different positions: initial, medial, or final. In the sixth century, the Arab language did not possess the pointing or diacritical marks of modern Arabic. These marks are used to both distinguish some consonants from one another and determine the insertion of short vowels into words. The lack of pointing made it impossible to distinguish between consonants such as b from t or th, f from q, j from h and kh, s from d, r from z, s from sh, d from dh, and t from z. Different words could also be formed by inserting the marks for short vowels in different locations. This had several implications for understanding written text from this period. Either the individual had to (1) be present when the words were spoken so they would understand the context, (2) be told what was said by a trustworthy transmitter (referred to as isnad), or (3) derive the meaning from the text itself.

Without these marks, it was possible to develop a great number of variant readings from the same written text. These variant readings were not simply grammatical differences in tense, person, or subject-verb agreement. Instead their insertion produced phrases and statements with different meanings from the same source text. Literally thousands of different variant readings could be and, as we will see later, were created from the same written text. Variations were produced simply by differing which marks were used and where they were placed. Different sets of rules developed to apply these marks to the text. Also as we will see later, the Medinan codex selected by Uthman as the true Qur'an had unpointed text without the orthographic marks for short vowels. These characteristics of the Arabic language had implications for the eventual derivation of the text's meaning.

Here is one quick example from the *Answering Islam* website that provides insight into the formation of and relationship between some words that are relevant to the current topic. While Arabic is read from right to left, these examples use English and are presented left to right. They are meant as an example only. A three-letter infinitive verb forms the root for many different words. Depending on the source one uses to help discern the Arabic language, the meaning of these derived words may or may not be related. For example, one Arabic root is SLM. From this root we get the infinitive salama, which means "the way of security" or "the path of safety." All of the words in the diagram below are derived from this same infinitive.

SLM

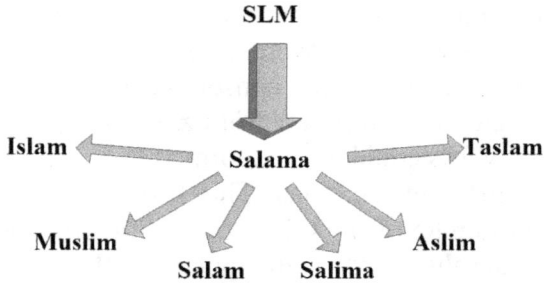

The meaning of each of these words is discussed below.

> **Islam**: submission to the will of Allah
>
> **Muslim**: one who submits to the will of Allah
>
> **Salam**: peace
>
> **Salima**: to be saved or escape from danger
>
> **Aslim**: [see below]
>
> **Taslam**: [see below]

On the surface there does not appear to be any direct relationship between the words above. Despite these surficial differences, at another level, I believe that a relationship exists between these words that can only be brought out by understanding cultural differences. First, the words *Islam* and *Muslim* involve an external action between two objects, one in submission to the other. I think it is no different for the Arabic word for peace. This is important to understand, so we are going to spend a moment on the topic. Some of the material below repeats ideas expressed earlier in this chapter.

In Western culture, we usually assume peace to be the normal state, and it is at times interrupted by conflict. This is characterized by the following quote from Augustine: "Peace is the end sought for by war. For every man seeks peace by waging war, but no man seeks war by making peace."[10] He goes on to say even they who intentionally interrupt the peace do not hate peace, but only want a peace that suits them better. This notion assumes that peace is the normal state. Peace happens when a people turns to God as they obey divine law: love God and your fellow man. When man turns to himself, he is more likely to harm others by his actions as he has turned from self-sacrifice to self-interest: "For he sees that peace cannot be maintained unless all the members of the same domestic circle be subject to one head, such as he himself is in his own house."[11] Man turns from virtue to vice.

As noted earlier, the environment in the Arabian peninsula was very different. It was harsh and unforgiving. There were two basic groups of people. One settled mostly around oases and generally farmed. The second– nomadic—raised livestock such as camels and goats, and generally existed in small groups numbering two dozen or less. For this second group in particular, life was often lived on the edge. If the rains didn't come, or someone took your grazing land, or raided your camp to take your stuff—because they did not have enough—you likely died. Things could and did change rapidly.

Unlike the rest of the known world in the sixth century, Arabia relied on tribal rule. A group's leader was responsible for his clan's or tribe's welfare. The code of conduct called *muruwa* was followed and represented the Arabic idea of manliness and honor. This honor was maintained or increased based upon individual actions, such as whether your tribe's wealth or status increased. The outcomes were what mattered. Killing another was okay if it was seen as bettering the tribe. Retaliation for insults or raids was required to maintain honor. Inaction would result in loss of prestige and honor. The welfare of the tribe came first and foremost.

It was an environment where there was seldom enough for everyone. Raids were used to acquire what was needed, and sometime to break life's monotony (for sport). Alliances were created for mutual protection, but they were subject to change as conditions often changed. Again, whatever increased a tribe's wealth and/or honor was good. That which decreased either was bad. In such an environment, conflict was the norm, and peace the interlude between conflict. I am not saying than one culture is better than the other, or that one is right and the other wrong, but merely that in some ways they were very different and in some respects the opposite of each other.

This notion is not just my thoughts, but are confirmed by other sources. A couple of years ago, I met a man named Georges Houssney. He is a Lebanese Christian whose family came to America with the Islamization of Lebanon. He has performed Muslim outreach for most of his life. He describes Arabs as follows:

> Al Jahiz (a famous Arab scholar of the ninth century), described the Arab as "temperamental, easily provoked to anger for the meanest reason, ready to kill if his honor has been hurt." The Arab temperament is not much different today. You see this in the streets, marketplace, and movie theaters, where it is common for people to pick a fight over almost anything. Yet Arabs can also be quite humorous and easy-going. Just as quickly as their tempers flare up, they will often almost instantly turn from yelling to joking, smiling, and shaking hands.[12]

This brings us to the meaning of the words *Aslim* and *Taslam*. Toward the end of his life, Muhammad would sign the letters he sent to groups demanding they accept Islam with the closing "Aslim Taslam." This phrase has two equivalent meanings: surrender and you will be safe, and submit or face death. Again, submission would bring peace—the kind of peace purchased by Augustine's city of man.

In my opinion, these words are all related. They all involve the act of one object/person submitting to another, thereby achieving a type of safety/security. They represent how *the way of safety is obtained through submission*. We will return to this aspect of culture later when we discuss the formation of some of Islam's tenets.

Arabic Practices

It is difficult to ascertain many of the customs and practices within Arabic culture prior to Muhammad. Why? Because the early caliphs ordered all things pre-Muhammad that did not support Islam to be destroyed, a practice still continuing today. This included literature, poetry, history, and art. What we know primarily comes from a few non-Arabic sources.

Below are a few common pre-Islamic practices from Arab culture that we know about. With the exception of the first two items, all of these practices carried over into Islam. Verses within the Qur'an prohibited the practice of female infanticide. Verses related to the Zaynab affair changed the status of adopted children. They were no longer considered to be the offspring of those who adopted them. Finally, the status of women within Islam is today very clear, a position sanctioned by verses from within the Qur'an and other Islamic sources.

1. Female infanticide (a pagan practice also performed within the Roman Empire, but reduced as the influence of Christianity grew).

2. Children who were adopted, culturally and legally, became the offspring of the person adopting them.

3. Child weddings to girls as young as 8 or thereabouts.

4. Multiple wives.

5. Frequent blood feuds and payment of blood-wit (a fine or penalty for shedding injuring another).

6. Use of tribal leaders as arbiters.

7. The owning of slaves.

8. The tribe or clan was paramount in society, but these ties were beginning to fade and be replaced by economic mutual interests in the sixth century.

9. The role and status of women is unclear. Some sources suggest they were treated as property. Other sources indicate that property was passed through the female's family, that they participated equally with their men in taking care of their clan, and that females contracted to be wives for a specific period of time. Muhammad's first wife Khadija was a widow who had significant wealth of her own. She hired Muhammad to be in charge of some of her caravans as a business manager, caravans which she appears to have funded. One of the bases for their eventual marriage was Muhammad's success in managing her caravans.

In the next chapter, we will begin our study of Islam's development by looking at Islam's source documents and their development.

Chapter 2

Islam's Documents and Their Development

This chapter focuses on Islam's religious document development. At Muhammad's death, the Qur'an had not yet been written down. In fact, the word *Qur'an* means "the reading" or "the recital." It is likely that the Qur'an was never intended to be in written form. Islam's doctrines and documents developed over a period of about three hundred years.

This chapter will cover the development of its primary sources. Chapters 3 and 4 cover some important doctrinal development, especially from a Judeo-Christian perspective. Chapter 5 provides a comparison of those doctrines to Judeo-Christian tenets, and Chapter 6 provides a historical overview of this ideology's implementation from its inception to the twentieth century. It is during the first three hundred years, and particularly during the Abbasid Dynasty, that Islam's core beliefs hardened into those we know today. This chapter focuses on the development of the Qur'an, hadith, sunna, shari'a, and sirat.

As we saw in the previous chapter, Muhammad added nothing new from a theological perspective. Instead he borrowed from every religion that existed within the Arabian Peninsula. One can find borrowings from Judaism, Christianity, Zoroastrianism, gnosticism, and paganism. What is interesting is that almost all of the "Christian" borrowings come from either gnosticism or heretical sects. From that perspective alone, Islam's understanding of Christianity cannot be compatible with what the Bible teaches, as what it incorporated came from false sources.

The timeline below provides an overview of Islam's document development and the extent to which that development began with the Abbasid Dynasty. Definitions for the Islamic terms mentioned above follow the timeline. Note Islam marks its beginning with Muhammad's migration from Mecca to Medina and not from when he received his first revelation in 610 AD.

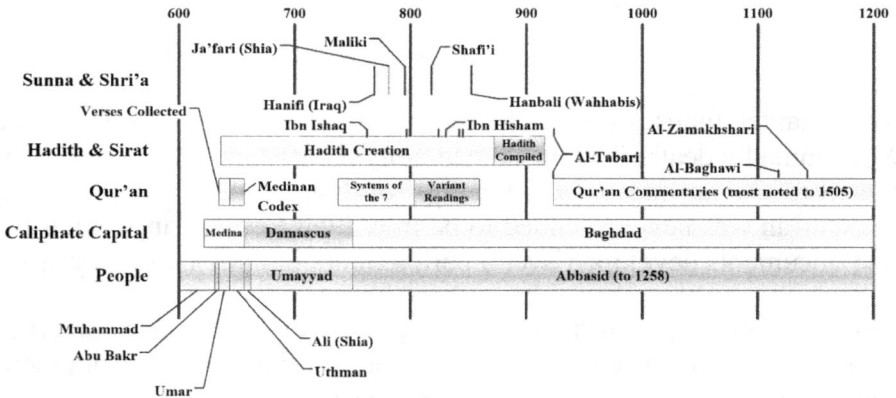

Figure 2-1: Timeline of Islam's Development

The lighter shaded item within the sunna and shari'a row is Shia specific, and the lines roughly indicate when the Islamic schools of jurisprudence began. The lines atop the hadith creation bar are the approximate times the sirat were written. Only generally accepted writings are shown, and a few of those are named. The lines atop the Qur'an bar indicate some commentary writers. Al-Tabari both edited Ibn Ishaq's sirat and wrote one of the earliest Qur'an commentaries.

For those who do not know, after Muhammad's death one group of followers wanted a successor chosen from his inner circle. A second group wanted someone chosen from his blood-line. These respectively developed over time into the Sunni and Shia denominations within Islam.

Definitions

1. **Qur'an**: The reading or recital. Within Islam, God's full and final revelation to man.

2. **Hadith**: A story. Oral tradition later written down as to what Muhammad supposedly did, said, or approved of. Second in authority to the Qur'an.

3. **Sunna**: Written traditions about Muhammad's conduct, considered authoritative and the basis for shari'a.

4. **Sirat**: The way. Biographies of Muhammad's life and actions. Also, the bridge one is to cross to reach paradise on the day of judgement.

5. **Shari'a**: The path. Code of Islamic jurisprudence, but also more. "By the Shari'ah of God is meant everything legislated by God for ordering man's life."[1].

The Qur'an

As mentioned above, it is likely that the Qur'an was never intended to be written down. It did not exist as a written collection at Muhammad's death in 632. However, within a year most of his early followers were dead, particularly after the battle at Yamamah that was part of the Apostate Wars. With their death, the Qur'an was in danger of being lost as many of Muhammad's early followers who knew it no longer lived.

There are several contradictory stories related to collecting the Qur'an verses. One of them regards the development of several different codices and Uthman (the third caliph) selecting the Medinan codex as the official consonantal text of the Qur'an. Other texts came from places including Mecca, Basra, Damascus, and Kufa. Research indicates additional codices were created (see below), and that written texts did not appear before the eighth century.[2] The text in these codices was unpointed, meaning that the marks distinguishing between certain consonants were not present. In addition, these texts did not contain the markings indicating where short vowels were inserted. Different variant readings of the same consonantal text were possible by choosing what marks to insert and where to insert them.

From Charles Adams in the *Encyclopedia of Religion:*

> It must be emphasized that far from there being a single text passed down inviolate from the time of Uthman's commission, literally thousands of variant readings of particular verses were known. ... The variants affected even the Uthmanic codex, making it difficult to know what its true original form may have been.[3]

> Although Muslims of the present time generally have forgotten the very existence of these variant versions of the Qur'an ... Arthur Jefferies has listed fifteen primary codices (i.e., from the Companions) and a large number of secondary ones.[4]

During the Umayyad and early Abbasid periods, the variant readings of individual verses grew, and over time various centers developed their own traditions for inserting these marks. As noted in Chapter 1, there were three ways to understand unpointed Arabic texts as noted in the first chapter. First, being present at the event. The Abbasid dynasty began almost 120 years after Muhammad's death. No one was left who had lived before Muhammad's death. Second, getting the information from a reliable transmitter. I mentioned above that variant readings were already in place and being used, and as we'll see in a moment, there were also many fabricated hadith created during the previous Umayyad Dynasty. So many hadith were fabricated that al-Bukhari selected just 2–4 percent of the hadith he reviewed as authentic, and there are questions regarding some of those as we will also see later. Hadith content were also contradictory. Finally, we have the unpointed text's nature as mentioned above. Only the third method, interpreting meaning from the text itself, was left, and this was done by clerics applying both consensus and reasoning.

Consensus comes from the word *ijma*, meaning agreement. It is derived from this saying attributed to Muhammad: "Allah has granted you protection from three things: Your Prophet lays no curse upon you, lest you perish; the party of falsehood among you will never triumph over the party of truth; you will never agree on a false doctrine."[5] Consensus means "all that is approved by the sense of the community of believers is correct, and can lay claim to obligatory acknowledgment, and it is correct only in the form that the sense of the community, the consensus, has given it. Only such interpretations and applications of the Qur'an and sunna are correct as are accepted by consensus."[6] Consensus was applied not only to the Qur'an and sunna, but the hadith and by extension shari'a as well.

But whose consensus? It is not simply that of the masses, but with all of the fabricated hadith and variant readings, limiting ijma to the consensus of Muhammad's companions or the early Medinan leaders also was not possible.[7] An approach acknowledging clerical authority was ultimately settled upon: "At last a formula was found and *ijma* defined as the concordant doctrines and opinions of those who are in a given period the acknowledged doctors of Islam. They are the men with the power 'to bind and to loosen'; it is their office to interpret and deduce law and theological doctrine, and to decide whether law doctrine are correctly applied."[8] This principle gave Islam the potential to change over time through those who were acknowledged to be its existing spiritual leaders.

This is very different from Christianity. Scripture does not change. Someone may at times come upon some new understanding of it, as noted by Augustine, but the meaning itself does not change. It is a guidepost set by God to which we are to return. Within Islam, what it encounters and considers to be good can be integrated into it—and has. For a simple example, one has only to look at the prohibition against drinking wine in the Qur'an, and the clerical changes incorporated into this prohibition to all but remove it over the course of several centuries.

But consensus alone did not determine, interpret, or apply Islam's doctrines. Reason was also used, and Greek philosophy— particularly that of Aristotle—exerted a strong influence on Islam. This can be seen in Islam's view of Allah, which is firmly anchored in the neoplatonic ideas of Plotinus. Plotinus was a pagan who despised Christianity, and his writings were widely read and accepted within Augustine's time, over two hundred years before Muhammad's first revelation. These writings were edited and written down by his student Porphyry in *The Enneads*. Augustine countered many of Plotinus and Porphyry's thoughts and ideas in *The City of God*.[9] Muslims refer to Allah as God, but both terms are used throughout this book as the notions they represent are not the same. A high-level comparison covering some aspects of God, Plotinus's The One, and Allah are shown below. These differences will be explored more fully in Chapter Five.

	God	The One	Allah
Sovereignty	Creator	Creator	Creator
Nature	Single Being w/ complex Nature	Simple Unity, beyond Being	Simple Unity, pure Will
Actions	Intrinsic	Extrinsic	Extrinsic
Can He be known?	Yes - Reason & Faith	Knowable only through complete submission	No - Inscrutable
Man's Nature	Free	Slave	Slave
Basis for Obedience	Love	Mysticism	Fear
Man's Will	Free Will	Imposing one's will on another	Predestination
Man's Purpose	Know Creator	Submit to Creator	Obey Creator
Day of Resurrection	Yes	Not Mentioned	Yes

The Mu'tazalites within Islam are credited with bringing Hellenistic thought into Islam during the latter Umayyad period; two of their main tenets were divine justice and the unity of God. Their rationalist thought brought them into conflict with their day's established belief. For much of the first half of the 9th century, the caliphs supported their views. This was the time of the *Mihnah*, the Islamic Inquisition. Their intolerance and doctrine resulted in the rejection of their beliefs, but they still had a lasting influence through the rationalism they brought to Islam.

Variant readings continued to increase for several more centuries. It was not until the 10th century, about 300 years after Muhammad's death, under Islamic scholars led by Ibn Mujahid that a single system of consonants was canonized and a limitation placed on vowel insertion. Seven systems were accepted by Ibn Mujahid, each traced through two different transmitters, leading to fourteen accepted variant readings. These seven systems and their accepted transmitters are as follows:

1. Nafi of Medina according to Warsh and Qalun

2. Ibn Kathir of Mecca according to al-Bazzi and Qunbul

3. Ibn Amir of Damascus according to Hisham and Ibn Dhakwan

4. Abu Amr of Basra according to al-Duri and al-Susi

5. Asim of Kufa according to Hafs and Abu Bakr

6. Hamza of Kufa according to Khalaf and Khallad

7. Al-Kisai of Kufa according to al-Duri and Abul Harith[10]

The above texts serve as the basis for the Qur'an used today, but while the contents are not exactly the same, all of them are accepted. From Charles Adams again:

It is of some importance to call attention to a possible source of misunderstanding in regard to the variant readings of the Quran. The seven [variants] refer to actual differences in the written and oral text, to distinct versions of Quranic verses, whose differences, though they may not be great, are nonetheless real and substantial. Since the very existence of variant readings and versions of the Quran goes against the doctrinal position toward the Holy Book held by many modern Muslims, it is not uncommon in an apologetic context to hear the seven [variants] explained as modes of recitation; in fact the manner and technique of recitation are an entirely different matter.[11]

What appears to have happened in this instance is that the community, being unable to agree on a single reading, accepted diversity as the norm and proclaimed all of the seven (or ten or fourteen) to be correct.[12]

The Qur'an was a collection of revelations, with no context and no sense of history, so other sources were needed to supply those: the hadith and sirat. The accepted hadith collections came to codify the Qur'an and bring some consistency to Islam. From Goldziher:

As the hadith would have it, believers had already harassed the Prophet by pointing out dogmatic contradictions in the Qur'an. Such discussions (according to the hadith) stirred him to anger. "The Qur'an," he says, "was not revealed with the purpose that you might seize on one part of it to strike at another, as the nations of the past did with the revelations of their prophets. Rather, in the Qur'an one thing confirms another. You should act according to what you understand of it; you should accept on faith what is confusing to you."[13]

We now come to another significant difference between Christianity and Islam. Within Christianity, we are to question because it is a part of our purpose to have a deepening personal relationship with God. We can only do that by questioning and learning more about Him on our journey. This type of questioning is discouraged within Islam. When reading the Qur'an, one can only accept what is presented. It is not to be questioned.

It should be noted that there are hadith that contradict Goldziher's passage above, and inconsistent verses within the Qur'an resulted in Muhammad's abrogating them. So in summary, there were initially different Qur'anic texts, with many variant readings, that reasoning and consensus was needed to determine Islam's doctrines, and that reasoning has its basis in pagan thought. Finally, any confusing verses should simply be accepted on faith; there should be no questioning of what is in the Qur'an. Any contradictions are due to changes in Allah's revelations, with later verses changing, or abrogating, earlier ones.

The Hadith

The Sunni generally accept six hadith collections as authentic. Most of these were not written until the latter half of the ninth century, and they were not canonized until the fourteenth century. The leading ones were written by al-Bukhari and Muslim ibn al-Hajjaj, sometimes referred to as the "Sound Ones." As noted earlier, hadith were originally oral stories, and relied on a train of trustworthy transmitters (isnad). Again, many hadith were fabricated during the Umayyad and Abbasid periods. Each hadith compiler devised his own criteria for evaluating hadith and determining its soundness.

Fabricating hadith was not considered bad in itself, if the fabrications improved Islam's ethics or brought it more consistency. The following saying, attributed to Muhammad, indicated that fabrications would happen: "After my death more and more sayings will be ascribed to me, just as many sayings have been ascribed to previous prophets (without their having really said them). When a saying is reported and attributed to me, compare it with God's book. Whatever is in accordance with that book is from me, whether I really said it or no."[14] "Muhammad said" came to mean it was right, unassailable, desirable, and that Muhammad himself would agree with it. This approach was consistent with Arabic culture as described in the last chapter.

Hadith's subject matter was not limited to religion:

> Not only law and custom, but theology and political doctrine also took the form of hadith. Whatever Islam produced on its own or borrowed from the outside was dressed up as hadith. In such form alien, borrowed matter was assimilated until its origin was unrecognizable. Passages from the Old and New Testaments, rabbinic sayings, quotes from apocryphal gospels, and even doctrines of Greek philosophers and maxims of Persian and Indian wisdom gained entrance into Islam disguised as utterances of the Prophet.[15]

To give these sayings authority, everything needed to come from Muhammad, and the companions were seen as the best source for learning Muhammad's will: "Conduct and judgment were considered correct and their legitimacy was established if a chain of reliable transmission ultimately traced them back to a Companion who could testify that they were in harmony with the Prophet's intentions."[16] This authority was needed for each matter:

> The Prophet's authority was invoked by every group for every idea it evolved: for legal precepts couched in the form of tradition, as well as for maxims and teachings of an ethical or simply edificatory nature. Through solid chains of tradition, all such matters acquired an unbroken tie to the "Companions" who had heard those pronouncements and statutes from the Prophet or had seen him act in pertinent ways. It took no extraordinary

discernment on the part of Muslim critics to suspect the authenticity of much of this material.[17]

In his *Muslim Studies (Volume 2)*, Goldziher demonstrated "that a vast number of hadith accepted even in the most rigorously critical Muslim collections were outright forgeries from the late 8th and 9th centuries—and as a consequence, that the meticulous isnad which supported them were utterly fictitious."[18] Joseph Schacht and R.S. Humphreys extended Goldziher's work.

> Humphries sums up Schacht's theses [on the hadith] as: (1) that isnad going all the way back to the Prophet only began to be widely used around the time of the Abbasid Revolution—i.e., the mid-eighth century; (2) that ironically, the more elaborate and formally correct an isnad appeared to be, the more likely it was to be spurious. In general he concluded, *no* existing hadith could be reliably ascribed to the Prophet, though some of them might ultimately be rooted in his teaching.[19]

From the above, many accepted hadith were forgeries, the isnad used to support them came later, and more convincing isnad were more likely to be false.

In addition to using different criteria, there is also doubt about the hadith text's authenticity: "For example, at one point there were a dozen different Bukhari texts, and apart from these variants, there were deliberate interpolations. As Goldziher warns us, 'it would be wrong to think that the canonical authority of the two [collections of Bukhari and Muslim ibn al-Hajjaj] is due to the undisputed correctness of their contents and is the result of scholarly investigations.' Even a tenth-century critic pointed out the weaknesses of two hundred traditions incorporated in the works of Hajjaj and Bukhari."[20]

Islam's documents have not undergone the kind of scrutiny the documents of other religions have received. Instead its doctrines are accepted by tradition and faith. Rituals play a critical role in Arabic culture and over time grow in importance: "On the strength of such traditions, certain customs in ritual and law were established as the usage of the authoritative first believers of Islam, and as having been practiced under the Prophet's own eyes. As such, they acquired a sacred character."[21] These are called *sunna*, sacred custom. The form in which such usage is stated is *hadith*, tradition. The two concepts are not identical. Hadith is the documentation of sunna, which is where we head next.

The Traditions (Sunna)

The sunna are traditions for how one is to live, based upon Muhammad's example. These traditions are derived from Islam's sources—the Qur'an and hadith—but the sunna was not new. A sunna existed before Islam and was part of Arabic culture. Islamic traditions replaced many of the traditions that existed prior to Muhammad.

> When the Arabs accepted Islam—which had commanded them to break with their authentic sunna—they brought the concept of sunna with them. From that time forth it became the main pillar of the Islamic view of law and religion. There was, naturally, one essential modification: in Islam one could not draw one's precedents from the pagan sunna. Its point of departure was shifted; its source now consisted in the doctrines, conceptions, and practices of the oldest generation of Muslims, founders of an entirely different sunna from what the original Arab one had been.[22]

The hadith included cultural, legal, political, and religious concepts. The Abbasid viewed themselves as secular rulers and princes of Islam; everything became tied to religious doctrine and the divine law that underlay it. Increasing importance was paid to those who studied and practiced the traditions:

Since state, law, and the administration of justice were to be ordered and built up according to the precepts of religion, preference had to be given to people who practiced and studied the *sunna*, or who used scholarly methods to ascertain the divine law. ... Not only the rules for the ritualistic aspects of life were now based on religious law, but also the institutions of the state. The administration of justice in all kinds of transactions, down to the simplest statutes of civil law, must fulfill the requirements of the divine law. Consequently those requirements must be discovered down to the minutest detail. This was the age of the development and fixing of the law, the age of fiqh and of the scholars of jurisprudence.[23]

In summary, reasoning and consensus was used to create new traditions based upon Islam's documents, these superseded historic Arab traditions and became the source of Islamic law. This influence was not limited to just religion, but was incorporated into all aspects of life. *Islam is all*.

Shari'a

Islamic law's first development took place under the early caliphs and Umayyad. The initial military expansion and swift turn to consolidation contributed to changing the Islamic community. Conditions shifted often, and many changes required new regulations as few were referred to or implied by the Qur'an. Unlike the West, where law is separate from a society's religious sphere, every aspect of life comes under Islamic law as noted earlier. Human and divine law are one, with all law having its basis in the Qur'an and hadith, as embodied in the sunna. This leads to significant difference between Sunni and Shia. The Sunni do not view the Shia as dissenters due to their differences in law, but instead due to differences in the sunna each sect follows.[24] The Sunni look to sources coming from Muhammad's companions, while the Shia look to Muhammad's family.

During its early development,

> Hadiths were carried and handed about; new postulates and rules were derived from received material. On occasion the results were contradictory. Points of view and methods also led to differences. Some lawyers deferred to hadith. Gradations between these opposing tendencies gave rise to scholarly factions and schools that differed mostly in particular details of legal rulings, but were also at variance on some points of method. But contradictory hadiths would furnish contradictory answers to a question. One would have to determine in such cases which hadith outweighed the other. Because of the dubiousness of proof from hadith, other lawyers wanted freedom in legal reasoning, and refused to be much inconvenienced by received material. Deeply rooted local usage and customary law could not be simply done away with. Gradations between these opposing tendencies gave rise to scholarly factions and schools that differed mostly in particular details of legal rulings, but were also at variance on some points of method.[25]

These became Islam's schools of jurisprudence that were noted in the timeline at the beginning of this chapter.

Islamic law developed in several phases. In its early stages, the Islamic state showed some tolerance to the conquered people as there were no regulations in place for dealing with their more ancient culture, religions, and customs. The Umayyad also were more concerned with accumulating land and wealth than in applying religious doctrine. They needed the conquered people's assistance in sustaining order and in generating a revenue stream sufficient to maintain the caliphate's large army. These conditions did not last when the Abbasid assumed power; the shift toward religion had implications for law.

Clerics found it more difficult to rely on fraudulent hadith in developing legal opinions, especially as different groups with differing viewpoints had developed contradictory hadith. Once again, the same classical reasoning as outlined earlier was applied to law's development. Hadith were incorporated when they seemed to offer a firm footing, but only if there were a justifiable method of arriving at the end.

Outside influences also found their way into Islamic law. According to Goldziher, "Islamic jurisprudence shows undeniable traces of the influence of Roman law both in its methodology and in its particular stipulations."[26] This shift led to the concept of fiqh, the Islamic science of religious law: "A science which, perverted by casuistry, was soon to become disastrous for religious life and religious learning."[27]

Goldziher indicates that this change was associated, at least in part, with the rise of the Abbasid. While Islam asserts this shift purified its religion, human history has shown repeatedly that combining both the state and religious spheres results in the corruption of both.[28] Islam's position comes from believing that a collective consensus protects their community from error.

> We shall have occasion to study more closely the application of this principle as a criterion of orthodoxy. We shall see that only the continued effectiveness of this principle, throughout the history of Islam, explains that certain religious phenomena gained the stamp of orthodoxy because they had gained general acceptance, although in theory they should have been ensured as being contrary to Islam.[29]

So, like before, we have Islamic law coming from Islam's sources, and similar reasoning being applied. In addition, this consensus developed in a rapidly expanding geographic area, where Islam was in the minority position, and it relied on the native people for the caliphate's income.

The laws' development was often used to relieve perceived religious burdens: "The jurists pressed their ingenuity into service to find means of evasion whenever the literal text of the Qur'an would have led to an oppressive situation for the believers. Liberal interpretation of the text would often lighten a burden, or explain it away entirely."[30] Goldziher illustrated using the prohibition against drinking wine and the application of reasoning to that prohibition in order to relieve this burden. By the middle of the ninth century, "Although outright permission of the 'water of the grape' was out of the question, they [legal scholars] furnished the legal conscience of the believers with diverse means of relief, and of these means even well-intentioned people widely availed themselves."[31] This focus on searching into law, using sophistry, led to a form of legalism that stamped Islam.

The Sirat

There are seven principle sirat for information on Muhammad's life. The earliest biography is Ibn Ishaq's *Sirat Rasul Allah,*[32] written around the beginning of Abbasid rule. A complete original copy of this work does not exist: it was ordered destroyed as it presented Muhammad in an uncomplimentary light. The version that survives today is one that was edited by Ibn Hisham almost one hundred years later. Al-Tabari (10th century) also quotes from Ibn Ishaq and these quotes have been incorporated into the English version. Although this work is not the original, it still presents a compelling view of Islam's belief development. The other biographies were all written in the late eighth to ninth centuries. The development of Islam's beliefs is the subject of the next chapter.

Summary

The relationship between Islam's sources can be shown as in the diagram below. The application of reasoning and consensus to the interpretation of the Qur'an, the development of the sunna, and the selection and codification contained within the hadith, all resulted in a closed system of divine orientation. It was from this closed system that its legal system was derived. The biographies (sirat) add some context and a sense of history to the Qur'an's content.

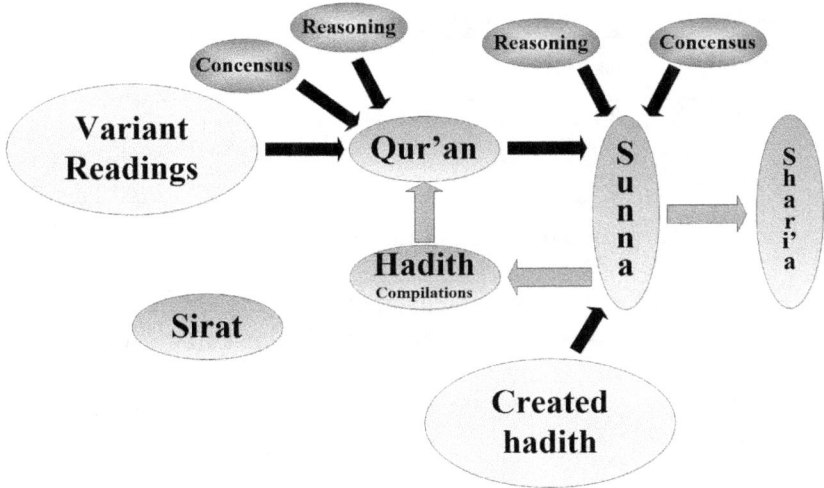

Figure 2-2: Relationship Between Islam's Sources

Biblical Consistency

Before we close this chapter, we need to do a brief comparison between Islam's development from the previous sections to the Bible itself. One claim that Islam's followers make is that the Bible has been corrupted. More about that in chapter four.

Norman Geisler cites the information below on some of the classical texts coming from the ancient world.[33]

Author/Book	Written	Earliest Copy	Time Gap	# of Copies	Accuracy
Homer, *Iliad*	800 BC			643	95%
Herodotus, *History*	480-425 BC	c. 900 AD	c. 1,350 yrs	8	?
Plato	400 BC	c. 900 AD	c. 1,300 yrs	7	?
Demosthenes	300 BC	c. 1100 AD	c. 1,400 yrs	200	?
Caesar, *Gallic Wars*	100–44 BC	c. 900 AD	c. 1,000 yrs	10	?
Livy, *History of Rome*	59 BC–17 AD	Partial (4th) Most (10th)	c. 400 yrs c. 1,000 yrs	1 19	? ?
Tacitus, *Annals*	100 AD	c. 1100 AD	c. 1,000 yrs	20	?

There are several things to note about these works.

1. In most cases there are at least a thousand years between the time these works were written and the earliest manuscript that we have for them. There are few instances of sources for materials dating from that ancient world that are older than the tenth century.

2. In most cases the number of copies in existence number less than two dozen.

3. With the exception of the *Iliad*, there are so few manuscripts that it is difficult to assess their accuracy.

In contrast to the above we can compare the manuscripts from the New and Old Testaments.

Author/Book	Written	Earliest Copy	Time Gap	# of Copies	Accuracy
New Testament	50-100 AD	c. 114 (Fragment) c. 200 (Books) c. 250 (Most of NT) c. 325 (NT)	c. 50 yrs c. 130 yrs c. 180 yrs c. 255 yrs	5,366	>99%

There are a mere 50 years between the date of the earliest fragment from the New Testament and the date it was written, and only approximately 250 years between its writing and the compilation of manuscripts for the entire New Testament. There are also many more copies of manuscripts, over 5,000, and more being found almost every year. The accuracy among these manuscripts is also over 99%.

You will often hear today that there are hundreds of thousands of errors in the New Testament manuscripts. This comes down to how one defines an error. Every stray mark on a manuscript, every misspelling, every variant is counted as an error. It counts not just as an error on one manuscript, but on every manuscript on which it occurs. For example, if there is a misspelling of one word in one verse, and that error appears on 1,999 other manuscripts, it is not just counted as one error but 2,000 errors. In effect, the Bible is penalized for having so many manuscripts available.

In regards to these errors, the noted Biblical scholar Philip Schaff said the following. "Only about 400 of the 100,000 or 150,000 variations materially affect the sense. Of these, again, not more than about fifty are really important for some reason or other; and even of these fifty not one affects an article of faith or a precept of duty which is not abundantly sustained by other and undoubted passages, or by the whole tenor of Scripture teaching."[34]

As already alluded to, this is very different from the number of variant readings occurring within Islam's documents. The same level of scrutiny has yet to be applied to these documents as has been applied to the Bible.

There are three additional items that need to be pointed out about these manuscripts. First, the canonization of the New Testament occurred in the fourth century, so it makes sense that we would have manuscripts from at least that period onward. Second, even if every manuscript disappeared today, the entire New Testament—with the exception of eleven verses—could be reconstructed entirely from the writings of the early church fathers. This is amazing. Third, it is quite likely we would have older manuscripts yet today, but the ancient library of Caesarea was destroyed by Islam in 638 and its contents lost.

All the above apply to the New Testament, but what about the Old Testament? Until the twentieth century, the earliest manuscripts dated to about the ninth century. But beginning in the 1940s, the Dead Sea Scrolls were found in Qumran. Portions of all Old Testament books were found, with the exception of Ruth. Entire texts, and in some cases multiple texts, were found for some books such as Isaiah.

These texts date from the first or second century BC. They confirm the contents of the Biblical Old Testament, and also confirm that the Old Testament passages within the New Testament come from the Greek Septuagint translation. In addition, many of the people, places, and events occurring within the Old Testament have been confirmed by archeology.

While Islam says that the Bible has been corrupted, that simply is not the case. We can trace the contents of today's translations to these manuscripts. So if a current day translation is doubted, we have available to us interlineal Bibles written in both Hebrew and Greek to use as reference. Finally, there are three sets of passages within the Qur'an that are relevant to both the Bible and Torah. The passages come from Pickthall's translation of the meaning of the Qur'an. The references are to sura and verse. We will come back to this in Chapter 4, but relevant verses from the Qur'an include the following:

First, the truth comes from God.

> Say: We believe in Allah and that which is revealed unto Us and that which was revealed unto Abraham, and Ishmael and Isaac, and Jacob, and the tribes, and that which Moses and Jesus received, and that which the Prophets received from their Lord. We make no distinction between any of them, and unto Him we have surrendered. (S2.136)

Second, scripture and the Torah come from God and are the truth.

> Lo! We did reveal the Torah, wherein is guidance and a light, by which the Prophets who surrendered (unto Allah) judged the Jews, and the rabbis and the priests (judged) by such of Allah's Scripture as they were bidden to observe, and thereunto were they witnesses. So fear not mankind, but fear Me. And barter not My revelations for little gain. Who judges not by that which Allah has revealed: such are disbelievers.
>
> And we prescribed for them therein: a life for a life, and eye for an eye, a nose for a nose, and ear for an ear, a tooth for a tooth, and for wounds retaliation. But who forgoes it (in the way of charity) it shall be expiation for him. Who judges not by that which Allah has revealed: such are wrongdoers.
>
> And We caused Jesus son of Mary to follow in their footsteps, confirming that which was (revealed) before him, and We bestowed on him the Gospel wherein is guidance and a light, confirming that which was (revealed) before it in the Torah a guidance and an admonition unto those who ward off (evil). (S5.44-46)

If Muhammad doubts the revelations he is receiving, he is to ask those who received God's revelations before him.

> And if you (Muhammad) are in doubt concerning that which We reveal unto you, then question those who read the Scripture (that was) before you. Verily the Truth from your Lord has come unto you. So be not you of the waverers. (S 10.94)

These passages place Islam in an inconsistency from which there is no escape. For Muhammad to be a Prophet, all of his revelations must be true. All parts of the Old and New Testament date to at least the early part of the fourth century, almost three hundred years before the first revelation in the Qur'an. Therefore, the entirety of the Bible and Torah must be accepted by Islam as truth and are not corrupted. However, it is not surprising that this conclusion would have been reached. As we saw in the last chapter, most of the "Christian" borrowings within Islam came from either gnostic or heretical sources.

We will now turn to the development of Islam's doctrines.

Chapter 3

Islam's Doctrines

This chapter will look at Muhammad's life and teachings. The discussion won't cover all Islam's tenets or their development, but it will include the tenets relevant to some of Islam's core beliefs and how those changed over time. But first a little bit about the sources for this information. As Muhammad was born at a relatively recent time when compared to the founders of other major religions, one might think that there are relatively more works written about him, his life, and his teachings. However, that is not the case. Instead we only know about him from the Islamic sources mentioned in the previous chapter.

The contents for this chapter use two primary sources: (1) M. Pickthall's *The Meaning of the Glorious Qur'an*[1] and (2) A. Guillaume's translation of Ibn Ishaq's *Sirat Rasul Allah*.[2] It is important that another text such as the sirat be used in conjunction with the Qur'an in order to provide context for its verses. References for both sources in the remaining part of this book are indicated by either a sirat paragraph number (number only), or a Qur'an verse (numbers preceded by an "S").

It is a generally held belief among traditional Islamic followers that the Qur'an cannot be translated from Arabic into another language. This is problematic, as most of the world's Muslim population does not speak Arabic. Pickthall's original writing has been revised and updated by Islamic clergy, and is generally accepted by Muslims as providing an accurate literal translation of the Qur'an. Ibn Ishaq's sirat is one of the earliest and most comprehensive biographies of Muhammad's life. The version that we have today comes from copies of his work that were later edited by Ibn Hisham and Al-Tabari. Even though these works are Islamic sources, they are still quite revealing regarding Islam's basic tenets and their evolution, provided they are taken with an appropriate grain of salt. Even Ibn Ishaq used phrases such as "it is alleged" and "only God knows the truth" in describing some events within his biography.

Muhammad's Early Life

There is very little known about Muhammad's early life. He is thought to have been born about 570 AD within the Hashim clan of the Quraysh tribe. Muhammad's father was named "Abdullah" (meaning "servant of Allah" or "slave of Allah"), and he died before Muhammad was born. Muhammad lived the first few years of his life with his mother, Amina, and his grandfather. His mother died when he was six, and his grandfather died two years later. After the death of his grandfather, one of Muhammad's uncles named Abu Talib became his guardian. Abu Talib was apparently fond of Muhammad and took good care of him. The sirat says that Muhammad went on at least one caravan to Syria with his uncle, and that while he was in Syria he met a monk named Bahira. It is said that this monk identified Muhammad as being a prophet of his people, but no documentation exists for this claim outside of Islam.

Very little else is known about his youth until he married his first wife Khadija when he was about twenty-five years of age. She was the mother of all but one of Muhammad's children. Only his daughters lived to adulthood. Khadija was also a distant cousin of Muhammad, a not uncommon occurrence within the cultures of that period, and also one of the best born women of Mecca. She was apparently a very wealthy widow, and used to hire men for her caravans. She hired Muhammad to manage her caravan. It is said that Muhammad doubled the value of the property that she had entrusted to him. She proposed marriage to

Muhammad, and he accepted. During her lifetime, Muhammad had no other wives.

Islam's Development in Mecca

Muhammad received his first vision in 610 at about the age of forty. He had taken to withdrawing for extended periods of solitary contemplation during Ramadan, a practice performed by many Arabs during this period. The sirat says that the angel Gabriel came to him in a vision while he slept and demanded that Muhammad read some writing that was presented to him. Muhammad did not initially believe the vision, but instead thought he had either become a poet or was possessed. Both of those states were often viewed within his culture as indicating one was not in their right mind. He also thought initially that he had been visited by a demon. He sought to take his own life but was barred from doing so by the vision. His wife Khadija and her cousin Waraqa convinced Muhammad that his vision was real after he returned home.

Muhammad did not preach publicly for three years after this first vision. During that time about two dozen converted to Islam, most from Mecca's lower social classes. They initially prayed together in seclusion. The Quraysh did not "withdraw or turn against" Muhammad until he began to speak against their gods. Hostility grew between the people of Mecca and Muhammad and his followers. Muhammad's uncle, Abu Talib, protected him from harm, but Muhammad was subject to many insults.

Muhammad was offered money, honor, sovereignty, and the opportunity to be cured from his ghost by the Quraysh; all in an effort to heal the rift within the community. He refused. He was then asked to perform a miracle. He stated that was not his purpose.

The persecution of Muhammad's followers became so bad that about 83 men and their families migrated to Abyssinia, where they stayed for a period of time. The sirat says that Muhammad became very concerned about the divide between the people of Mecca. After a period of meditation, he received what are referred to as the Satanic verses. The three entities referred to in this revelation are the daughters of the pagan god Hubal.

> "By the star when it sets your comrade errs not and is not deceived, he speaks not from his own desire," and when he reached His words "Have you thought of al-Lat and al-Uzza and Manat the third, the other," Satan, when he was meditating upon it, and desiring to bring it (*sc.* reconciliation) to his people, put upon his tongue "these are the exalted Charaniq (exalted birds) whose intercession is approved."[3]

This revelation temporarily healed the rift between Muhammad and those who did not follow his teachings. It was at this time that his followers returned from Abyssinia. The above revelation was shortly abrogated by another that annulled what Satan had suggested. At this time the persecution of Muhammad's followers grew even more intense.

Sometime later Muhammad spoke of being taken on a night journey to Jerusalem while he slept.[4] From there he travelled through the seven heavens where he met Adam and many of the prophets, including Abraham, Moses, and Jesus. Muhammad related his experience to the people of Mecca, and it is said that many of them did not believe him. It is also said that some of his followers left Islam after hearing the story.

Two additional events occurred a short time later in about 619: both his wife Khadija and Abu Talib died in the same year. With both his closest support and protection gone, Muhammad began to offer his teachings to the people at fairs. In 621, a delegation came to Mecca from Yathrib (Medina) during its fair and learned Islam from Muhammad. They were from the Ansar clan. A larger group returned the following year and offered him protection. They wished to have him arbitrate the tribal feuds in Medina.

With his uncle Abu Talib gone, and his replacement by another uncle that was not as supportive, his clan's support became unpredictable. His followers began to emigrate from Mecca to Medina in about 622. It was after receiving the offer of assistance from the Medinan delegation that Muhammad received a revelation giving him permission to fight against those who wronged him and treated him badly.[5]

> The apostle had not been given permission to fight_or allowed to shed blood before the second Aqaba. He had simply been ordered to call men to God and to endure insult and forgive the ignorant...
>
> When Quraysh became insolent towards God and rejected His gracious purpose, accused His prophet of lying, and ill treated and exiled those who served Him and proclaimed His unity, believed in His prophet, and held fast to His religion, He gave permission to His apostle to fight and to protect himself against those who wronged them and treated them badly. (313)

Islam's Early Teachings

Up to this time the main tenets of Islam were as follows. Note the references for each item are representative and do not include all references for that item.

1. Worship Allah alone (S 72.18)

2. Pray towards Jerusalem[6]

3. Peace, to each their religion (S 109, S 43.88-9)

4. Care for the widows, orphans, and the needy (S 76.8-10)

5. Salvation by works (S 101.6-9)

6. There will be a day of judgment (S 37.19-26)

7. Muhammad was the last of God's prophets that began with Moses (150)

By this time, the five pillars of Islam were also being taught. These are the shahada (creed of belief), salat (prayer), zakat (alms), swam (fast during Ramadan), and the hajj (pilgrimage to Mecca). The unofficial sixth pillar of jihad had not yet been added. An approximate timeline that includes some significant events occurring during Muhammad's life is included as Appendix A.

Islam Moves to Medina

With the migration from Mecca, Islam's tenets began to change and become more oriented toward regulating life and relations. This section's focus will be on the additions and changes to the tenets outlined in the last section. Medina was home to three Jewish and eight Arab clans, including the Ansar who had pledged their loyalty to Muhammad. The Jewish clans were the Banu Qaynuqa, the Banu Nadir, and the Banu Qurayza, and each had formed alliances with the various Arab clans.

The Medina Constitution

One of Muhammad's first actions in Medina was to create an agreement referred to as the Constitution of Medina. Muslims point to this document as the world's first constitution. Below are some of its contents. Note that Medina is still referred to as Yathrib at this point.

> This is a document from Muhammad the prophet (governing the relations) between the believers and Muslims of Quraysh and Yathrib (Medina), and those who followed them and joined them and labored with them. They are one community (umma) to the exclusion of all men....

Believers shall not leave anyone destitute among them by not paying his redemption money or blood wit in kindness.

A believer shall not take as an ally the freedman of another Muslim against him. The God-fearing believers shall be against the rebellious of him who seeks to spread injustice, or sin or enmity, or corruption between believers; the hand of every man shall be against him even if he be a son of one of them. A believer shall not slay a believer for the sake of an unbeliever, nor shall he aid an unbeliever against a believer. God's protection is one, the least of them may give protection to a stranger on their behalf. Believers are friends one to the other to the exclusion of outsiders. To the Jew who follows us belong help and equality. He shall not be wronged nor shall his enemies be aided ... The believers must avenge the blood of one another shed in the way of God ... Whosoever is convicted of killing a believer without good reason shall be subject to retaliation unless the next of kin is satisfied (with blood-money)....

The Jews shall contribute to the cost of war so long as they are fighting alongside the believers. The Jews of the B.'Auf are one community with the believers (the Jews have their religion and the Muslims have theirs) ... The contracting parties are bound to help one another against any attack on Yathrib. If they are called to make peace and maintain it they must do so; and if they make a similar demand on the Muslims it must be carried out except in the case of a holy war. (341 – 344)

This document laid out the foundation for the following additions to Islam:

1. All Muslims are members of a single brotherhood (umma).

2. Distinctions are made between believers and non-believers in terms of their rights and obligations.

3. Believers are obliged to avenge the blood of another believer, and not to assist a non-believer against a believer.

4. The Jewish clans were to contribute to the costs of war and to fight alongside the believers, with one exception in the case of a holy war. These conditions laid the initial foundation for the later formation and treatment of the dhimmis (protected peoples). These conditions would change with subsequent revelations.

While the agreement was drawn up between Muhammad's followers and the Medinans, as noted above there were also provisions for the Jewish clans, even though they did not participate in the discussions or agree with the document's contents.

Relations with the Jews and the Hypocrites

Relations with the Medinan Jewish clans worsened, and they began to annoy Muhammad with questions of a religious nature. One of the rabbis is said to have converted to Islam and was denounced by the Jewish clans. The sirat asserts that this rabbi declared Muhammad's appearance as a prophet was foretold in the Torah (354). This has become a basis for claims by Muslims that Jews and Christians have altered their scriptures in order to discredit Muhammad. We looked at that charge in the previous chapter and will come back to it in the next. There also arose a defection of some of the early Muslim converts (the Hypocrites) who began to work with the Jewish clans against Muhammad (355–400). Sura 63 is devoted entirely to denouncing the hypocrites, and sura 2 also contains verses relevant to the events from this time.

During this period, Muhammad wrote a letter to the Jews of Khaybar, stating that he was the apostle of God and urging them to accept his teachings. Muhammad urged them to search their scriptures to see if they should believe him: "If you do not find that in your scripture then there is no compulsion on you" (376-7). The Jews responded in the only way they could and did not accept Muhammad as a prophet.

The Christian Delegation from Najran

A delegation of Christians came from Najran to discuss theology with Muhammad. Judging the beliefs associated within this group by the sirat, it is likely that they were gnostics. This conclusion is suggested by the fact that the story from the Gospel of Thomas where Jesus breathed into some clay birds is mentioned. This delegation arrived about the same time as the letter was sent to Khaybar and the disputes between the Jews and Muhammad noted above. Muhammad stated the delegation was in error and attempted to correct their belief. Some of these corrections included the following:

1. Your assertion that God had a son, your worship of the cross, and your eating of pork hold you back from submission [to God]. (403)

2. A revelation that Jesus himself would deny the doctrine of the trinity. "And when Allah says: O Jesus, son of Mary! Did you say unto mankind: Take me and my mother for two gods besides Allah? He says: Be glorified! It was not mine to utter that to which I had no right." (S5.116)

3. Jesus was not God as he could not do all that God did. "All that I withheld from Jesus and gave him no power over it. Have they not an example and a clear proof that if he were a God all that would be within his power." (406)

4. The creation of Jesus was no different from the creation of Adam. Jesus was not divine and was not crucified; it only appeared to them that he was slain. (409)

5. Christians had received these beliefs because they had strayed from what Jesus actually taught. (410)

6. Muhammad called for both Jews and Christians to become Muslims and accept his teachings, and the restoration of the original message of Jesus. (405 and 410)

7. Believers should not choose those outside your community as intimate friends. "They will spare no pains to corrupt you longing to ruin you." (388)

It was also at this time that the direction for prayer was changed from Jerusalem to Mecca (427). Muhammad began to criticize the Jews for not accepting his teachings.

Raid During Rajad

Initially Muhammad and his followers were supported by the Ansar, but this condition could not last. The cultivatable land was already in use and his followers did not have the wealth necessary to support themselves. Muhammad organized raids against caravans traveling to Mecca to collect booty and take captives to be held for ransom. These were unsuccessful at first but finally succeeded when a caravan was attacked during the month of Rajab. Historically this was a period when no fighting was to occur. The raiding party was faced with the choice of fighting during the last day of Rajab, or letting the caravan go another day which would allow it to reach the sanctuary of Mecca. It chose to attack during Rajab.

After the attack, Muhammad received the following revelation concerning the event: "They will ask you about the sacred month, and war in it. Say, war therein is a serious matter, but keeping people from the way of God and disbelieving in Him and in the sacred mosque and driving out His people therefrom is more serious with God" (S2.216-7 and 425). "If you have killed in the sacred month, they have kept you back from the way of God with their unbelief in Him" (425).

This event set several more precedents.

1. Muhammad was not only attacking during a month considered sacred when no bloodshed was to take place, but he was also attacking his own tribe. These raids, along with the conditions of the Medinan Constitution noted previously, set the stage for replacing the bonds of kinship with the bonds of belief.

2. Raiding and taking booty had been a part of nomadic life for a long time. The above revelation made these actions good and lawful as they helped Islam.

3. Expediency in the advance of Islam trumps morality. This point cannot be emphasized enough. While the call to morality within Islam exists, a higher priority is placed on actions which spread Islam. The ends justify whatever means are used, as long as the outcome is viewed as being good for Islam.

The Battle of Badr

A large caravan was returning to Mecca from Syria. Muhammad called for volunteers to raid it, and about 300 warriors set out from Medina. The Meccans learned of the plans and set out with a much larger force to intercept and destroy Muhammad. The caravan feared an attack and went straight to Mecca. Some of the Quraysh returned to Mecca when they learned the caravan was safe, but the rest rode on to meet Muhammad's party. They were routed by Muhammad at Badr. About 75 Meccans died and another 70 were taken prisoner. Muhammad took one fifth of the booty as had been prescribed for him in a previous revelation (425) and proclaimed that the angels had assisted the Muslims in the fight because of their piety.

From Ibn Ishaq's sirat, the prisoners were held for ransom. A quarrel broke out over how to distribute the booty. When Muhammad set out on the raid, it was with the belief that either the party or its property was to be his. As part of the sura that came down regarding the quarrel, it is recorded that "when God promised you that one of the parties should be yours, and you wanted to have the one that was not armed [i.e., booty and not war]... God wanted to establish the truth by His words, and to cut off the uttermost part of the unbelievers" (476-477). When Muslims met unbelievers in battle, they were not to turn their backs on them (477), and they were to fight them until there was no more persecution, and religion, all of it, shall belong to God (480). In other words, they were to fight until either their enemies surrendered and accepted Islam, or were dead. If an unbeliever ceased to fight they would be pardoned, but if they returned to fight the Muslims again that "the example of the ringleaders has been made," that is, those who had been killed at Badr (480).

Muhammad was reproached by Allah for taking booty, something that he said no prophet had been allowed before him. Muhammad received a revelation that "booty was made lawful to me as to no prophet before me; and I was given the power to intercede; five privileges accorded to no prophet before me. God said, 'It is not for any prophet (before thee) to take prisoners from his enemies until he has made slaughter in the earth.'... God desires the next world, i.e., their killing them to manifest the religion which He wishes to manifest and by which the next world may be attained" (484).

The hadith of Sahih Muslim presents this event somewhat differently. After the battle, an argument ensued over what to do with the prisoners. Abu Bakr stated they were kin and should be released after receiving a ransom. Umar disagreed and thought they should be executed. Muhammad initially sided with Abu Bakr. The next day Muhammad was distraught, saying he had received a revelation that Allah had sided with Umar and scolding Muhammad for taking booty instead. However, since Muhammad had previously been allowed to take booty, he was forgiven. Muhammad took revenge on several prisoners who had belittled him in Mecca, having them beheaded for their remarks against him.

Some of the precedents coming from this event include the following:

1. Piety will bring victory. I will reinforce you with a thousand angels, one behind the other. (477)

2. Beheading of enemies taken in war, and the taking of captives only after war has ceased.

    a. Now when you meet in battle those who disbelieve, then it is smiting of the necks until, when you have routed them, then making fast of bonds; and afterward either grace or ransom till the war lay down its burdens. (S47.4)

    b. The killing of nonbelievers serves to manifest the religion Allah wished to create and facilitates attaining paradise after death.

The Banu Qaynuqa

After the Battle of Badr, the scope and frequency of the raids increased. Muhammad received the following revelation: "And if you fear treachery from any folk, then throw back to them (their treaty) fairly" (S8.58). He assembled the Qaynuqa in the marketplace and addressed them saying, "O Jews, beware lest God bring upon you the vengeance that He brought upon Quraysh and become Muslims. You know that I am a prophet who has been sent–you will find that in your scriptures and God's covenant with you" (545).

The Qaynuqa could not comply, and Muhammad laid siege to them until they asked for an unconditional surrender. At that time some of the Muslims that had alliances with the Qaynuqa came forward to plead on their behalf. Muhammad wanted to put all of the men to death, but one of Muhammad's followers caught him by the collar of his robe until he agreed to deal with them mercifully. They were allowed to leave as long as they left all of their property behind. (545–546)

At this time, Muhammad received several new revelations, reinforcing that Muslims should have relationships only with other Muslims and that the hypocrites—those who had been followers of Muhamad, but had turned away from Islam—should be punished.

1. Take not Jews and Christians as friends. They are friends one of another. (S5.51)

2. In regard to the Jews specifically, "And because of their breaking their covenant, We have cursed them and made hard their hearts. They change words from their context and forget a part of that whereof they were admonished." (S5.13)

3. If the hypocrites, and those in whose hearts is a disease, and the alarmists in the city do not cease, We verily shall urge you on against them, then they will be your neighbours in it but a little while. Accursed, they will be seized wherever found and slain with a (fierce) slaughter. (S33.60-1)

The Assassination of Ka'b

The options for those nonbelievers living in Medina became conversion, expulsion, or death. Muhammad next turned his attention to several enemies. The first was a Jewish poet Ka'b bin Al-Ashtaf, who had composed verses lamenting the Quryashi loss at Badr and insulting Muslim women. Muhammad asked, "Who is willing to kill Ka'b bin Al-Ashtaf who has hurt Allah and his Apostle?" A Muslim volunteer offered to kill him, and Muhammad replied, 'Do so if you can.' After fasting for three days, the volunteer did not know if he could fulfill his commitment as he would have to tell lies to accomplish it. Muhammad answered, 'Say what you like, for you are free in the matter.'"

The volunteer went to Ka'b and complained about Muhammad, asking for Ka'b's help in breaking away from Islam. They struck a deal and the Muslim returned to Ka'b's house that night with others, where they proceeded to slay him and presented his head to Muhammad. The Jews were outraged, but Muhammad reminded them that the Muslims were provoked by Ka'b's actions. "There was no Jew in Medina that did not fear for his life." (550-553). After the murder of Ka'b, Muhammad issued the command to "Kill any Jew that falls into your power" (553).

Later on, Muhammad asked for someone to kill the poetess Asima and the aged poet Abu Afak. Asima was killed in her sleep after composing verses against Muhammad and Islam. Muhammad asked, "If there was no one to rid him of this daughter of Marwan." Muhammad praised her killer and assured him that "two goats won't butt their head about her." The next day her entire family converted to Islam (996). Abu Afak had composed verses against Muhammad and the way he attempted to control others' lives. Muhammad asked, "Who will deal with this rascal for me?" One of the Muslims went out and slayed the poet (995). In all it appears there were thirty to forty individuals whose deaths were either ordered or supported by Muhammad.

New precedents:

1. That which advances Islam is good, including lies, deceit, and murder.

2. Disparaging remarks against Muhammad or Islam are punishable by death.

The Battle of Uhud

The Meccans assembled an army of about 3,000 men to attack the Muslims. Muhammad led an army of about 1,000 and met them at the mountain of Uhud. Some of the Muslims had asked Muhammad if they needed the help of their Jewish allies. Muhammad replied they were not needed. The Muslims were routed at Uhud and Muhammad was wounded. Muhammad swore revenge when the body of an uncle was found that had been mutilated by a Meccan woman who was taking revenge for her family being killed at Badr.

In reaction to Muhammad's oath, the Muslims also swore revenge on the Meccans. Muhammad stated he would not take revenge on his uncle's killer if he became a Muslim. The person who killed his uncle converted to Islam. Muhammad asked him to recite how he had killed his uncle, which the convert did. After the story was completed,

Muhammad told him to never let the convert see him again if he wanted to live (555 – 606).

Precedents established by this event include the following:

1. Any attack calls for swift and fierce revenge.

2. Muslims will hesitate to kill other Muslims but not hesitate to kill nonbelievers.

3. Losses are due to not obeying Allah. Whatever occurs, the answer is always that more Islam is needed. (Also S3.130-2)

The Banu Nadir

After returning to Medina, Muhammad went to the Nadir to ask for their help in paying the blood wit for several men. They agreed, and the sirat says that some of the Nadir later plotted to kill Muhammad. Muhammad was warned of their intent and returned to Medina. He marched against the Nadir and ordered that their palm-trees should be cut down and burned. Some of their Arab allies told the Nadir to "Stand firm and protect yourselves, for we will not betray you" (653). However, their allies did not come to the aid of the Jews.

When some of the Nadir reminded the b. Auf of the alliance that the two tribes had, the Jews were told, "Hearts have changed, and Islam has wiped out the old covenants" (Tabari). The Nadir asked Muhammad to spare them by deporting them with only the property they could carry on their camels, except for their weapons. The Nadir's property became the personal property of Muhammad (652–56). This action later became the basis for *fay*, property administered by the state for the *umma's* benefit.

The Battle of the Ditch and the Banu Qurayza

The Meccans learned that they had not ended Muhammad's rule in Medina. They were approached by representatives of the last remaining

Jewish tribe within Medina, the Qurayza, to form an alliance against Muhammad. They also approached the Ghatafan tribe with the same offer. Both agreed to march against Muhammad in support of the Qurayza. Muhammad learned of the planned attack and ordered a trench be dug around the city of Medina.

The Muslims were pressed into service in order to dig the trench. During this time, Muhammad had visions of taking other territories beyond Arabia. The Quraysh and Ghatafan came against Medina with an army of more than 10,000, and they were met by a Muslim army of about 3,000. The attackers were unable to penetrate the defenses, but the Muslims were also unable to break the siege. At this time, Muhammad heard reports that the Qurayza were supporting the attackers. He sent spies to determine if the Jews had actually broken the agreement they had with Muhammad. The people he sent reported that the situation was worse than expected.

A Ghatafan convert to Islam approached Muhammad and offered to do whatever he ordered. The apostle said, "You are only one man among us, so go and awake distrust among the enemy to draw them off us if you can, for war is deceit" (681). The individual was able to create distrust among the allies and the Arabs withdrew when they could not penetrate Medina's defenses.

After the siege was broken, Muhammad turned his attention to the last Jewish tribe remaining in Medina. He besieged them for twenty five days, after which they agreed to submit to Muhammad's judgment on the condition that their fate be determined by a member of their allies. Muhammad selected a man from the clan, who gave the following decision: "Then I give judgement that the men should be killed, the property divided, and the women and children taken as captives" (689).

Muhammad had trenches dug in the marketplace. The men were brought out five or six at a time and beheaded. "There were 600 or 700 in all, though some put the figure as high as 800 or 900" (690). Torches were lit so that the executions could be completed in one day. Muhammad chose to comfort himself with Rayhana, whose husband and all male relatives had been executed just hours before. He offered to marry her, but she refused (693). A revelation was received sanctioning the Qurayza's punishment (S33.25-28).

Muhammad taught that nobility lay in forgiveness and that restraining anger and pardoning men was well-doing. However, he failed to practice this. Instead, he promoted the following:

1. Using any means necessary to advance Islam, including deception and lies.

2. Creating betrayal and then avenging the acts in order to further his aims.

3. Fighting those who did not accept Muhammad's teachings or his being a prophet, and any captives taken having no rights unless they converted to Islam.

4. Solidified the use of these methods through a revelation from Allah that Muslims should imitate him. "Surely in the Messenger of Allah you have a good example for him who looks unto Allah and the last Day, and remembers Allah much." (S33.21 and 695)

The Raid on the Al Mustaliq

Muhammad received word that a tribe related to the Quraysh, the Al-Mustaliq, was gathering to attack him at Medina. Muhammad went out and attacked them first, taking much of their property, women, and children. Muhammad's men wanted the women for themselves but also wanted to hold them for ransom as well. The Qur'an already allowed Muslims to have intercourse with women taken in battle if they were being taken as slaves, but they could not also claim ransom for them. Muhammad lifted the prohibition against having intercourse with women to be held for ransom: "It does not matter if you do not do it, for every soul that is to be born up to the Day of Resurrection will be born" (hadith of Al-Bukhari).

The following arises from this event:

1. When a woman is taken captive her previous marriage becomes annulled.

The Armistice with Mecca

Before the raid on Khaybar (see below), the Quraysh sent a representative to Muhammad to make peace. The Treaty of Hudaybiyya was to last for ten years, and it allowed the Muslims to go on pilgrimage to Mecca during Ramadan. An additional term of the agreement was that any Meccan going to Medina without their guardian's permission was to be returned to Mecca, while any Muslims going to Mecca were not. The Muslims were shocked and upset, but Muhammad received several revelations supporting his decision and the treaty.

Before too long, a woman named Umm Kulthum came from Mecca to become a Muslim. Her two brothers came to take her back, but Muhammad refused. He had received a revelation that Allah forbade returning her to Mecca. In reality, this event broke the treaty, but Muhammad decided to send his followers against the oasis of Khaybar shortly after this time. He went on the pilgrimage to Mecca in 629 with some of his followers. Shortly thereafter, he had the occasion he needed to attack Mecca. Some allies of Mecca skirmished with some of Muhammad's allies. He marched on Mecca in 630 with an army of about 10,000 men. The city surrendered on the condition that they would be spared.

The following is from the sirat:

> The apostle had instructed his commanders when they entered Mecca only to fight those who resisted them, except a small number who were to be killed even if they were found beneath the curtains of the Ka'ba. Among them was 'Abdullah b. Sa'd.... The reason he ordered him to be killed was that he had been a Muslim and used to write down revelation; then he apostatized and

returned to Quraysh.... Uthman b.'Affan hid him until
he brought him to the apostle after the situation in Mecca
was tranquil, and asked that he might be granted
immunity. They allege that the apostle remained silent
for a long time till finally he said yes. When Uthman had
left he said to his companions who were sitting around
him, "I kept silent so that one of you might get up and
strike off his head!" One of the Ansar said, "Then why
didn't you give me a sign, O apostle of God?" He
answered that a prophet does not kill by pointing" (818–
819).

The following principles evolved from these actions:

1. Treaties between Muslims and nonbelievers are to last no longer
    than ten years. It is no coincidence that the recent agreement
    with Iran only lasts ten years.

2. Treaties were only to be made with nonbelievers when Muslims
    were in the weaker position, allowing them to get strong enough
    to defeat their enemies. Again, this is no coincidence in
    connection with the recent treaty with Iran.

3. Apostates were to be killed. Also from the Qur'an, "They long
    that you should disbelieve even as they disbelieve, that you may
    be upon a level (with them). So choose not friends from them till
    they forsake their homes in the way of Allah; if they turn back
    (to enmity) then take them and kill them wherever you find
    them, and choose no friend nor helper from among them"
    (S4.89).

The Jews of Khaybar

Muhammad moved against Khaybar with about 1,600 men. None of
Khaybar's allies decided to come to their aid. The forts fell one at a time
until the Muslims took Khaybar itself. Many of the Nadir who had fled
Medina earlier had migrated to Khaybar. The Jewish leader who had

custody of the Nadir's treasure was brought to the apostle "who asked him about it. He denied that he knew where it was.... The apostle gave orders that the ruin was to be excavated and some of the treasure was found. When he asked him about the rest he refused to produce it, so the apostle gave orders to ... 'Torture him until you extract what he has,' so he kindled a fire with flint and steel on his chest until he was nearly dead. Then the apostle delivered him to Muhammad b. Maslama and struck off his head" (763-764).

The people of Khaybar were exiled. Some date farmers requested that they be allowed to remain on their farms and offered to give Muhammad half of their crops. He accepted on the condition that the Jews would only be allowed to stay as long as the Muslims allowed it. This marked the beginnings of what would become dhimmitude (protected people). Dhimmi means both "protected" and '"guilty." They were protected because they had received genuine revelations. They were guilty because they had corrupted those teachings and rejected Muhammad as a prophet.

A woman slave that Muhammad had taken at Khaybar poisoned some meat that was fed to him and his companions. He did not die, but one of his companions did. This occurred in about 628.

The Push for Arabia

After the fall of Mecca, Muhammad learned that the Thaqif tribe was gathering an army to attack him. This tribe was historically a rival of the Quraysh. Muhammad met them with an army of about 12,000. They met near Hunayn. Initially the Thaqif routed the Muslims, but the Muslims were able to turn the tide at great loss of life to both sides. Muhammad then took the town of Ta'if itself. He was lenient with the Thaqif and favored some of the recent converts in an attempt to cement relationships with them. Some of the Muslims complained to him about the booty distribution. "The prophet was angry and said, 'If justice is not to be found with me then where will you find it?'" (884).

Later Muhammad sent letters to the rulers of the great powers surrounding Arabia, calling them all to Islam. He made one final attack against the Byzantine at the city of Tabuk. At this time, the murders of the last two poets mentioned earlier occurred. In regards to going to war for Islam, Muhammad received the following revelation: "Those who believe in Allah and the Last Day ask no leave of you lest they should strive with their wealth and their lives. Allah is Aware of those who keep their duty unto Him. They alone ask leave of you who believe not in Allah and the Last Day, and whose hearts feel doubt, so in their doubt they waver" (S9.44-5).

Muhammad received a revelation that commanded the Muslims to fight against the Jews and Christians until they accepted Islam. Christians and Jews were viewed as guilty peoples as they had corrupted the teachings given to them and rejected Muhammad as a prophet. (S9.29) Because of their false beliefs and hoarding, they are not the equal of Muslims and will burn in Hell (S9.30–5). Also, due to their disbelief, they will not be guided by Allah.

> How shall Allah guide a people who disbelieved after their belief and (after) they bore witness that the Messenger is true and after clear proofs (of Allah's sovereignty) had come unto them? And Allah guides not wrong-doing folk. As for such, their reward is that on them rests the curse of Allah and of angels and of men combined. There will they abide. Their doom will not be lightened, neither will they be reprieved. (S3.86-8)

With Muhammad's victories, clans and tribes from all over Arabia came to pay tribute. The nonbelievers were to be offered the opportunity to convert to Islam. If they refused they were to pay tribute. If they refused that, the Muslims were to go to war against them (956).

Muhammad became ill a short time later and died in 632. His last words were said to have been, "Let not two religions be left in the Arabian peninsula" (1021). This is also reflected within the Qur'an by the following two verses. First, "Fight them so that there be no more seduction, and the religion is Allah's" (S2.193). Second, "Fight against such of those who have been given the Scripture as believe not in the Allah nor the Last Day, and forbid not that which Allah has forbidden by His Messenger, and follow not the religion of truth, until they pay the tribute readily, being brought low" (S9.29).

With the Medinan revelations, Islam changed from a religion of inclusion and sacrifice to an ideology based upon division, fear, and intimidation. Finally, below is a table containing the changes to Islam's tenets after the migration to Medina. What is most striking is that these changes all occurred in only ten years.

We will next look at some concepts derived from Islam's teachings.

Meccan tenets			Changes
• To each their religion		C	• Captives (pagans) given choice of conversion or death
		I	• Apostates killed
		K	• People of the Book to be offered chance for conversion
• Peace		B	• Unbelief cause of hatred & struggle
		D	• Beheading enemies in war
		G	• Don't hesitate to kill non-Muslims • Swift revenge for Muslim's death
		K	• Fight until only Islam remains
• Worship Allah alone			
• Pray – toward Jerusalem		B	• Pray toward Mecca
• Care for the widows, orphans, needy			
• There will be a day of judgement			

	Medinan Tenets		Changes
A	• Diff. between believers & non-believers (ties of religion)	H	• Captives have no rights
		K	• Dhimmitude formalized
		L	• Jews & Christians less than Muslims
A	• Hypocrites evil	E	• Hypocrites to be killed
B	• Christian doctrine in error	E	• Do not take Jews or Christians for friends • Jews under curse for changing doctrine

Medinan Tenets		Changes	
C	• That which advances Islam is good (expediency foremost)	E	• Break treaties if fear treachery
		H	• Advancing Islam by any means necessary is okay • Create betrayal is okay
D	• Piety brings victory • Killing manifests religion that Allah wishes to manifest	G	• Losses due to lack of obedience (more Islam is always the answer)
F	• Slander & provocation punishable by death		
G	• Islam replaces what was before • Non-Muslim property becomes Muslim property	H	• Marriages nullified
H	• Muhammad to be imitated (Sunna)		
I	• Treaties to last maximum of 10 years • Made only when in weak position		
J	• Wealth managed for umma (fay) basis for Islamic charity		

Table Key to chapter sections:

A - Medina Constitution
B - Najran Delegation and Letter to Khaybar
C - Ramadan Raid
D - Battle of Badr
E - Banu Qaynuqa
F - Assassinations
G - Battle of Uhud and the Banu Nadir
H - Battle of the Trench and Raid on Al-Mustaliq
I - The treaty with Mecca
J - Khaybar Raid
K - The Final Push

Chapter 4

Islamic Concepts

Much of this chapter's content comes from *Do You Want to Be Free.*[1] Its focus was the relationship between faith and governance, and the same discussion is equally relevant here. The next chapter then looks at some differences between Judeo-Christian beliefs and Islamic tenets, and some inconsistencies within Islamic tenets themselves. More information on this chapter's topics can be found in the above resource.

Who Is God?

This chapter will look at some of the key passages from the Qur'an and sirat which address the questions within Islam about who is our Creator, what is man, can they have a relationship, and if so, what would that relationship look like? We will also look at what the Creator expects of man, His laws, etc. In this section we will refer to the Creator as Allah. As we will see, the God of Christianity and Judaism cannot be Allah.

Understanding The One and The Many

The concept of Allah within Islam is grounded in neoplatonic thought, as alluded to earlier by Goldziher. The writings of Plotinus had a significant influence on Islam. To understand these thoughts, one must first understand what is meant by the terms "the one" and "the many" appearing in platonic philosophy. Don't worry. We won't go very deep into the subject, but you do need a basic knowledge to help understand this chapter's contents.

When discussing Platonic philosophy, there are two concepts that must be understood. The first concerns what is meant by the ambiguous terms "the one" and "the many." The second is the theological concepts of divine immanence versus transcendence. Within early Christian writings that leveraged platonic thought, these philosophical and theological issues were mixed together. The following is summarized from Chapter 1 of E. F. Osborn's book *The Philosophy of Clement of Alexandria.*[2]

The philosophical concept of the meaning of the one comes from Plato's *Parmenides*. What do we mean when we say that a thing "is one"? Is it a simple unity from which nothing can be made from the things that are left, or is it a complex whole of many parts? In the dialogue, a simple unity can only be described in negative terms, in terms of what it is not. The hypothesis for a simple unity is "if the One is to be One, it will neither be a whole nor have parts" (137d).[3] Further properties of a simple unity are the following:

1. It will "have neither a beginning, nor an end nor a middle." (137d)

2. "It is also without shape; for it partakes of neither round nor straight." (137e)

3. It is "not anywhere, if it is neither in itself nor in another." (138a)

4. It is "neither at rest nor in motion." (139b)

5. It "can't be either different from another or the same as itself." (139e)

6. It is "neither like nor unlike another or itself." (140b)

7. It is "neither equal nor unequal to itself or another." (140b)

8. "It has no share of time, nor is it *in* any time." (141d)

9. "Therefore it is not named or spoken of, nor is it the object of opinion or knowledge, nor does anything that is perceive it." (142)

A complex unity, on the other hand, can be described in positive terms, that is, in terms of what it is. The hypothesis for a complex unity is "If One is ... the one that is, must it not itself, since it is one being, be a whole, and the parts of this whole be oneness and being" (142d). A complex unity therefore has both unity and being. An example of a complex unity would be you, the reader. You have many parts, but you are a single human being. Further properties of a complex unity are the following:

1. It is "unlimited in multitude." (144)

2. It is "both one and many, a whole and parts, and limited and unlimited in multitude." (145)

3. It has "a beginning, and end, and a middle." (145 b)

4. "It would partake of some shape ... either straight or round, or some shape mixed from both." (145b)

5. "Insofar as it is a whole, is in another; but insofar as it is all parts, it is in itself." (145e)

6. "Since it is itself always both in itself and in a different thing, must always be both in motion and at rest." (146)

7. It "will be like and unlike the others—insofar as it is different, like, and insofar as it is the same, unlike." (148c)

8. It "both touches and does not touch the others and itself." (149d)

9. It "is both equal to, and greater and less than, itself and the others." (151b)

10. It "will be equal to, and more and fewer than, itself and the others in number." (151e)

11. It has a "past, present, and future ... there would be knowledge and opinion and perception of it." (155d)

These two hypotheses "present us with a pattern of two unities—a unity which is simple, bare, one and nothing but one, and a unity which is infinitely complex, one and many."[4]

The second issue is the one of transcendence versus immanence. Is God transcendent, by which is meant remote from the world and beyond the reach of human knowledge? Or is He immanent: is He present in, and maybe even identical with, the world? In Middle Platonism, to which Clement and the other early church fathers were responding, the two issues were blended, with single unity being transcendent and complex unity being immanent. However, the blending of these two concepts varied according to each philosopher.

This allowed for a very different view of God than the one that developed within Islam. Plotinus and his student Porphyry lived during the third century. Plotinus believed that there must be a single simple unity above each and every complex unity; there must be a "one" above each and every instance of "the many." Applying this thought to the maker of the universe meant that there must be a single simple transcendent unity above everything else, and this unity was the cause of existence for everything that has ever been created. This single simple unity left no room for the blending of one/many and transcendence/immanence that appears in the early Christian writings. More about this in Chapter 5. This difference lays out the basic idea and is the driver for the following description of Allah's characteristics.

Allah's Characteristics

In their book *Answering Islam,* Geisler and Saleeb develop the following list of characteristics to describe Allah: absolutely one, absolutely sovereign, absolute justice, absolute mercy, absolute will, and absolutely unknowable.[5] We will use this same list to classify passages describing Allah from Pickthall's book on the meaning of the Qur'an[6] and add an additional characteristic of having absolute knowledge. All references are to the sura and verses within the Qur'an. Islamic tradition has it that the words from the Qur'an are generally Allah's being related through the angel Gabriel to Muhammad.

Absolutely One

> Say: He is Allah, the One!
> Allah, the eternally Besought of all!
> He begets not nor was begotten,
> And there is none comparable to Him. (S112)

> Your God is One God; There is no god save Him, the Beneficent, the Merciful. (S2:163)

> Allah has said: Choose not two gods. There is only One God. So of Me, Me only, be in awe. (S16:51)

> Lo! Allah pardons not that partners should be ascribed unto Him. He pardons all save that to whom He will. Who ascribes partners unto Allah has wandered far astray. (S4:116)

Absolutely Sovereign

> The Originator of the heavens and the earth! When He decrees a thing, He says unto it only; Be! And it is. (S2:117)

> Allah! There is no God save Him, the Alive, the Eternal. Neither slumber nor sleep overtakes Him. Unto Him belongs whatever is in the heavens and whatever is in the earth. Who is he that intercedes with Him save by His leave? He knows that which is in front of them and that which is behind them, while they encompass nothing of His knowledge save what He will. His chair includes the

heavens and the earth, and He is never weary of preserving them. He is the Sublime, the Tremendous. (S2:255)

Unto Allah (belongs) whatsoever is in the heavens and whatsoever is in the earth; and whether you make known what is in your minds or hide it, Allah will bring you to account for it. He will forgive whom He will and He will punish whom He will. Allah is Able to do all things. (S2:284)

He it is Who created the heavens and the earth in truth. On that day when He says: Be! It is. His word is the truth, and His will be the Sovereignty on the day when the trumpet is blown. Knower of the invisible and the visible, He is the Wise, the Aware. (S6:73)

He is Allah, than whom there is no other God, the Sovereign Lord, the Holy One, the Peace, the Keeper of Faith, the Overwhelming, the Majestic, the Compeller, the Superb. Glorified be Allah from all that they ascribe as partner (unto Him). (S59:23)

All that is in the heavens and all that is in the earth glorifies Allah; unto Him belongs sovereignty and unto Him belongs praise, and He is Able to do all things.

He it is Who created you, some of you are disbelievers and some of you are believers, and Allah is Seer of what you do. (S64:1-2)

Absolute Will

And if We had so willed, We could have given every soul its guidance, but the word from Me concerning evildoers took effect: that I will fill Hell with the jinn and mankind together. (S32:13)

As for the disbelievers, whether you warn them or you warn them not it is all one for them; they believe not. Allah has sealed their hearing and their hearts, and on their eyes there is a covering. Theirs will be an awful doom. (S2:6-7)

For him are angels ranged before him and behind him who guard him by Allah's command. Lo! Allah changes not the condition of a folk until they (first) change that which is in their hearts; and if Allah wills misfortune for a folk there is none that can repel it, nor have they a defender beside Him. (S13:11)

Absolutely Unknowable

Vision comprehends Him not, but He comprehends (all) vision. He is the Subtle, the Aware. (S6:103)

They ask you of the (destined) Hour, when will it come to port? Say: Knowledge thereof is with my Lord only. He alone will manifest it at its proper time. It is heavy in the heavens and the earth. It comes not to you save unawares. They question you as if you could be well informed thereof. Say: Knowledge thereof is with Allah only, but most of mankind know not. (S7:187)

If Allah afflicts you with some hurt, there is none who can remove it save Him; and if He desires good for you, there is none who can repel His bounty. He strikes with it whom He will of His bondmen. He is the Forgiving, the Merciful. (S10:107)

Had it been possible for a Qur'an to cause the mountains to move, or the earth to be torn asunder, or the dead to speak, (this Qur'an would have done so). Nay, but Allah's is the whole command. Do not those who believe know that, had Allah willed, He could have guided all

mankind? As for those who disbelieve, disaster ceases
not to strike them because of what they do, or it dwells
near their home until the threat of Allah come to pass.
Lo! Allah fails not to keep the appointed time. (S13:31)

Absolute Justice

Wait they for nothing else then that Allah should come
unto them in the shadows of the clouds with the angels?
Then the case would be already judged. All cases go
back to Allah (for judgment). (S2:210)

And your Lord has said: Pray unto me and I will hear
your prayer. Lo! Those who scorn My worship, they will
enter Hell, disgraced. (S43:60)

This is the Day of Decision. We have brought you and
the men of old together.
If now you have a wit, outwit Me. (S77:38-39)

Again, what will convey unto you what the Day of
Judgment is!
A day on which no soul has power at all for any (other)
soul. The (absolute) command on that day is Allah's.
(S82:18-19)

Absolute Mercy

Say (O Muhammad, to mankind): If you love Allah,
follow me; Allah will love you and forgive you your sins.
Allah is Forgiving, Merciful.

Say; Obey Allah and the Messenger. But if they turn
away, Lo! Allah loves not the disbelievers (in His
guidance). (S3:31-32)

Unto Allah belongs whatsoever is in the heavens and
whatsoever is in the earth. He forgives whom He will,

and punishes whom He will. Allah is Forgiving, Merciful. (S3:129)

Say: Unto whom belongs whatsoever is in the heavens and the earth? Say: Unto Allah. He has prescribed for Himself mercy, that He may bring you all together to a Day whereof there is no doubt. Those who ruin their own souls will not believe. (S6:12)

And ordain for us in this world that which is good, and unto You. He said: I smite with My punishment whom I will, and My mercy embraces all things, therefore I shall ordain It for those who ward off (evil) and pay the poor due, and those who believe Our revelations; (S7:156)

Absolute Knowledge

Say (unto them): Would you teach Allah your religion, when Allah knows all that is in the heavens and all that is in the earth, and Allah is Aware of all things? (S49:16)

On the day when Allah will raise them all together and inform them of what they did. Allah has kept account of it while they forgot it. And Allah is Witness over all things.

Have you not seen that Allah knows all that is in the heavens and all that is in the earth? There is no secret conference of three but He is their fourth, nor of five but He is their sixth, nor of less than that or more but He is with them wheresoever they may be and afterward, on the Day of Resurrection. He will inform them of what they did Lo! Allah is Knower of all things. (S58:6-7)

Lo! Your Lord is best aware of him who strays from his way, and He is best aware of those who walk aright. (S68:7)

Plotinus's Thoughts Applied to Allah

Neo-Platonic philosophy was firmly in place during the Middle Ages. Indeed, Augustine wrote extensively against the writings of Plotinus and his student Porphyry. Hellenistic philosophy has already been noted as having a strong influence on Islam's development. Islamic monotheism is rooted in Neo-Platonism. Allah is an absolute simple unity, so absolute it leaves no room for distinctions as provided by Plato, Clement, or Augustine. Allah is transcendent in nature and pure will. Therefore, He cannot be known by man. As Allah is pure will, He is also extrinsic—outside of nature and the natural order. He can therefore only be known from His actions. While the names given to Him within Islam are what he causes, they are not a part of His nature. Indeed, with this concept, Allah is the only one capable of causing anything, and therefore must be the cause of everything. Finally, Allah has absolute knowledge of all things, which is consistent with being the cause of all things.

This logic can also be summarized as follows.

> Allah is absolutely One, He is only absolute will.
> As Allah is only absolute will, He has no Being.
> As Allah has no Being, He has no essence (nature).
> As Allah has no essence, He has no essential attributes.
> As Allah has no essential attributes, any attempts to depict Him are blasphemy.

As Allah has no being, essence, or nature, the real question becomes not "Who is Allah?" but instead "What is Allah?"

Problems with Plotinus's Ideas

Plotinus puts forth three primary hypostases: the One, the Intellect, and the Soul, in that order. The One is a simple transcendent unity, while the Intellect and Soul are complex unities. This One is above speech, above intellect, and above consciousness, but it gives all of that, and more, to us. But in the words of St. Thomas, "How can one give what it has not got?" Plotinus' explanation is that the One is an "infinitely overwhelming power." This approach does not solve the problem of how a simple unity can produce many things which it does not possess. The result is a mysticism that Plotinus expressed as follows: "This is what one must do if one is going to philosophize about the One ... one must become Intellect and entrust one's soul to and set it firmly under Intellect, that it may be awake to receive what that sees, and may by this Intellect behold the One."[7]

In comparing Clement and the Christian writer Philo with Plotinus, E. F. Osborn writes the following:

> Despite the clarity and penetration of Plotinus's account, there appear to be certain inconsistencies. Perception, life, and consciousness are attributed to the One. It is the power of all things and identical with the Good. These are an indication of a readiness to talk about the One which is not consistent with its ineffability... The inevitable result is that his successors postulate some still more mysterious principle behind the Monad.
>
> When we turn to Plotinus's account of the One as first cause and producer of all things, we find again an acute awareness of the problems involved. The One is above speech, thought, and sensation, yet it gives these things to us. How can the one give them to us if it does not have them? How can it have them and yet be simple?... Plotinus then gives us an explanation in terms of power. The One is an infinitely great power. It must have produced everything because nothing else has the power to do this and because what produces must be simpler than the thing it produces. Plotinus is not as satisfied with this explanation when he has finished as he was when he began.... To say that the One is a great power, is the Good, or is an overflowing perfection, to place a One-many as a second first principle, does not explain the

> puzzle.... It is disappointing that despite a clear statement of the problem Plotinus really does imagine that he shows how the many proceed from the One.
>
> From this comparison of Clement, Philo, and Plotinus it would appear that in Clement's treatment of the problems arising from the ineffability and creative activity of the One the most consistent account given. Clement is more ready to accept the consequences of the ineffability of the one and the inexplicability of the method of creation. It is possible that Clement was less inclined to put forward bad solutions of philosophical problems because the existence of the problem was less painful to him than it was to Philo and Plotinus.[8]

Clement found his solution in both the need for faith and reason, instead of reason alone. We will talk more about Clement's view of the one and many in Chapter 5 before discussing some differences between Christianity and Islam.

Allah's Nature

Islam's construct of what Allah is has several consequences, especially in light of the Qur'an's contents. These include the nature of the Qur'an itself, abrogation, truth, good and evil, and hope. We will look at each of these topics before continuing with creation. The questions raised in this section will be discussed again in the next chapter.

The Qur'an

> And (it is) a Qur'an that We have divided, that you may recite it unto mankind at intervals, and We have revealed it by (successive) revelation. (S17:106)
>
> Lo! We have appointed it a Qur'an in Arabic that you may understand. And lo! In the Source of Decrees, which We possess, it is indeed sublime, decisive. (S43:3-4)

That (this) is indeed a noble Qur'an
In a Book preserved
Which none touches save the purified
A revelation from the Lord of the Worlds. (S56:77-80)

Nay, but it is a glorious Qur'an
On a guarded tablet. (S85:21-22)

Tradition has it that the Mother of the Book is Allah's eternal word. It is Allah, but separate from Him. "The great Sunni authority, Abu Hanifa, expressed the orthodox belief that 'the Qur'an is the word of God, and is His inspired word and revelation. It is a necessary attribute of God. It is not God, but still is inseparable from God.' Of course, 'It is written in a volume, it is read in a language ... but God's word is uncreated.'"[9] This is the same kind of distinction made by Clement to distinguish the Father and the Logos. However, the Neo-Platonic concept of Allah leaves no room for such a distinction, as discussed in the previous section. More about this in Chapter 5.

Abrogation

Such of Our revelations as We abrogate or cause to be forgotten, we bring (in place) one better or the like. Do not you know that Allah is Able to do all things? (S2:106)

Over time some of the revelations changed. When questioned by his followers, Muhammad replied with the verse above. As such earlier verses within the Qur'an may be abrogated by later verses. The implication is that while Allah has absolute knowledge, His will can change over time. Why would this be if He has absolute knowledge?

Truth

Say: We believe in Allah and that which is revealed unto Us and that which was revealed unto Abraham, and Ishmael and Isaac, and Jacob, and the tribes, and that

which Moses and Jesus received, and that which the
Prophets received from their Lord. We make no
distinction between any of them, and unto Him we have
surrendered. (S2:136)

And unto you have We revealed the Scripture with the
truth, confirming whatever Scripture was before it, and a
watcher over it. So judge between them by that which
Allah has revealed, and follow not their desires away
from the truth which has come unto you. For each We
have appointed a divine law and a traced out way. Had
Allah willed He could have made you one community.
But that He may try you by that which He has given you
(he has made you as you are). So vie one with another in
good works. Unto Allah you will all return, and He will
then inform you of that wherein you differ. (S5:48)

We send not down the angels save with the Truth, and in
that case (the disbelievers) would not be tolerated.
Lo! We even We, reveal the Reminder, and lo! We surely
are its Guardian.
We surely sent (messengers) before you among the
factions of the men of old. (S15:8-10)

Truth comes from Allah. The Bible and Torah also came from Allah and
are therefore truth.

Lo! We did reveal the Torah, wherein is guidance and a
light, by which the Prophets who surrendered (unto
Allah) judged the Jews, and the rabbis and the priests
(judged) by such of Allah's Scripture as they were
bidden to observe, and thereunto were they witnesses. So
fear not mankind, but fear Me. And barter not My
revelations for a little gain. Who judges not by that which
Allah has revealed: such are disbelievers.

And we prescribed for them therein: a life for a life, and eye for an eye, a nose for a nose, and ear for an ear, a tooth for a tooth, and for wounds retaliation. But who forgoes it (in the way of charity) it shall be expiation for him. Who judges not by that which Allah has revealed: such are wrongdoers.

And We caused Jesus son of Mary to follow in their footsteps, confirming that which was (revealed) before him, and We bestowed on him the Gospel wherein is guidance and a light, confirming that which was (revealed) before it in the Torah a guidance and an admonition unto those who ward off (evil).

Let the People of the Gospel judge by that which Allah has revealed therein. Who judges not by that which Allah has revealed; such are evildoers.

And unto you have We revealed the Scripture with the truth, confirming whatever Scripture was before it, and a watcher over it. So judge between them by that which Allah has revealed, and follow not their desires away from the truth which has come unto you. For each We have appointed a divine law and a traced out way. Had Allah willed He could have made you one community. But that He may try you by that which He has given you (He has made you as you are). So vie one with another in good works. Unto Allah you will all return, and He will then inform you of that wherein you differ.

So judge between them by that which Allah has revealed, and follow not their desires, but beware of them lest they seduce you from some part of that which Allah has revealed unto you. And if they turn away, then know that Allah's will is to smite them for some sin of theirs. Lo! Many of mankind are evildoers. (S5:44-49)

> Say: O People of the Scripture! You have nothing (of
> guidance) till you observe the Torah and the Gospel and
> that which was revealed unto you from your Lord. That
> which is revealed unto you (Muhammad) from your Lord
> is certain to increase the contumacy and disbelief of
> many of them. But grieve not for the disbelieving folk.
> (S5:68)

The Gospel confirms that which was revealed in the Torah. However, truth is not changeless as Allah's will can change through abrogation. The result is that truth is no longer a one and many as described by Clement as some truths cease to be and other new ones are created at given points in time, even though Allah has absolute knowledge.

A further implication is that Allah must not care for all men. In the words of Clement, "For either the Lord does not care for all men; and this is the case either because He is unable (which is not to be thought, for it would be a proof of weakness), or because he is unwilling, which is not the attribute of a good being.... Or He does care for all."[10] This position has implications for the view of good and evil and the virtue of hope as noted below.

<u>Good and Evil</u>

> And (remember) when your Lord said unto the angels:
> Lo! I am creating a mortal out of potter's clay of black
> mud altered.
> So, when I have made him and have breathed into him of
> My spirit, do you fall down, prostrating yourselves unto
> him.
> So the angles fell prostrate, all of them together
> Save Iblis. He refused to be among the prostrate.
> He said: O Iblis! What ails you that you are not among
> the prostrate?
> He said: I am not going to prostrate myself unto a mortal
> whom You have created out of potter's clay of black mud
> altered.

He said: Then go you forth from hence, for surely you
are outcast.
And lo! The curse shall be upon you till the Day of
Judgment.
He said: My Lord! Reprieve me till the day when they
are raised.
He said: Then lo! You are reprieved
Till an appointed time.
He said: My Lord, Because You have sent me astray, I
verily shall adorn the path of error for them in the earth,
and shall mislead them every one. (S15:28-39)

Allah must be the source of both good and evil. As stated above, the
names of Allah are ascribed to what He causes, but are not a part of His
nature. Earlier verses state that Allah inflicts both hurt and good through
His will. He causes both good and evil. He could therefore just as easily
be called Evil as Good. Note that Iblis within the Qur'an is Satan.

Hope

If Allah willed, He could have brought them all together
to the guidance—So be not you among the foolish ones.
(S6:35)

And whomsoever it is Allah's will to guide, He expands
his bosom unto Islam, and whomsoever it is His will to
send astray, He makes his bosom close and narrow as if
he were engaged in sheer ascent to the sky. Thus Allah
lays ignominy upon those who believe not. (S 6:125)

But the Messenger and those who believe with him strive
with their wealth and their lives. Such are they for whom
are the good things. Such are they who are the successful.
(S 9:88)

(True) believers are those only who believe in Allah and
His Messenger and afterward doubt not, but strive with

> their wealth and their lives for the cause of Allah. Such
> are the sincere ones. (S 49:15)
>
> Establish prayer at the two ends of the day and in some
> watches of the night. Lo! Good deeds annul ill deeds.
> This is a reminder for the mindful. (S 11:114)

Allah's will alone is the guiding force as to whether one is saved or
condemned, and He does not desire to turn everyone to His path. For
those who are guided, it is their external acts alone (deeds) which lead
to their salvation. Obedience is all that is required.

Creation

> He it is Who created the heavens and the earth in six
> Days; then He mounted the Throne. He knows all that
> enters the earth and all that emerges therefrom and all
> that comes down from the sky and all that ascends
> therein; and He is with you wheresoever you may be.
> And Allah is Seer of what you do.
> His is the Sovereignty of the heavens and the earth and
> unto Allah (all) things are brought back.
>
> He causes the night to pass into the day, and He causes
> the day to pass into the night, and He is Knower of all
> that is in the breasts. (S57:4-6)
>
> Are you the harder to create, or is the heaven that He
> built?
> He raised the height thereof and ordered it;
> And He made dark the night thereof, and He brought
> forth the morn thereof.
> And after that He spread the earth,
> And produced therefrom the water thereof and the
> pasture thereof,

> And He made fast the mountains,
> A provision for you and for your cattle.
> But when the great disaster comes,
> The day when man will call to mind his (whole) endeavor,
> And Hell will stand forth visible to him who sees,
> Then, as for him who rebelled
> And preferred the life of the world,
> Lo! Hell will be his home. (S79:27-39)

Allah made all of creation and existed before creation.

Who is Man?

> Does man think that he is to be left aimless?
> Was he not a drop of fluid which gushed forth?
> Then he became a clot; then (Allah) shaped and fashioned
> And made of him a pair, the male and female
> Is not He (who does so) able to bring the dead to life? (S75:36-40)

Allah is the creator of all things. There are several different versions of how man was created within the Qur'an. One is mentioned above and another in the preceding section on good and evil. Man is a creation of Allah.

Predestination

> And every man's augury have We fastened to his own neck, and We shall bring forth for him on the Day of Resurrection a book which he will find open.
> (And it will be said unto him): Read your book. Your soul suffices as reckoner against you this day. (S17:13-14)

> And if We had so willed, We could have given every soul
> its guidance, but the word from Me concerning evildoers
> took effect: that I will fill Hell with the jinn and mankind
> together. (S32:13)

> No disaster befalls in the earth or in yourselves but it is
> in a Book before We bring it into being—Lo! That is
> easy for Allah. (S57:22)

Not only does Allah have absolute knowledge, but all outcomes have
been predetermined by His will. There is no free choice or free will.
There are also several passages related to free will within the Qur'an,
but the side advocating predestination won the argument a long time
ago. Today most Islamic scholars cite predestination as tradition.

Man's Purpose

As Allah is pure will, man cannot be created in His image. Allah is
beyond all nature, being and essence. Man's only purpose is to worship
Allah, but how can one worship what they cannot know?

> I created the jinn and humankind only that they might
> worship Me. (S51:56)

> There is none in the heavens and the earth but comes unto
> the Beneficent as a slave. (S19:93)

> The (faithful) slaves of the Beneficent are they who walk
> upon the earth modestly, and when the foolish ones
> address them answer: Peace. (S25:63)

> If Allah took mankind to task by that which they deserve,
> He would not leave a living creature on the surface of the
> earth; but He reprieves them until an appointed term, and
> when their term comes then surely (they will know that)
> Allah is ever Seer of His slaves. (S35:45)

> A spring wherefrom the slaves of Allah drink, making it
> gush forth abundantly,
> Because they perform the vow and fear a day whereof
> the evil is wide-spreading,
> And they feed with food the needy wretch, the orphan
> and the prisoner, for love of Him,
> (Saying): We feed you for the sake of Allah only. We
> wish for no reward nor thanks from you. (S76:6-9)

Man's sole purpose is to worship Allah. There is no sense of relationship between Allah and man as He is inscrutable, only strict obedience to His will is required. Good is not performed for the sake of another, but because it is commanded by Allah.

Submission

> If you punish them, lo! They are Your slaves, and if You
> forgive them (lo! They are Your slaves). Lo! You, only
> You are the Mighty, the Wise. (S5:118)

> He is the Omnipotent over His slaves, and He is the
> Wise, the Knower. (S6:18)

> He is the Omnipotent over His slaves. He sends
> guardians over you until, when death comes unto one of
> you. Our messengers complete their terms (through
> death), and they neglect not. (S6:61)

Man is his creator's slave. This idea comes from Plotinus. In Christian thought freedom (free will) is God's gift, necessary to fulfilling our purpose, and a positive attribute. Plotinus viewed freedom as the negation of a negative, as your primary state of being is to be coerced, a slave to another. Freedom in this view is what you have when you are not being coerced. This view carries over into Islam and is one reason why a western style republican form of government will never work in an Islamic society. These views are not only contradictory but incompatible.

No Need for the Cross

> And because of their saying: We slew the Messiah, Jesus
> son of Mary, Allah's messenger - they slew him not nor
> crucified him, but it appeared so unto them; and lo! those
> who disagree concerning it are in doubt thereof; they
> have no knowledge thereof save pursuit of a conjecture;
> they slew him not for certain. But Allah took him up unto
> Himself. Allah was ever Mighty, Wise. (S4.157-8)

> They indeed have disbelieved who say: Lo! Allah is the
> Messiah, son of Mary. Say: Who then can do aught
> against Allah, if He had willed to destroy the Messiah
> son of Mary, and his mother and everyone on earth?
> Allah's is the Sovereignty of the heavens and the earth
> and all that is between them. He createth what He will.
> And Allah is Able to do all things. (S5.17)

Orthodox Islam does not recognize original sin. Therefore there is no
reason for the cross. These beliefs come from gnostic heresy and include
(1) Jesus did not die on the cross, (2) another took his place, (3) Jesus
was taken directly into heaven, and (4) he will die after his second
coming in the end days.

Within Islam, there is no original sin as Adam and Eve's transgression
was forgiven after they repented. As there is no original sin, there is no
fallen nature. As there is no fallen nature, there is no need for salvation.
As there is no need for salvation, there is no need for a savior. The
concept of grace does not exist. Instead one is saved by doing good
works.

Salvation

> Lo! As for those who believe and do good works, for
> them is a reward enduring. (S41:8)

Save those who believe and do good works, for theirs is
a reward enduring. (S84:25)

Lo! Those who believe and do good works, theirs will be
Gardens underneath which rivers flow. That is the Great
Success. (S85:11)

Then, as for him whose scales are heavy (with good
works),
He will live a pleasant life.
But as for him whose scales are light,
The Bereft and Hungry One will be his mother (Hell).
(S101:6-9)

By the token of time (through the ages)
Lo! Man is in a state of loss,
Save those who believe and do good works, and exhort
one another to truth and exhort one another to endurance.
(S103)

Man's salvation is based upon the good works that he performs, but this
must be subject to Allah's will in the form of predestination. You cannot
have it both ways. That position is illogical.

Man's Nature

And Allah has favored some of you above others in
provision. Now those who are more favored will by no
means hand over their provision to those (slaves) whom
their right hands possess, so that they may be equal with
them in respect thereof. Is it then the grace of Allah that
they deny? (S16:71)

The believers are nothing else than brothers. Therefore
make peace between your brethren and observe your
duty to Allah that you may obtain mercy.

O you who believe! Let not a folk deride a folk who may
be better than they (are), nor let women (deride) women
who may be better than they are; neither defame one
another, nor insult one another by nicknames. Bad is the
name of lewdness after faith. And who turns not in
repentance, such are evildoers.

O you who believe! Shun much suspicion; for lo! Some
suspicion is evil. And spy not, neither backbite one
another. Would one of you love to eat the flesh of his
dead brother? You abhor that! And keep your duty (to
Allah). Lo! Allah is Relenting, Merciful. (S49:10-12)

O you who believe! When you contract a debt for a fixed
term, record it in writing. Let a scribe record it in writing
between you in (terms of) equity. No scribe should refuse
to write as Allah has taught him, so let him write and let
him who incurs the debt dictate, and let him observe his
duty to Allah his Lord, and diminish nothing thereof. But
if he who owes the debt is of low understanding, or weak,
or unable himself to dictate, then let the guardian of his
interests dictate in (terms of) equity. And call to witness,
from among your men, two witnesses. And if two men
be not (at hand) then a man and two women, of such as
you approve as witnesses, so that if the one errs (through
forgetfulness) the other will remind her. And the
witnesses must not refuse when they are summoned. Be
not averse to writing down (the contract) whether it be
small or great, with (record of) the term thereof. That is
more equitable in the sight of Allah and more sure for
testimony, and the best way of avoiding doubt between
you; save only in the case when it is actual merchandise
which you transfer among yourselves from hand to hand.
In that case it is no sin for you if you write it not. And
have witnesses when you sell one to another, and let no
harm be done to scribe or witness. If you do (harm to

them) lo! It is a sin in you. Observe your duty to Allah. Allah is teaching you. And Allah is Knower of all things. (S2:282)

Allah charges you concerning (the provision for) your children: to the male the equivalent of the portion of two females, and if there be women more than two, then theirs is two-thirds of the inheritance, and if there be one (only) then the half. And to his parents a sixth of the inheritance, if he has a son; and if he has no son and his parents are his heirs, then to his mother appertains the third; and if he has brothers then to his mother appertains the sixth, after any legacy he may have bequeathed, or debt (has been paid). Your parents or your children: you know not which of them is nearer unto you in usefulness. It is an injunction from Allah. Lo! Allah is Knower, Wise. (S4:11)

Men are in charge of women, because Allah has made the one of them to excel the other, and because they spend of their property (for the support of women). So good women are the obedient, guarding in secret that which Allah has guarded. As for those from whom you fear rebellion, admonish them and banish them to beds apart, and scourge them. Then if they obey you, seek not a way against them. Lo! Allah is ever High Exalted, Great. (S4:34)

Bear unto the hypocrites the tidings that for them there is a painful doom.

Those who choose disbelievers for their friends instead of believers! Do they look for power at their hands? Lo! All power appertains to Allah.

He has already revealed unto you in the Scripture that, when you hear the revelations of Allah rejected and derided, (you) sit not with them (who disbelieve and mock) until they engage in some other conversation. Lo! In that case (if you stayed) you would be like unto them. Lo! Allah will gather hypocrites and disbelievers, all together, into Hell. (S4:138-140)

O you who believe! Choose not disbelievers for (your) friends in place of believers. Would you give Allah a clear warrant against you?

Lo! The hypocrites (will be) in the lowest deep of the Fire, and you will find no helper for them. (S4:144-145)

Lo! Those who believe, and those who are Jews, and Sabaeans, and Christians—Whosoever believes in Allah and the Last Day and does right—there shall no fear come upon them neither shall they grieve. (S5:69)

O you who believe! Choose not your fathers nor your brothers for friends if they take pleasure in disbelief rather than faith. Whoever of you takes them for friends, such are wrongdoers. (S 9:23)

Lo! Allah defends those who believe. Lo! Allah loves not each treacherous ingrate. (S22:38)

All men are not created equal. Some Muslims are more favored by Allah. Muslim men are placed over Muslim women. Muslims are placed over other Peoples of the Book (Jews, Christians, and Zoroastrians). The Peoples of the Book are placed over those who have not received the Creator's revelations at all. This refers to everyone else.

Virtue

America's Founders believed that in order for a society to be successful, its people must be moral. This conclusion was arrived at based upon both the history and religious material they studied. For a people to be moral, they must be virtuous. Virtue is also necessary for us to fulfill our purpose of knowing our Creator. All virtues start with faith and end with acts of charity performed out of love.[11] So by acquiring virtue we not only fulfill His Law, but our purpose as well.

In regards to morality, the following revelation is found within the Qur'an: "Surely in the Messenger of Allah you have a good example for him who looks unto Allah and the last Day, and remembers Allah much" (S33:21). Many of the early Meccan revelations urged people to take care of the poor, the widows, and the orphans. In the later Medinan sura, we find the following:

1. In regards to following treaties which are entered into, "And if you fear treachery from any folk, then throw back to them (their treaty) fairly. Lo! Allah loves not the treacherous." (S8:58)

2. In keeping with no bloodshed during Rajad and not attacking one's own tribe, "Warfare is ordained for you, though it is hateful unto you, and it may happen that you hate a thing which is good for you, and it may happen that you love a thing which is bad for you. Allah knows, you know not. They question you (O Muhammad) with regard to warfare in the sacred month. Say: Warfare therein is a great (transgression), but to turn (men) from the way of Allah, and to disbelieve in Him and in the Sacred Mosque, and to expel its people from it, is a greater sin with Allah: for persecution is worse than slaughter. And they will not cease from fighting against you till they have made you renegades from your religion, if they can. And who becomes a renegade and dies in his disbelief; such are they whose works have fallen both in the world and the Hereafter. Such are rightful owners of the Fire: they will abide therein forever." (S2:216-217)

3. In a story within the Qur'an, Moses goes on a journey and finds one of Allah's slaves. Moses asks if he can accompany him. They first come to a boat where the slave of Allah

makes a hole in the hull. They continue their journey and next meet a lad, who is slain by the man Moses is accompanying. Finally, they come to a town and ask for food, but they are refused as guests. Before they leave the town they find a wall to the point of falling into ruin and the man accompanying Moses repairs the wall.

Moses questioned the man when they parted. The man responded,

This is the parting between you and me! I will announce unto you the interpretation of that you could not bear with patience. As for the ship, it belonged to some poor people working on the water, and I wished to mar it, for there was a king behind them who is taking every ship by force. And as for the lad, his parents were believers and We feared lest he should oppress them by rebellion and disbelief. And We intended that their Lord should change him for them for one better in purity and nearer to mercy. And as for the wall, it belonged to two orphan boys in the city, and there was beneath it a treasure belonging to them and their father had been righteous, and your Lord intended that they should come to their full strength and should bring forth their treasure as a mercy from your Lord; and I did it not upon my own command. Such is the interpretation of that with which you could not bear. (S18:78-82)

The story advocates preemptive actions, even murder if it furthers Allah's cause. The means used to achieve an end do not matter, only the ends achieved do.

4. Several poets created verses which were insulting to Muhammad. These included Asima bint Marwan, Abu Afak, and Ka'b ibn al-Ashraf. After Muhammad received the following revelation, "It is not for any prophet to have captives until he has made slaughter in the land" (S8:670), he asked his followers who would rid him of them. When

questioning the person who had volunteered to kill Ka'b, Muhammad said, "'all that is incumbent upon you is that you should try.' He (Muhammad b. Maslama) said, 'O apostle of god, we shall have to tell lies.' He answered, 'Say what you like, for you are free in the matter.'"[12] Also, upon hearing that Asima bint Marwan had been killed, Muhammad said, "'You have helped god and His apostle, O 'Umayr!' When he asked if he would have to bear any evil consequences the apostle said, 'Two goats won't butt their heads about her.'"[13]

5. In the battle of the trench, Muhammad sent a Ghatafan who had converted to Islam to his own tribe who was laying siege to Medina with the following charge: "You are only one man among us, so go and awake distrust among the enemy to draw them off us if you can, for war is deceit."[14]

6. Muhammad had adopted a former slave named Zayd. In that time when a person was adopted they took the father's name and took on the same status as a natural born child. Muhammad had married him to one of his cousins, Zaynab. She was said to be about thirty-five but still very beautiful. It was an unhappy marriage. One day Muhammad came by Zayd's home to see him. He knocked on the door, but Zayd was not there. Zaynab met Muhammad in a state where she was not fully dressed, but asked him in as "he was as a father and mother to her. Muhammad declined but the wind lifted the curtain, evidently, while she was hurriedly dressing. He fled in some confusion, muttering something which she did not quite catch. All she heard was: 'Praise be to Allah the Most High! Praise be to Allah who changes men's hearts!'"[15]

Zaynab heard Muhammad's words and told them to Zayd. Zayd went to Muhammad and offered to divorce Zaynab so that Muhammad could marry her. A short time later, Muhammad had the following revelations: "Allah has not assigned unto any man two hearts within his body, nor has he made your wives whom you declare (to be your mothers) your mothers, nor has he made those whom you claim (to be your sons) your sons. This is but a saying of your mouths. But Allah says the truth and He shows the way. Proclaim their real parentage. That will be more equitable in the sight of Allah. And if you know not their fathers, then (they are) your brethren in the faith, and your clients. And there is no sin for you in the mistakes that you make unintentionally, but what your hearts purpose (that will be a sin for you). Allah is Forgiving. Merciful." (S33:4-5)

"And it becomes not a believing man or a believing woman, when Allah and His Messenger have decided an affair (for them), that they should (after that) claim any say in their affair; and who is rebellious to Allah and His Messenger, he surely goes astray in error manifest. And when you said unto him on whom Allah has conferred favor and you have conferred favor: Keep your wife to yourself, and fear Allah. And you did hide in your mind that which Allah was to bring to light, and you did fear mankind whereas Allah had a better right that you should fear Him. So when Zayd had performed the necessary formality (of divorce) from her, We gave her unto you in marriage, so that (henceforth) there may be no sin for believers in respect of wives of their adopted sons, when the latter have performed the necessary formality (of release) from them. The commandment of Allah must be fulfilled. There is no reproach for the Prophet in that which Allah makes his due. That was Allah's way with those who passed away of old and the commandment of Allah is certain destiny." (S33:36-38)

These last revelations had two impacts. First, an adopted child was no longer viewed as being equivalent to a natural born child. Second, the marriage to Zaynab by Muhammad before would have been viewed as taboo as he would have been marrying his son's wife. The revelation was exactly what he needed in order to marry Zaynab. A hadith is credited to Aisha regarding some who doubted that Muhammad had revealed all of the verses Allah had revealed to him. She is credited with saying, "If the Prophet had concealed anything of the revelation, it would have been those verses he ought to have kept hidden."[16]

The above are just a few examples. As these are later verses within the Qur'an, they abrogate earlier revelations. The result is the potential for a strictly "ends justifies the means" point of view.

Summary

Allah is one, but we can see the influence of Neo-Platonic thought as this One is so absolute that it leaves no room for any distinctions. It is Allah's absolute power which is the cause of all things. The mysticism that developed within Neo-Platonism as a result of this absoluteness is also present, and it creates several inconsistencies in the nature of Allah's will and word. This view of a Creator leads not to man's free choice, but instead to a predestined fate over which he has no control. He can have no relationship with his Creator; he is merely a slave from whom only obedience is expected. This does not lead to hope but instead to despair. In addition, all man is not created with an equal nature. Some are simply more favored by Allah, and others have more rights based upon worldly attributes such as their religious beliefs and gender.

The next chapter takes the constructs developed in this chapter and compares them to Christian principles, and also examines some inconsistencies within Islam arising from the ideas just discussed.

Chapter 5

Comparisons

This chapter is likely the most controversial in the book, and likely to be considered blasphemy by a follower of Islam. However, it is simply based upon the facts we've discussed up to this point. This information must be understood in order to effectively engage Muslims, and engagement is necessary in order to create understanding and change. I think Georges Houssney has it right:

> Our purpose in engaging Muslims is not to defeat a belief system, or challenge a culture, or bring down a civilization. We don't seek to sow dissension, or overturn traditions out of disrespect. No, our motive is the same as Paul's: "I have become all things to all men so that by all possible means I might save some. I do all this for the sake of the Gospel, that I may share in its blessings."[1]

We engage in order to reach others. We'll begin this chapter by looking at the early church father's view of God and man, and use that information to make comparisons to the ideas within Islam that were presented in the last couple of chapters. Again, it is just the facts and where those facts take us. With this information it is clear that Allah and God cannot be the same. Some implications of these differences are discussed before closing with some comparisons coming directly from the Qur'an and Bible. But before we begin, we'll do a quick review of the previous chapter's contents that we'll leverage throughout this discussion.

Review of Allah's Unity

From the last chapter, Allah is the Creator, a unity so simple that it is nothing but pure will. There is no being, nature or essence. Man's sole purpose is to worship Allah; man is simply Allah's slave. If one were to diagram this relationship, it would look like the following.

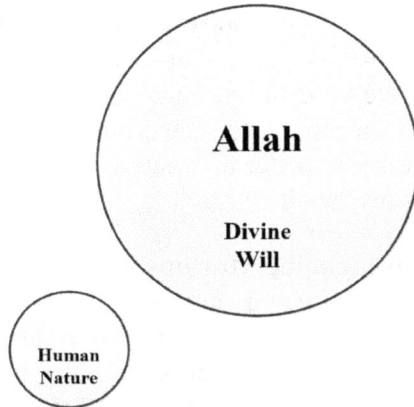

There is no intersection between divine and human nature. They are separate and distinct. As Allah is pure will, He is the cause of all things, but the things He causes are extrinsic as He is outside of nature. He is named by His actions, but they are not a part of Him. Characteristics ascribed to Him are absolute and include the following:

1. Absolutely One
2. Absolutely Sovereign
3. Absolutely Unknowable
4. Absolute Justice
5. Absolute Mercy

6. Absolute Will

7. Absolute Knowledge

Early Christian View of God

Most of the quotes in this section come from Clement of Alexandria. He lived in the second and early third century, over 1,700 years ago and 300 years before Muhammad. He addressed the problem faced in both understanding God and responding to the pagan platonic thought prevalent at the time.[2] He lays out the problem as follows.

> The professed aim of our philosophy ... leads through Wisdom, ... to the Rule of all, —a Being difficult to grasp and apprehend, ever receding and withdrawing from him who pursues. But He who is far off has ... come very near ... He is in essence remote ... But He is very near in virtue of that power which holds all things in its embrace ... For the power of God is always present, in contact with us, in the exercise of inspection, of beneficence, of instruction. ... God is not to be known by human wisdom ... For God is not in darkness or in place, but above both space and time, and qualities of objects.[3]

Clement is laying out his balance between the transcendent and the immanent. God is transcendent and therefore One. He also cannot be known by us through human wisdom and is outside of time and space, a simple unity. It is His power which is immanent and it appears to be a complex unity as there are different positive attributes being associated with that power. So what does Clement say about God?

First, that "God is one."[4] As our Creator is transcendent, He has been spoken of "in enigmas, and symbols, and allegories, and metaphors, and such like tropes."[5] Clement noted, however, that most men think our Creator to be like themselves. They fail to notice that our Creator "has bestowed on us ten thousand things in which he does not share."[6] These things include birth, food, growth, long life, and our bodies. All such references are not literal and should be interpreted symbolically.

But that does not mean that we cannot have some understanding of Him. We know our Creator through a process of confession, contemplation, and analysis, stripping away "not what He is but what He is not."[7] This stripping away includes all form, motion, position, place, throne, and notions of right hand or left. "The First Cause is not then in space, but above both space, and time, and name, and conception."[8]

This process indicates that "In reasoning, it is possible to divine respecting God"[9] by moving within the world of thought. However, reason alone is not enough. "Should one say that Knowledge is founded on demonstration by a process of reasoning, let him hear that first principles are incapable of demonstration; for they are known neither by art nor sagacity ... Hence ... the first cause of the universe can be apprehended by faith alone."[10] We also must know Him by faith. The knowledge of our Creator comes not from man, but by His power through the Logos, for "the grace of knowledge is from Him by the Son."[11]

Clement finds this line of thought difficult because it is hard to exhibit the absolutely first and oldest principle. The Creator cannot be expressed as He is not genus, difference, species, an individual, number, event, nor that which is caused by an event. "No one can rightly express Him wholly. For on account of His greatness He is ranked as the All, and is the Father of the universe. Nor are any parts to be predicated of Him. For the One is indivisible; wherefore also it is infinite, not considered with reference to inscrutability, but with reference to its being without dimensions, and not having a limit. And therefore it is without form and name."[12] Even though no one can fully or correctly express the Creator, *He is not inscrutable*.

So why do we use names to describe Him? "We speak not as supplying His name; but for want, we use good names, in order that the mind may have these as points of support, so as not to err in other respects. For each one by itself does not express God; but all together are indicative of the power of the Omnipotent."[13] *The names we do use are good and keep us from going further astray as we are limited in our ability to understand Him, and what we can understand of Him lies within the mind.* "For the God of the universe, who is above all speech, all conception, all thought, can never be committed to writing, being inexpressible even by His own power."[14]

Clement asserts there is a Father and Son (Logos). Both are God, a unity. He also presents two different themes of the Father and the Son. One theme is the emphasis on the unity of the Father and the Son, as in the following passages.

1. "The Son in the Father, and the Father in the Son."[15]

2. "Our Instructor is like His Father God ... the Word who is God, who is in the Father ... and with the form of God is God."[16]

3. "But nothing exists, the cause of whose existence is not supplied by God. Nothing, then, is hated by God, nor yet by the Word. For both are one—that is, God."[17]

4. "And His justice is shown to us by His own Word from there from above, whence the Father was. For before He became Creator He was God."[18]

5. "He Himself being one, the Son of the Father, who is truly one, the beginning and the end of time."[19]

The preceding thoughts all stress the Creator's unity. There is only One Creator. Clement draws a contrasting theme indicating that there is a distinction between the Son and the Father. Yet, even within the distinction, the Son is still one with the Father—there is still unity. The distinctions that Clement expresses are that the Son is (1) the power of the Creator, (2) the image of the Creator, but still one with Him, (3) the Creator of all creation, and (4) the key to what we can know about our Creator.

1. "God then, being not a subject for demonstration, cannot be the object of science, but the Son is wisdom, and knowledge, and truth, and all else that has affinity thereto. He is also susceptible of demonstration and of description ... And the Son is neither simply one thing as one thing, nor many things as parts, but one thing as all things; whence also He is all things. For He is the circle of all powers rolled and united into one unity."[20]

2. "But the nature of the Son, which is nearest to Him who is alone the Almighty One, is the most perfect, and most holy, and most potent, and most princely and most kingly and most beneficent. ... For from His own point of view the Son of God is never displaced; not being divided, not severed, not passing from place to place, being always everywhere, and being contained nowhere, complete mind, the complete paternal light; all eyes, seeing all things, hearing all things, knowing all things, by His power scrutinizing the powers. ... He, the paternal Word ... For the Son is the power of God, as being the Father's most ancient Word before the production of all things, and His Wisdom."[21]

3. "He, the Son, is,... the cause of all good things, being the first efficient cause of motion – a power incapable of being apprehended by sensation. ... Being, then the Father's power, He easily prevails in what He wishes, leaving not even the minutest point of His administration unattended to."[22]

4. "And as the Lord is above the whole world, yea, above the world of thought, so the name engraven on the plate has been regarded to signify ... it is the name of God that is expressed; since as the Son sees the goodness of the Father, God the Saviour works, being called the first principle of all things which was imaged forth from the invisible God first, and before the ages, and which fashioned all things which came into being after itself."[23]

5. "And as the unoriginated Being is one, the Omnipotent God; one, too, is the First-begotten, 'by whom all things were made, and without whom not one thing ever was made.'"[24]

6. "'Now the just shall live by faith,' which is according to the covenant and the commandments; since these, which are two in name and time, given in accordance with the [divine] economy—being in power one—the old and the new, are dispensed through the Son by one God."[25]

7. "For the gates of the Word being intellectual, are opened by the key of faith. No one knows God but the Son ... through whom alone God is beheld."[26]

The Son is immanent as he can be described by us. The Father is transcendent as He is outside of human thought and inexpressible directly.

But how is this possible? Clement cites both Father and Son as being the First Principle and Creator, but he says that they are First Principle and Creator in different senses of the word, similar to the four causes discussed in Aristotle's *Metaphysics*.[27]

1. "Wherefore the Word is called the Alpha and the Omega, of whom alone the end becomes the beginning, and ends again at the original beginning, without any break....

   Now God, who is without beginning, is the perfect beginning of the universe, and the producer of the beginning. As, then He is being, He is the first principle of the department of action, as He is good, of morals; as He is mind, on the other hand, He is the first principle of reasoning and of judgment. Whence also he is Teacher, who is the only son of the Most High Father, the Instructor of men."[28]

2. "The timeless and unoriginated First Principle, and Beginning of existence – the Son – from whom we are to learn the remoter Cause, the Father, of the universe, the most ancient and the most beneficent of all."[29]

From the above our Creator is the source of all existence, morality, and knowledge. The distinctions that Clement lays out are not always consistently maintained. This goes back to his statements about our inability to accurately name or write about our Creator. These only serve to act as "points of support" for our limitations.

So we have a God who is One. He has Being, Essence, Nature. While He is One, He is a combination of transcendence and immanence. He has been described as a single essence containing three persons. This can be diagramed as follows.

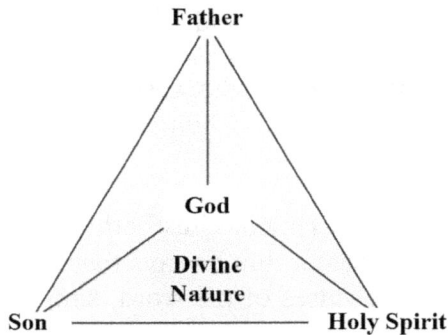

God is our Creator, and *He is Good*. Clement notes that doing good and doing wrong are opposites, and they are not compatible. "To do wrong, then, is not good, for no one does wrong except for some other thing; and nothing that is necessary is voluntary. To do wrong, then is voluntary, so that it is not necessary. But the good differ especially from the bad in inclinations and good desires. For all depravity of soul is accompanied with want of restraint; and he who acts from passion, acts from want of restraint and from depravity."[30] Doing wrong is voluntary and driven by internal factors.

In discussing good, Clement cites Plato saying there are two goods. "Further, Plato the philosopher says that the end is twofold: that which is communicable, and exists first in the ideal forms themselves, which he also calls "the good"; and that which partakes of it, and receives its likeness from it, as is the case in the men who appropriate virtue and true philosophy."[31]

The first good is our Creator as follows:

> For assuredly He does not hate anything, and yet wish that which He hates to exist. Nor does He wish anything not to exist, and yet become the cause of existence to that which he wishes not to exist. Nor does He wish anything not to exist which yet exists. If, then, the Word hates anything, He does not wish it to exist. But nothing exists, that cause of whose existence is not supplied by God. Nothing, then, is hated by God, nor yet by the Word. For both are one—that is, God.... If then He hates none of the things which He has made, it follows that He loves them. Much more than the rest, and with reason, will He love man, the noblest of all objects created by Him, and a God-loving being. Therefore God is loving; consequently the Word is loving.

> But he who loves anything wishes to do it good. And that which does good must be every way better than that which does not good. But nothing is better than the Good. The Good, then, does good. And God is admitted to be good. God therefore does good. And the Good, in virtue of its being good, does nothing else than do good. Consequently God does all good. And He does no good to man without caring for him, and He does not care for him without taking care of him. For that which does good purposely, is better than what does no good purposely. But nothing is better than God. And to do good purposely, is nothing else than to take care of man. God therefore cares for man, and takes care of him.... But the good is not said to be good, on account of its being possessed of virtue ... but on account of its being in itself and by itself good."[32] "For there is one good, the Father."[33]

This has the following implications for His creation: "God is good on His own account, and just also on ours, and He is just because He is good. And His justice is shown to us by His own Word from there from above, when the Father was. For before He became Creator He was God; He was Good."[34] Even before creation, *our Creator was and has always been good. He is also just because He is good.*

It is also because our Creator was good that creation was made. "For God, being good, on account of the principal part of the whole creation, seeing he wishes to save it, was induced to make the rest also; conferring on them at the beginning this first boon, that of existence. For that to be is far better than not to be, will be admitted by every one. Then, according to the capabilities of their nature, each one was and is made, advancing to that which is better."[35]

But our Creator is not only good in and of Himself, but his good is active in creation. In Clement's writing, this active good is Providence. This is the second good Plato referenced. "For God is the cause of all good things; but of some primarily, as of the Old and the New Testament; and of others by consequence, as philosophy. Perchance, too, philosophy was given to the Greeks directly and primarily, till the Lord should call the Greeks."[36]

Within Christianity, we have a God who is One—three persons in a single essence—and He is Good. *He is good not only in Himself, but His good is active in creation - resulting in even our bad decisions being turned to His Good.* This is Providence.

Man's Nature, Purpose and Freedom

If the Creator created everything, then let's start with asking about creation and man's nature. Why was man made? "For if the heavenly bodies are not the works of men, they were certainly created for man."[37] It is not creation itself which is to be worshipped but its Creator. While creation was created for man, it was created for a specific use. "No one is a stranger to the world by nature, their essence being one, and God one. But the elect man dwells as a sojourner."[38] We have a common nature and must choose to be travelers, using what we need while keeping our eyes on the ultimate destination. This life only offers the way toward that ultimate goal.

So why then was creation created for man? What made man different from the rest of creation? "The other works of creation He made by the word of command alone, but man He framed by Himself"[39] in His image. We were given life in a very special way, either because this was in itself desirable or because it was desirable on account of something else. The Son is the image of the Father, and in the creation of man "there is now a third divine image, made as far as possible like the Second Cause, the Essential Life."[40] Man is the image of the Son. But this is not meant as a physical resemblance. "For conformity with the image and likeness is not meant of the body ... but in mind and reason."[41] This is repeated in another form. "For the image of God is His Word ... the image of the Word is the true man, the mind which is in man."[42] Why? Because "man is made principally for the knowledge of God."[43] Just as the Son is in the Father, and the Father in the Son; "God in man, and man in God."[44]

Man has a special place within creation. Man was created as the image of an image. This image is not physical, but inward, our mind and reason. *While this image is remote, there is nothing else in all creation that is closer.* So what are the implications of that nature?

<u>Implications from Man's Nature</u>

Clement says there are several implications arising from that special place. They are (1) the need to know one's self, (2) we all have an equality of nature, (3) we all have choice, and (4) we all have been given freedom. This of course is not a complete list but are the things relevant to the topic at hand. Passages reflecting each of these points follow below.

As to the first point, "It is then, as appears, the greatest of all lessons to know one's self. For if one knows himself, he will know God; and knowing God, he will be made like God, not by wearing gold or long robes, but by well doing, and by requiring as few things as possible."[45] We were made to know God, and by knowing Him we fulfill our purpose. This knowing is not evident by how we look, but instead by how we act and live. For "by thus receiving the Lord's power, the soul studies to be God; regarding nothing bad but ignorance, and action contrary to right reason."[46]

But if we were made to know our Creator, how do we do that? "Prayer is, then, to speak more boldly, converse with God."[47] As the image of the Son, we have a basis for a relationship with our Creator. Through prayer we can communicate and build a relationship with Him, as it is our mind by which we have that image. By faith, obtaining knowledge, and applying reason, we complete our purpose and acquire some understanding of our Creator.

As to the second point, Clement very clearly states that we are all equal as God's creation. "Suffice it for me to say that the Lord of all is God; and I say the Lord of all absolutely, nothing being left by way of exception."[48] It does not matter whether he is Jew, Gentile, or barbarian.[49] "For God is not only Lord of the Jews, but of all men."[50] Neither is there a difference between the sexes, for "the virtue of man and woman is the same. For if the God of both is one, the master of both is also one."[51] This does not mean there are not physical differences, but that in their nature "there is sameness, as far as respects the soul, she will attain to the same virtue (as man)."[52]

As for those who would say otherwise, Clement responds, "For either the Lord does not care for all men; and this is the case either because He is unable (which is not to be thought, for it would be a proof of weakness), or because He is unwilling, which is not the attribute of a good being.... Or He does care for all, which is befitting for Him who has become Lord of all."[53]

In regards to choice, our purpose is to know our Creator and we have been given mind and reason as our likeness to Him. In discussing faith and free choice, Clement asserts that we are given reason in order to live rationally and rightly for the Word of the Father is wisdom. How does one live rightly? According to Clement, there are four levels. At the first, and lowest, level are "those who manage well the things which occur each day."[54] The second level consists of "those who behave becomingly and rightly to those who approach them."[55] At the third level are "those who have command of their pleasures."[56] Finally, the "fourth—and this is the greatest—those who are not corrupted by prosperity."[57]

It is only because some choose to dispute and not believe that all "do not attain to the perfection of the good. For neither is it possible to attain it [faith] without the exercise of free choice."[58] Not only is the existence of free choice necessary to establish faith, it is also necessary for choosing good. "For this was the law from the first, that virtue should be the object of voluntary choice."[59] Further that "the preference and choice for truth is voluntary."[60] It is voluntary "since to obey or not is in our own power."[61] If we do not choose good, "The Lord clearly shows sins and transgressions to be in our own power."[62]

Truth and obedience are also voluntary. "'Transgressions catch a man; and in the cords of his own sins each one is bound.' And God is without blame."[63] For "the individual man is stamped according to the impression produced in the soul by the objects of his choice ... the cause lay in his choosing, and especially in his choosing what was forbidden. God was not the cause."[64] We alone are responsible for our own choices and those choices leave their imprint on our soul. This is free will.

This free will is not only voluntary, but knowledge is required to exercise it. "Choice and avoidance are exercised according to knowledge; so that it is not pleasure that is the good thing, but knowledge by which we shall choose a pleasure at a certain time, and of a certain kind."[65] However not all actions are voluntary. Towards involuntary action, Clement states that "What is involuntary is not a matter for judgment. But this is twofold—what is done in ignorance, and what is done through necessity." [66]

Free will is freedom. It is the ability, as individuals, to choose our own actions without coercion. It was given by our Creator. Freedom is necessary to fulfill our purpose, but requires knowledge for its proper use. We must each use this gift to the best of our ability. In his *Exhortation*, Clement says, "He (the Creator) offers freedom, you flee into bondage; He bestows salvation, you sink down into destruction; He confers everlasting life, you wait for punishment."[67] "Although visited with ignominy and exile, and confiscation, and above all, death, he will never be wrenched from his freedom, and signal love to God."[68] This freedom from our Creator is enduring, and cannot be taken away through any trial, even at the point of death. Further, we have a choice as to whether we accept that freedom or not. *It is our choice.*

So from the material in the last several sections, we have the following on man and his relationship with God. Man was made in God's image. This is an inward image and not a physical one. Man was intended to know God through a personal relationship with Him, and that is only possible through the Word: Christ, God who became man. We are to know Him as our purpose is to become good as He is Good, to the extent that each one of us is able, realizing this goal is up to each of us through the gift of freedom we have been given.

The relationship between God and man can be shown as follows:

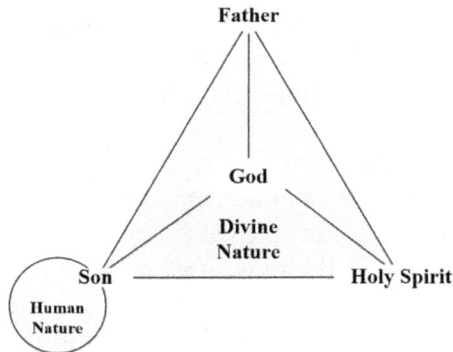

There is only one single point of intersection between divine and human nature, and that is Christ. Of course this is an analogy, so it only takes us so far, but for the purposes of this discussion, I think that it communicates the essential differences that exist on the topic.

Belief

We just saw that in Christianity freedom is (1) a gift from God, (2) a positive attribute, and (3) essential to our purpose. Within Islam, however, freedom is the negation of a negative; it is what one has when one is not being coerced. This is because the view of man's nature within Islam is one of being coerced: a slave.

We see the same in regards to belief. In Christianity, belief is a positive expression. Consider when one is baptized. Normally their is a profession of faith as to who God is, acceptance of the relationship between God the Father and Christ, and surrendering their life to Him. Within Western thought, belief and disbelief are opposites.

But this is not the case in Arabic culture:

> Belief and disbelief ... are two unrelated words, *iman* and *kufr*. For example, I found it fascinating that Abul A'la Mawdudi (an influential Sunni Pakistani scholar), in explaining the Islamic belief system, did not start with belief. Rather he wrote first about *kufr*, which means denial or concealment. He defined a Muslim not by belief in Allah, but by saying that a Muslim is one who does not deny Allah. He went on to add that to not deny Allah is to believe in him.[69]

The upshot is that within Islam everyone is a Muslim, some just do not know it yet. This is why it is incumbent on all Muslims to offer another the opportunity to accept Allah. A refusal to accept this is to become an infidel (*kafir*).

Virtue and Morality

As we are all God's creation, we all have the same virtuous nature. This does not mean we are born virtuous. Virtues must be acquired. Virtues are voluntary and connected to faith,[70] and it is by acquiring virtue that we partake of "the good." But what is virtue? It is defined as moral uprightness, righteousness.

Clement starts with discussing truth: "One speaks in one way of the truth, in another way the truth interprets itself. The guessing at truth is one thing, and truth itself is another. Resemblance is one thing, the thing itself is another. And the one results from learning and practice, the other from power and faith."[71] Further, "The way of truth is therefore one. But into it as into a perennial river, streams flow from all sides."[72] There is both truth itself and many truths which resemble it. In regards to truth itself, Clement asserts that 'the Word is truth.'[73] "The instruction which is of God is the right direction of truth to the contemplation of God. ... As therefore the general directs the phalanx, consulting the safety of his soldiers, and the pilot steers the vessel, desiring to save the passengers; so also the Instructor [the Word] guides the children to a saving course of conduct."[74]

As to the truths that resemble the truth, "so while the truth is one, many things contribute to its investigation. But its discovery is by the Son. If then we consider, virtue is, in power one. But it is the case, that when exhibited in some things, it is called prudence, in others temperance, and in others manliness or righteousness. By the same analogy, while truth is one, in geometry there is the truth of geometry; in music, that of music; and in the right philosophy, there will be Hellenic truth.... And each, whether it be virtue or truth, called by the same name, is the cause of its own peculiar effect alone."[75] Virtue and truth are one and the same thing, and again we have the same framework as with our Creator and good. We have again another instance of the one and the many. By understanding truth we understand virtue. Virtue is the means by which we approach the Truth.

"Now, inasmuch as there are four things in which the truth resides— Sensation, Understanding, Knowledge, Opinion—intellectual apprehension is first in the order of nature; but in our case, and in relation to ourselves, Sensation is first, and of Sensation and Understanding the essence of Knowledge is formed; and evidence is common to Understanding and Sensation. Well Sensation is the ladder to Knowledge; while Faith, advancing over the pathway of the objects of sense, leaves Opinion behind, and speeds to things free of deception, and reposes in the truth.... For knowledge is a state of mind that results from demonstration; but faith is a grace which from what is indemonstrable conducts to what is universal and simple, what is neither with matter, nor matter, nor under matter."[76] For "sight, and hearing, and the voice contribute to truth, but it is the mind which is the appropriate faculty for knowing it."[77] Knowledge comes from reason and demonstration, but faith is not demonstrable. It is the mind which alone can know truth.

The special way in which we have been made allows us to learn virtue. "Above all, this ought to be known, that by nature we are adapted for virtue; not so as to be possessed of it from our birth, but so as to be adapted for acquiring it."[78]

In regard to how truth is acquired, "philosophy, being the search for truth, contributes to the comprehension of truth; not as being the cause of comprehension, but a cause along with other things, and co-operator; perhaps also a joint cause."[79] Philosophy is one way to discover truths that are demonstrable.

The false should not persuade us from pursuing the truth.

> On account of the heresies, therefore, the toil of discovery must be undertaken; but we must not at all abandon [the truth]. For, on fruit being set before us, some real and ripe, and some made of wax, as like the real as possible, we are not to abstain from both on account of the resemblance. But by the exercise of the apprehension of contemplation, and by reasoning of the most decisive character, we must distinguish the true from the seeming.
>
> And as, while there is one royal highway, there are many others, some leading to a precipice, some to a rushing

> river or to a deep sea, no one will shrink from travelling
> by reason of the diversity, but will make use of the safe,
> and royal, and frequented way; so, though some say this,
> some that, concerning the truth, we must not abandon it;
> but must seek out the most accurate knowledge
> respecting it. Since also among garden-grown vegetables
> weeds also spring up, are the husbandmen, then, to desist
> from gardening?[80]

Knowing truth is necessary to distinguish the true from the false. Virtue is useful, and it is by our efforts that we acquire them: "If one loves justice, its toils are its virtues. For temperance and prudence teach justice and fortitude; and [other] than these there is nothing more useful in life to men."[81]

As to why we need virtue, "to the whole human race, then, discipline and virtue are a necessity, if they would pursue after happiness."[82] "Now Plato the philosopher, defining the end of happiness, says that it is likeness to God as far as possible."[83] Virtue is necessary to achieve happiness and the pursuit of happiness ends by becoming as close as possible to the likeness of our Creator. This is our purpose. To become good as our Creator is the Good.

Christian Heresies

There have been any number of heresies identified by the Church over the years. Two early significant ones were the Monophysite and Nestorian heresies. These are shown in the diagrams below.

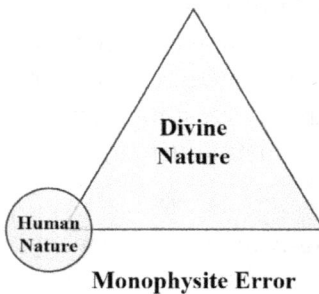

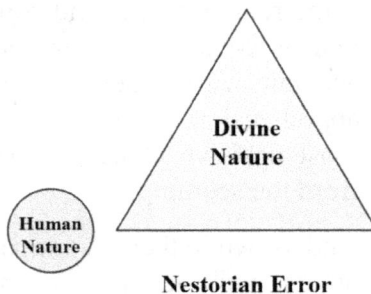

Monophysite Error   Nestorian Error

According to Norman Geisler,

> [T]he monophysite heresy confuses the two natures of Christ. This is not only heresy but is also an absurdity, since the divine nature of Christ is infinite and the human nature is finite. And it is impossible to have an infinite finite, an unlimited limited.

> The second diagram where the circle and triangle do not even touch is the Nestorian heresy, which posits two persons as well as two natures in Christ. If this were so, then when Christ sacrificed his life on the cross, it was not the person who is also divine, the Son of God, who died for us. In this case, the atoning sacrifice of Christ would have no divine value and could not be efficacious for our sins. Only if one and the same person, who is both God and man, dies on the cross for our sin can we be saved.[84]

If you ask a follower of Islam if they believe in Jesus, they will very likely say yes. Bear in mind what they are agreeing to is that he was a prophet of God, a good man. Whereas a Christian saying they believe in Jesus is confirming that they believe He is the Messiah, the Word, the only Son of the ever-living God.

It should not be surprising that the Nestorian heresy is very similar to the Islamic view of the relationship between man and his Creator. Remember that most of the "Christian" principles absorbed by Islam came from gnosticism and heretical sects. In addition to Christ being only a human being, he did not die on the cross because God would not let a prophet die such an ignoble death. Finally, man is not in need of redemption as there is no such thing as original sin, therefore Christ's death on the cross was not necessary.

One final point before closing this section. One of the most frequently asked questions when teaching about Islam goes along the lines of "Why would anyone want to convert to Islam?" I think that the preceding points are a key part of the answer. *Christianity requires a positive commitment to personal transformation.* For many people, this is very difficult to do. It requires effort and commitment on our part. Christian principles are fairly easy to understand, but are at times very difficult to live out.

But we live in an increasingly secular country. Islam offers a means of accepting an ideology with a religious component that doesn't require transformation—it only requires you to not disbelieve. Couple this with salvation by works. If one already views one's self as good/moral, *a powerful alternative vision for addressing one's spiritual needs that is easy is offered.* However, it is a false promise, one that is normally sold as merely a religion, without all of the ideology we've discussed being attached to it.

There is a document from the Muslim Brotherhood in North America that surfaced during the Holy Lands Foundation trial. That document confirms this approach. It outlines the group's plan for making the U.S. an Islamic State. There are two statements from that document that are relevant. These are the following:

> The general strategic goal of the Group in America ... is "Enablement of Islam in North America," meaning, establishing an effective and a stable Islamic Movement led by the Muslim Brotherhood which adopts Muslims' causes domestically and globally, and which works to expand the observant Muslim base, aims at unifying and directly Muslims' efforts, presents Islam as a civilization alternative, and supports the global Islamic State wherever it is.[85]

> We must possess a mastery of the art of "coalitions," the art of "absorption," and the principles of "cooperation.[86]

Its objective is furthered by deliberately suppressing the understanding of core Islamic doctrines. The following quote comes from Iranian-born Amil Imani's article "Islam's Useful Idiots."

The Useful Idiot may even engage in willful misinformation and deception when it suits him. Terms such as "Political Islam," or "Radical Islam," for instance, are contributions of the Useful Idiot. These terms do not even exist in the native parlance of Islam, simply because they are redundant. Islam, by its very nature and according to its charter—the Qur'an—is a radical political movement. It is the Useful Idiot who sanitizes Islam and misguides the populace by saying that the "real Islam" constitutes the main body of the religion; and, that this main body is non-political and moderate.

Regrettably, a large segment of the population goes along with these nonsensical euphemisms depicting Islam because it prefers to believe them. It is less threatening to believe that only a hijacked small segment of Islam is radical or politically driven and that the main body of Islam is indeed moderate and non-political.[87]

Summary

We've covered a lot of ground in this section. Below is a summary of some of the key points regarding God in Christianity.

1. God is One, but this unity consists of a single nature with multiple persons.

2. God has essence, being, nature. Therefore, His attributes tell us something about who He is. One attribute is that He is Good (read virtuous).

3. Man has been created in His image, an inward image. It is our purpose to know him and become like Him, to become good. This requires we have a relationship with Him through reading scripture, prayer, meditation, and living out His directives.

4. As He is Good (virtuous), we must each acquire virtue to become good. We are made in such a way that we are adapted for learning virtue. The gift of freedom provides us the opportunity to acquire virtue through education and learning, which is confirmed experientially by the choices we make.

5. We are to become good, using the skills, abilities, and talents we have each been given. While we all have the same purpose, we will likely all accomplish it a little differently as we do not have the same gifts.

Islamic Inconsistencies

Islamic monotheism is very different from the Christian perspective just described. Its blend of monotheism asserts,

> Allah has no Being, he is only absolute will.
> As Allah has no Being, he has no essence (or nature).
> As Allah has no essence, he has no essential attributes, nor can we know Him.
> As Allah has no essential attributes any attempts to depict Him are blasphemy.

The above view of our Creator raises a number of inconsistencies of a theological, metaphysical, moral, and logical nature. While this material is not an exhaustive list of inconsistencies, it does address the most serious of them concerning the nature of God and man, and the relationship (if any) between them. Many of the quotes in this section come from *Answering Islam*.

Islamic Monotheism

1. The above view of Allah is nominalistic and leaves no room for plurality. Nominalism is a doctrine that universals (abstract

concepts) exist only as names without a basis in reality. This raises several issues.

a. **Theological**: Islamic monotheism is inconsistent with its own view of the Qur'an.

The Qur'an is the uncreated and perfect expression of the mind of Allah. It is a part of Allah but separate from Allah. Allah's speech is an eternal attribute; it is uncreated. If His speech is an eternal attribute and not identical to Allah, then there is plurality within Allah.

According to the Muslim scholar Yusuf Ibish, "It (Qur'an) is not a book in the ordinary sense, nor is it comparable to the Bible, neither the Old or New Testament. It is an expression of Divine Will. If you want to compare it with anything in Christianity, you must compare it with Christ himself."[88]

b. **Logical**: Islam is inconsistent in its arguments for the unity of Allah and against the plurality of God.

The same argument used to affirm oneness within Allah, is denied to affirm the oneness of God within Christianity.

Muslims also misunderstand Christ's relationship with God. The phrases "only begotten," "Son of God," and "Son of Man" are taken to imply a physical act that is inconsistent with scripture. It takes a spiritual matter and relegates it to a physical plane. Instead, these terms refer to a special relationship between Christ and God the Father. There is a priority in rank implied, with Christ, God's Word, proceeding eternally from God the Father and submitting to His will.

2. Allah is absolute will and is not essentially just or loving. Instead He has chosen to be merciful (nominalism again). He could just as easily choose not to be merciful. There are at least two problems with this position.

   a. **Metaphysical**: Orthodox Islam claims that Allah is a necessary Being. He cannot not exist among other things as He is responsible for all creation. If He is necessary, then it is His nature to exist. He must have a nature or else He could not be by nature a necessary kind of Being. Orthodox Islam also believes that there are other attributes of Allah, such as self-existence, eternality, and uncreatedness. Essence is defined as essential attributes or characteristics of being.

      If these attributes are true, then Allah must have essence or else they would not be essential attributes. If Allah has essential attributes, then He cannot be just absolute will—He must have Being.

   b. **Moral**: If Allah is only will, without any real essence, then He does not do things because they are right—they are right only because He does them.

      S25.51: "If We willed, We could raise up a warner in very village."

      This is a serious moral problem as right and wrong become arbitrary. This leads Muslim scholars into great difficulty around concepts such as predestination, which the Qur'an both supports and rejects. Within Christianity, God is the source of not only existence, but also morality and knowledge. See item four below.

3. If Allah has no essence, then the Islamic view of Allah is a form of agnosticism. Agnosticism is defined as the doctrine that God is unknown and unknowable. At the core of Islam

is the notion one cannot know Allah but must simply obey Him. One is not to meditate on his essence but instead to submit to His will. Allah cannot be known by man. He is extrinsic and has no personal relationship, even with those who worship Him.

Fadlou Shehadi, commenting on the Muslim scholar Al-Ghazali says, "If God is a unique kind of being unlike any other being in any respect, more specifically, unlike anything known to man, it would have to follow by Ghazali's own principles that God is utterly unknowable. For, according to Ghazali, things are known by their likeness, and what is utterly unlike what is known to man cannot be known."[89] This presents several inconsistencies, several of which are noted below.

a. **Moral**: Allah is not essentially good but only called good because He does good. This is because He is named by His actions. If all actions come from Allah, then why is He not also called evil since He must also be the source of evil? Or faithless since He must also be the source of disbelief?

    If Islam says that there is something in Allah that is the basis for calling Him good, then it has admitted Allah's names do tell us something about His essence. This again refutes the nominalist view of who Allah is.

b. **Philosophical**: Neoplatonic thought teaches (1) the One is absolutely and indivisibly one, and (2) the One cannot be known except by a mystical experience relying on Intellect. This implies that there is no similarity between the One and what flows from it because the One is beyond Being. Thomas countered this argument in his writings. Effects must resemble their cause since "you cannot give what you have not got." You cannot produce what you do not possess.

From Thomas' argument, if Allah produces good, then He must be Good. If He produces Being, then He must have Being. If this is so, then Allah is intrinsic and the Islamic view of Allah based upon neoplatonic thought cannot be true. Objections to this idea usually confuse material or instrumental causes with efficient causes. A definition of each of these causes is as follows:

i.   Efficient cause: That by which something comes to be, as an artist's mind is the efficient cause of a painting.

ii. Instrumental cause: That through which something comes to be, such as a brush that an artist uses to create a painting.

iii. Material cause: That out of which something is made. An example of this is hot water that causes an egg to harden, but a candle to soften. These reactions are due to the material condition of the egg and candle, while the hot water is the same in both instances.

c. **Religious**: Religious experience within a monotheistic context by definition involves the relation between two persons: the worshiper and God. How can someone worship something about which they can know nothing? According to Ludwig Feuerbach, "Only when a man loses his taste for religion does the existence of God become one without qualities, an unknowable God."[90]

Some have deified Muhammad, as it is only through him that one can even hope to approach Allah. Muhammad is at times praised, such as, "If Muhammad had not been, then Allah himself would not have existed."[91] Muhammad himself taught against such views. This is an indictment of the theological bankruptcy of Islam.

Not only can you not make depictions of Allah, one cannot make depictions of Muhammad either—in his own words a mere man.

4. Islam cannot square up the need for atonement for sin with Justice.

God is infinite, but we are finite. We cannot harm God. The most we can do is to rebel against His sovereignty by breaking his laws, to sin. Committing sin requires punishment, or God is not just. Blood is required for atonement from sin. This is discussed in Leviticus 17:11: "For the life of the flesh is in the blood, and I have given it to you on the altar to make atonement for your souls; for it is the blood by reason of the life that makes atonement." This is reiterated in Hebrews 9:22.

It is only as believers in Christ that our sins have been atoned for, and justice has been meted out. His infinite payment atoned for the infinite weight of our sins. In Islam it is simply enough that your good deeds outweigh the bad. In addition, Allah can forgive whom he chooses to forgive. This is arbitrary and not justice.

5. The relationship between Allah and his creation is master and slave. Allah is absolutely sovereign. Orthodox Islam teaches the predestination of one's fate. This doctrine is a form of determinism.

   a. **Logical**: Allah is not logical as He performs contradictory actions. Islamic scholars will point out that these contradictions are not in Allah's nature, but instead in His will. Others create a distinction between what Allah does and what He allows His creatures to do by their free choice. This later position is not supported by orthodox Islam as it holds to predestination.

There are two problems with this position. First, for the above to be true, Allah must have a necessary essence or being. Second, the actions which flow from nature represent their source.

b. **Moral**: "Say: Nothing befalls us save that which Allah has decreed for us" (59.51). Allah could have saved everyone if He so chose, but He did not desire to do so! How can humans therefore be responsible for their own actions.

c. **Theological**: Allah is not only the source of good, but of evil. The Prophet said, "Adam and Moses argued with each other. Moses said to Adam, 'O Adam! You are our father who disappointed us and turned us out of Paradise.' Then Adam said to him, 'O Moses! Allah favoured you with His talk (talked to you directly) and He wrote (the Torah) for you with His own Hand. Do you blame me for action which Allah had written in my fate forty years before my creation?' So Adam confuted Moses, Adam confuted Moses, the Prophet added, repeating the statement three times" (Al-Bukhari hadith).

Al-Ghazali states, "He (Allah) willeth also the unbelief of the unbeliever and the irreligion of the wicked and, without that will, there would neither be unbelief nor irreligion." Further, "that we have no right to enquire about what Allah wills or does. He is perfectly free to will and to do what He pleases."[92]

d. **Metaphysical**: The ultimate conclusion is that there is only one agent within the universe: Allah, as He is the only one who can cause any action.

Aquinas wrote against this view in his *Summa contra Gentiles* to both deal with Islamic teachings in Spain and the Latin Averroism that had developed in the Middle

Ages. One Islamic creed states, "Allah Most High is the Creator of all actions of His creatures whether of unbelief or belief, of obedience or of rebellion: all of them are by the Will of Allah and His sentence and His conclusion and His decreeing."[93] The ultimate conclusion is that Islamic confessions of faith rise from "No God but God" and beyond "No one acts but God" to "No one has being but God.'"

Implications

Morality

There are several differences in regards to morality that can be derived from the above. While moral actions do matter within Islam, they can be placed below the expediency of advancing Islam, dependent on the individual's interpretation. Individuals can change their viewpoint at any point in their life, and each new generation must create its own interpretation of Islam's doctrines.

1. God is responsible for good. Man's turning away is the cause of evil. Allah is only the only one in existence who can cause things through His will. Therefore good and evil come from what He wills.

2. God is consistent. Through His providence, He has taken the bad decisions made by men and turned them to His good. Allah is inconsistent as His will changes over time. Right and wrong become a matter of what Allah wills and causes.

3. God has offered the opportunity for redemption to all man. Allah is capable of saving all mankind, but has chosen not to do so.

4. Man predestines himself through the decisions he makes. Allah has determined one's fate since before the beginning of time.

5. There is a relationship between God and His worshippers based upon love. There is no relationship between Allah and his followers as He cannot be known, only obeyed.

Man's Relationship to his Creator

Both Allah and God are responsible for the creation of everything that has ever been created. However, man's purpose differs significantly within Islam as man was created only to worship and obey Allah. Indeed Allah cannot be known as He is inscrutable.

> "I created the jinn and humankind only that they might worship Me." (S51, 56)

> "There is none in the heavens and the earth but comes unto the Beneficent as a slave." (S19, 93)

> "The (faithful) slaves of the Beneficent are they who walk upon the earth modestly, and when the foolish ones address them answer: Peace." (S25, 63)

Compare this again to the passage on creation and the logic Clement uses to demonstrate the type of relationship that must exist between God and man.

> For assuredly He [God] does not hate anything, and yet wish that which He hates to exist. Nor does He wish anything not to exist, and yet become the cause of existence to that which he wishes not to exist. Nor does He wish anything not to exist which yet exists. If, then, the Word hates anything, He does not wish it to exist. But nothing exits, that cause of whose existence is not supplied by God. Nothing, then, is hated by God, nor yet

by the Word. For both are one – that is, God. ... If then He hates none of the things which He has made, it follows that He loves them. Much more than the rest, and with reason, will He love man, the noblest of all objects created by Him, and a God-loving being. Therefore God is loving; consequently the Word is loving.

But he who loves anything wishes to do it good. But nothing is better than the Good. The Good, then, does good. And God is admitted to be good. God therefore does good. And the Good, in virtue of its being good, does nothing else than do good. Consequently God does all good. And He does no good to man without caring for him, and He does not care for him without taking care of him. For that which does good purposefully, is better than what does no good purposely. But nothing is better than God. And to do good purposely, is nothing else than to take care of man. God therefore cares for man, and takes care of him.... But the good is not said to be good, on account of its being possessed of virtue ... but on account of its being in itself and by itself good.

Man is made only to obey Allah, but God created man (and all creation) out of love, because *God is Good*.

Religion

Remember our definition for religion from Chapter 1. A religion is a particular system of beliefs, attitudes, emotions, behaviors, etc. that constitute man's relationship with some universal principle, power, or being. Its basis is a relationship between himself and that universal entity. That relationship requires faith on our part, the acceptance of truth without proof. In a word, belief.

But in Islam religion is "not merely belief."[94] "Religion actually means a way of life."[95] Belief is only the foundation and the way of life is defined by shari'a. Within Islam belief leads to compliance, to obedience and submission. It is imposed from the outside and accepted within.

Within Christianity, belief is transformational as one strives to become good. This transformation changes the heart, and therefore our actions. We strive to become good like God, to the extent we are able. This is accomplished through voluntary choice (freedom) in the acquisition of virtue, leading to performing acts of love (charity) that fulfill divine law. It is imposed by ourselves from within, and exhibited to the world by our actions.

One can argue that both Islam and Christianity are transformational, but once again while we may use the same word, the meaning behind the word is very different. One seeks acquiescence and the other change. This difference is demonstrated by a story of a Christian ('Adi Ibn Hatim) who fled to Syria during Muhammad's life. His sister and some of his people were taken as prisoners of war by Islam's followers. His sister went to 'Adi and invited him to Islam, and to come to Madinah. When 'Adi came to Muhammad:

> [He] was reciting the verse, "They (the People of the Book) have taken their rabbis and priests as lords other than God." 'Adi reports: "I said, 'They do not worship their priests." God's Messenger replied, "Whatever their priests and rabbis call permissible, they accept as permissible; whatever they declare as forbidden, they consider as forbidden, and thus they worship them."[96]

This story "makes it clear obedience to laws and judgment is a sort of worship,"[97] a form of legalism. From earlier, we saw that shari'a was derived from the sunna, which in turn was derived from the meaning of the Qur'an. All of which were derived by Islam's clerics using logic and consensus to derive the meaning from the original unpointed codex. How is this different from what Islam accuses Judaism and Christianity? While this at times has appeared within Christianity, it is not intended to be the focus. Instead the focus is to be on becoming good, acquiring virtue, because virtue is a will in conformity to God.

Both Islam and Christianity agree that God is one, but they do not agree on who God is. They both agree that God is the source of moral standards and knowledge, but not what those are because they do not agree on who God is. This difference has profound implications for man and his relationships with both God and his fellow human beings. It even affects his view of freedom, to which we turn next.

Freedom

Although some sects of Islam recognize free will, most do not. In regards to man's free will,

> And every man's augury have We fastened to his own neck, and We shall bring forth for him on the Day of Resurrection a book which he will find open. (And it will be said unto him): Read your book. Your soul suffices as reckoner against you this day. (S17, 13-14)

Good works matter within Islam, as they are necessary for salvation. But the basis for those actions is obedience and fear, not love, even for acts of charity.

> Then as for him whose scales are heavy (with good works), He will live a pleasant life. But as for him whose scales are light, The Bereft and Hungry One will be his mother (Hell). (S101, 6-9)

> Lo! Those who believe and do good works, theirs will be Gardens underneath which rivers flow. That is the Great Success. (S85, 11)

> A spring wherefrom the slaves of Allah drink, making it gush forth abundantly, because they perform the vow and fear a day whereof the evil is widespreading, and they feed with food the needy wretch, the orphan and the prisoner, for love of Him, (Saying): We feed you for the

sake of Allah only. We wish for no reward nor thanks
from you. (S76, 6-9)

These beliefs present us with another inconsistency within Islam. As all
things come about from Allah's will, then men cannot elect to do
anything except what Allah has willed, as both good works and bad have
been predetermined by Allah's will. Compare this to the writing below
by Clement on why bad things happen if God exists.

It was not He (our Creator) wished us to be persecuted ...
Accordingly, they unwillingly bear testimony to our
righteousness, we being unjustly punished for
righteousness' sake. But the injustice for the judge does
not affect the providence of God. For the judge must be
master of his own opinion—not pulled by strings, like
inanimate machines, set in motion only by external
causes. Accordingly he is judged in respect to his
judgment, as we also, in accordance with our choice of
things desirable, and our endurance.[98]

Governance

This leads to another moral dilemma within a society based upon
Islam's principles. The primary role of governance is that of
administering justice, which is the virtue of providing each man what is
due him. However, if all comes about by Allah's will, then how can
there be any justice outside of Allah's will? Can justice be achieved for
actions that are the result of another will? If not, mustn't one be resigned
simply to accept another's actions as right as those actions must have
their basis in Allah's will? In brief, can justice be achieved through any
human governance?

The Heritage Foundation's measure of Economic Freedom (for more
information see http://www.heritage.org/index/) provides one example.
Why this index? Because it offers an objective measure relevant to the
idea just presented. So what is economic freedom? From their website,
"Economic freedom is the fundamental right of every human to control

his or her own labor and property." Economic freedom is a measure of the degree of freedom an individual has in comparison to the notions of collectivism—at least in the area of using ones skills and property. The following areas are measured:

1. Rule of Law (property rights, freedom from corruption)

2. Limited Government (fiscal freedom, government spending)

3. Regulatory Efficiency (business freedom, labor freedom, monetary freedom)

4. Open Markets (trade freedom, investment freedom, financial freedom)

Composite measures for each country are created from the various area measures mentioned above. The index has been around for twenty years, so there is some trending information available as well. The country with the greatest economic freedom ranks number one on the list, and the country with the least economic freedom ranks last.

When correlating country's economic freedom rankings with the percentage of Islam's followers within their population, there is a negative correlation that is statistically significant at the .001 level. The higher the Islamic percentage within a country's population, the lower the level of economic freedom. This analysis included such bastions of freedom as North Korea, Cuba, Venezuela, and Burma, all of which have very low Muslim populations which should bias the results against finding non-Islamic countries ranking significantly higher.

This, of course, does not mean Islam is the cause, but merely that there is a correlation. However, I would assert that the collectivism inherent within Islam, when coupled with the differences in morality and fatalism also present, do lead to less freedom. In this respect, Islam is no different from the ancient state religion civilizations of Egypt, Babylon, Assyria, Greece, or Rome. These were not free societies either. Nor were they much different from the other "modern" forms of collectivism; whether it be communism, fascism, progressivism, or socialism. They all have the same root, and all produce the same fruit.

All Men are not Created Equal

Within Islam, while man was created by Allah, not all mankind has the same nature, and as not all have the same nature, not all have the same rights. There are several verses within the Qur'an for this area. Below are listed just a few.

> And Allah has favored some of you above others in provision. Now those who are more favored will by no means hand over their provision to those (slaves) whom their right hands possess, so that they may be equal with them in respect thereof. Is it then the grace of Allah that they deny? (S16, 71)

> Men are in charge of women, because Allah has made the one of them to excel the other, and because they spend of their property (for the support of women). So good women are the obedient, guarding in secret that which Allah has guarded. As for those from whom you fear rebellion, admonish them and banish them to beds apart, and scourge them. Then if they obey you, seek not a way against them! Allah is ever High Exalted, Great. (S4, 34)

> O you who believe! Choose not disbelievers for (your) friends in place of believers. Would you give Allah a clear warrant against you? Lo! The hypocrites (will be) in the lowest deep of the Fire, and you will find no helper for them. (S4, 144-5)

> Lo! Those who believe, and those who are Jews, and Sabaeans, and Christians—Whosoever believes in Allah and the Last Day and does right—there shall no fear come upon them neither shall they grieve. (S5, 69)

Judeo-Christian tenets point to all men having the same nature as all are descendants of Adam; therefore, all have the same basic rights given them by our Creator. Within Islam, the nature one possesses is based upon the group one is a part of, and therefore one's rights are also different. From the verses above there are differences in man's nature noted between several different groups: between believers in Allah and those who are not, differences between men and women, and even differences between those who believe in Allah.

We can also point to other examples. Within Islamic countries, non-Muslims generally cannot run for political office. They have fewer legal rights as they cannot bring suit against a Muslim, nor can a Muslim be charged for acts of violence against non-Muslims. Many types of jobs are also not open to non-Muslims. However, today even the lives of non-Muslims are at risk in Islamic countries. This is often portrayed in the media as something new—a high-jacking of Islam by extremists—but it is far from new. It is no different than what started to occur in the ninth and tenth centuries, only several hundred years after Muhammad's death, and indeed during Muhammad's life itself. More on this in the next chapter.

We've seen recent annihilations of the non-Islamic population of entire towns within Iraq by ISIS. And in 2010 *The Economist* reported on the last of the Jewish Arabs leaving their homeland in Yemen. This community had been part of the economically advanced trading ports within southern Arabia that existed at Muhammad's birth. They had their own legal system and architecture, and had lived in this area for over two thousand years. But no more. Their treatment by the Islamic population left them no choice but to leave, merely because of their religion. The same is happening in cities with historically large Jewish populations such as Beirut, Damascus, and Baghdad, and not only within Jewish communities, but Christian ones as well. We could go on with a discussion of homosexuality and the hypocrisy around alcohol consumption, but I think the point has been made.

Islam represents a form of elitism—collectivism—a belief in group rights and not individual rights or liberty. However, it does differ from other forms of collectivism in that the end is different. The end of a society with this foundation is based upon the expressed will of Allah as given through the revelations within the Qur'an. The church and the state are not separate; they are one, as are the military, law, civics, etc. All is Islam, and all exists to serve Allah, who is represented on the earth by the church and state, which are one. Those who believe one can bring democracy as we know it to an Islamic state simply do not know what they are talking about, or are not presenting the truth.

Truth and Knowledge

A brief word about knowledge. If God is the source of all creation, in order to know our purpose, and His will for us, then revelation is required for us to have knowledge of Him as He is First Cause. The knowledge which comes from Him must be Truth. Other truths may exist, but they must be consistent with His Truth. In the words of Clement again,

> One speaks in one way of the truth, in another way the truth interprets itself. The guessing at truth is one thing, and truth itself is another. Resemblance is one thing, the thing itself is another. And the one results from learning and practice, the other from power and faith.[99]

> The way of truth is therefore one. But into it as into a perennial river, streams flow from all sides.[100]

This presents several significant differences from one who holds to Islam's tenets. First, Allah is inscrutable; He cannot be known. We can only have knowledge of Him by His actions, but those actions are not a part of His nature. Second, Allah's will changes over time. There is no guarantee that His will on one day will be the same the next. So how can one know truth? Third, what relationship exists is in the form of master and slave; so understanding is not important—only acceptance and obedience matter.

The Use of Violence

One final area to look at is suicide bombers and violence in general. People willing to blow themselves up and take innocent people with them, all in the name of Islam. Why has this only occurred within Islam and various anarchist groups? We've previously touched on some of the fatalism within Islam. If one is born with his fate "fastened to his own neck" and no free will as Allah's will determines all, and ultimately Allah's judgment determining whether one enters heaven or hell— despite how one lives—then what hope does one have in life? At worst, death merely shortens the sentence of life and the injustice which this existence produces. In dying there is hope for better things in the life that is to come.

This view implies our Creator does not care about us. But is that position reasonable? Below again is the argument advanced by Clement.

> For assuredly He does not hate anything, and yet wish that which He hates to exist. Nor does He wish anything not to exist, and yet become the cause of existence to that which he wishes not to exist. Nor does He wish anything not to exist which yet exists. If, then, the Word hates anything, He does not wish it to exist. But nothing exists, that cause of whose existence is not supplied by God. Nothing, then, is hated by God, nor yet by the Word. For both are one—that is, God.... If then He hates none of the things which He has made, it follows that He loves them. Much more than the rest, and with reason, will He love man, the noblest of all objects created by Him, and a God-loving being. Therefore God is loving; consequently the Word is loving.

The violence within Islam is not new. Muhammad's life is said to provide the perfect example for how one is to live. Evidence of the violence within that life is well documented, some of which was presented in the previous chapter.

Jacques Maritain was a collectivist and friend of Saul Alinsky. There is little that I agree with Maritain about, but he wrote the following concerning societies without the connection of friendship among its members and where the absence of this connection leads. Although aimed at the problems occurring within fascism and communism that existed in his day, I believe his words apply equally well to Islam as it has the same basis as fascism and communism:

> If justice is first of all an essential requirement, it is as necessary condition which makes friendship possible, but this very friendship between citizens cannot prevail in actual fact within the social group if a stronger and more universal love, brotherly love, is not instilled in it and if civic friendship, itself becoming brotherhood, does not overflow the bounds of the social group to extend to the entire human race. Once the heart of man has felt the freshness of that terrible hope, it is troubled for all time. If it fails to recognize its supra-human origins and exigencies, this hope runs the risk of becoming perverted and of changing into violence to impose upon all "brotherhood or death."[101]

The kind of death that results in the execution of thirteen teens for simply watching a soccer game.

Summary

The following table compares some attributes/aspects of God and Allah.

	Christianity	Islam
God	Father	Master
Worshipper	Child	Slave
Motivation	Love	Fear
Requirement	Obedience	Submission
Involvement	Intrinsic: Man has a personal relationship with God	Extrinsic: Can only know of Allah by His actions
	Intimate God who is actively involved with mankind (theism)	Allah created the universe, but is detached from its affairs (deism)

	Christianity	Islam
"God Willing"	Hopeful	Fatalistic
Obtaining Heaven	Salvation, Grace	Earned by works
Nature	Triune: single Being with complex nature	Allah only: single Will without Being
	God can be known through the truth He has revealed in the Scriptures.	Allah defies all understanding and ability to know (agnosticism)
God's Nature *God doesn't change,* *Allah does*	James 1:17: "Every good thing given and every perfect gift is from above, coming down from the Father of lights, with whom there is no variation or 'shifting shadows.'"	S2.106 : "Such of Our revelations as We abrogate or cause to be forgotten, we bring (in place) one better or the like. Do not you know that Allah is able to do all things?"
God loves without limit, *Allah changes his affections*	John 3:16: "For God so loved the world that he have his one and only Son, that whoever believes in him shall not perish but have eternal life."	S32.13: "And if We had so willed, We could have given every soul its guidance, but the word from Me concerning evildoers took effect: that I will fill Hell with the jinn and mankind together."
God cannot lie, *Allah deceives*	Titus 1:2: "A faith and knowledge resting on the hope of eternal life, which God, who does not lie, promised before the beginning of time."	S8.30: "And when those who disbelieve plot against you (O Muhammad) to keep you in bands, or to kill you or to drive you forth; they plot, but Allah (also) plots; and Allah is the best of plotters."
Triune nature of God, Trinity is blasphemy	John 8:54: "Jesus replied, 'If I glorify myself, my glory means nothing. My Father, whom you claim as your God, is the one who glorifies me.'"	S5.73: "They surely disbelieve who say: Lo! Allah is the third of three; when there is no God save the One God. If they desist not from so saying, a painful doom will fall on those who disbelieve."
	John 1:1-2: "In the beginning was the Word, and the Word was with God, and the Word was God. He was with God in the beginning."	

	Christianity	Islam
God is a single Being with a complex nature, Christian Trinity is Three Gods	Matthew 28:19-20: "Therefore go and make disciples of all nations, baptizing them in the name of the Father and of the Son and of the Holy Spirit, and teaching them to obey everything I have commanded you. And surely I am with you always, to the very end of the age."	S5.116: "And when Allah says: O Jesus son of Mary! Did you say unto mankind: Take me and my mother for two gods beside Allah? He says: Be glorified! It was not mine to utter that to which I had no right. If I used to say it, then You know it. You know what is in my mind, and I know not what is in Your mind. Lo! You, only You, are Knower of Things Hidden."

Chapter 6

Islam's History

The Caliphate and Dhimmitude

This chapter provides a high level overview of about fourteen hundred years of history. It is not exhaustive, but it does contain many important developments related to Islam during the time after Muhammad's death. There are four periods that will be included. The first is the early caliphs that came from Muhammad's inner circle. They ruled for just over thirty years. They were followed by the Umayyad dynasty that ruled for almost one hundred years until about 750. The Umayyad were followed by the Abbasid dynasty that lasted until 1258. Finally, the Ottoman Empire rose from the ashes of the Abbasid during the fourteenth century and ruled until the early twentieth century when they were defeated in World War I as part of the Central Powers allied with Germany, Austria-Hungary, and others. At this time the various countries currently existing within the Middle East were created.

Myth Busting

The caliphate is often thought of as one long reign by a single Islamic empire. It is also portrayed as being a time of human enlightenment. As we will see in this chapter, neither is the case. But something else must also be understood. In many ways the history of the first caliphate varies little from the Christian kingdoms around it. What is different is the degree to which its actions were carried out against those they conquered and the length of time over which these actions occurred. Both were on a scale much greater than other places. It is these differences we must understand, because they are driven by the ideology discussed in the previous chapters, and that ideology still underlies events in today's Islamic countries.

It hasn't changed. It has only been silent for a century. After the First World War, Islam was not in a position politically or economically to pursue its previous course. We pray for peace, but it can only come with the removal or change of the ideology underlying Islam. There are some individuals who are pursuing this course. I pray that they are successful and that God is found by Islam along the way.

The First Caliphs and the Umayyad Dynasty

The spread of Islam after Muhammad occurred in two waves. The first wave includes the early caliphs, Umayyad and Abbasid Dynasties. It also includes the Fatimid and Seljuk Turk kingdoms that existed during this period. A timeline for these is shown below.

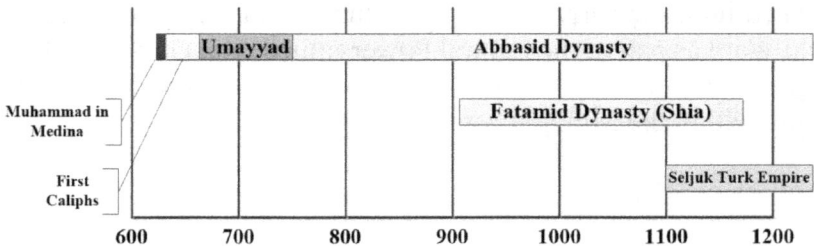

The First Wave

Muhammad left no successor at his death. From Ibn Ishaq's sirat, "Had it not been for what Umar said when he (Muhammad) died, the Muslims would not have doubted that the apostle had appointed Abu Bakr his successor; but he said when he died, 'If I appoint a successor, one better than I did so; and if I leave them (to elect my successor) one better than I did so.' So the people knew that the apostle had not appointed a successor and Umar was not suspected of hostility towards Abu Bakr."[1] Muhammad's followers met to discuss who would take his place even before his burial arrangements had been completed. Some argued that Muhammad's successor should be from his inner circle, and others argued that it should be someone from his blood-line. The first three caliphs came from Muhammad's inner circle, and the fourth was one of his nephews. The basis of the caliph's authority was only temporal, not spiritual. He ruled in the name of Islam and upheld Islamic teaching. Bear in mind at this time there was no written Qur'an, nor were there any official doctrines that had been derived yet by the clerics.

1. Abu Bakr (632–634): Abu Bakr was the father of Aisha, one of Muhammad's favorite wives. He was chosen by a group of the early converts on the basis of who the Muslims would follow. Khalid ibn-Walid (the Sword of Islam) became general of the army during Bakr's reign. The Wars of Apostasy were undertaken to more permanently cement the Arabs to Islam and enforce the payment of tribute. Islam expanded into Gaza and Caesarea.

    One tradition has it that Umar requested that the Qur'an be collected after the battle of Yamamah in 633, as many of Muhammad's early followers who were capable of reciting the Qur'an had died during this battle. Muhammad's scribe Zayd ibn Thatbit was appointed to collect and assemble all of the verses.

2. Umar (634–644): Persia and the Eastern Roman Empire had both been greatly weakened by their wars with each other. Umar brought Jerusalem under the control of Islam in 638, and by 641 he had conquered Iraq, Syria, Egypt, and Persia. Rome and Persia had fought each other for five hundred years at this point, but Persia was no more within ten years after Muhammad's death. The Arabs were aided by former Persian mercenaries and

military slaves who were taken in battle, many of whom had
been Monophysite Christians. It is not clear whether they were
attracted by the religious aspects of Islam, the cultural ties they
shared with the Arab invaders, or merely the potential of
collecting booty. These converts taught the Islamic leaders new
battle tactics and counter-measures, and one tribe led Islamic
forces through the Persian defenses. It was a blow from which
Persia never recovered. Umar was assassinated by one of his
Iraqi slaves in 644.

3. Uthman (644–656): Uthman consolidated his predecessor's
   conquests. He was the first caliph to come from the higher-order
   of Arab society. This put the Quryash back in control. His reign
   was marked by nepotism. Uthman was assassinated by rebels,
   marking the first of the rebellions against divine law. It was
   during Uthman's reign that the Medinan codex was selected as
   the official text of the Qur'an. All other codices and the variant
   readings based upon them were ordered to be destroyed. As we
   saw earlier, rules regarding the final use of diacritical marks and
   the insertion of vowels did not occur until the middle of the tenth
   century about three hundred years later.

4. Ali (656–661): Ali was one of Muhammad's nephews. He was
   disliked by Aisha, one of Muhammad's wives, who conspired
   with the Governor of Syria to overthrow him. The Governor of
   Syria and Uthman both belonged to the same tribe, the Umayya.
   Civil war ensued. Ali moved the caliphate's capital from Medina
   to Damascus. Ten thousand Muslims died at the ensuing Battle
   of the Camel, which the forces allied with Ali won. He was
   assassinated by one of his former supporters. This marked the
   end of rule by those closely associated with Muhammad and led
   to the formation of the Umayyad dynasty. Ali's death also
   deepened the rift between those who had supported a successor
   from Muhammad's inner circle (Sunni) and those who supported
   a successor from Muhammad's blood-line (Shia).

The Umayyad (661–750)

Mu'awiyah, the Governor of Syria, led the opposition against Ali. He made the position of caliph an inherited one. Ali's eldest son (Hasan) briefly opposed Mu'awiyah but then abandoned his claim. Hasan's brother Husayn went along with the decision as long as Mu'awiyah lived. He refused to recognize his son however, and in 680 he created an anti-caliph state in Iraq. Husayn was defeated and most of his family was killed. This sealed the split between Sunni and Shia. In 749, the family of the last Umayyad ruler, Marwan, was put to death with the exception of one son who fled to Spain.

The Umayyad concerned themselves with acquiring wealth and land. Tradition has it that they had little concern for religious doctrine. They surrounded themselves with palaces, poets, wine, etc. In addition, maintaining the armies required a large revenue stream to support them. Numerous revolts occurred in the later years of the dynasty, the result of internal power struggles. One of the uprisings led to the burning of the Kaaba in Mecca. Shiites, Berbers, and Kharijites all took up arms against the Umayyad, in part because of their second-rate standing in a society where all were supposed to be equal.

Early Development of the Qur'an and Hadith

Within his work *Why I Am Not a Muslim,* Ibn Warraq goes as far to state that "there is no such thing as *the* Koran; there never has been a definitive text of this holy book."[2] As has already been mentioned, there was no written collection of the Qur'an at Muhammad's death. In addition to the request made by Umar to Abu Bakr to collect the verses, other followers also attempted to collect the revelations and put them into a codex form. As previously mentioned, the Arabic text of this time was unpointed and contained no marks indicating short vowels. By the time of Uthman's reign, there existed codices within the centers of Mecca, Medina, Damascus, Kufa, and Basra. The consonantal text of these codices did not agree with each other, and the unpointed text made it impossible to distinguish between certain consonants (such as b from t from th, or s from d, for example). Uthman selected the Medinan codex in an attempt to standardize the consonantal text. This codex was selected in part because it was written in the dialect of Muhammad's tribe. Copies of the Medinan codex were sent to all of the cities mentioned above, with orders to destroy all the other codices.

However, variant readings continued to occur, in part because there were also no orthographic signs to indicate the presence of short vowels within the text. By the end of the Umayyad dynasty, there existed literally thousands of variant readings of some passages within the Qur'an. By the end of the Umayyad dynasty, clerics began to make rules to limit the number of variant readings that could be produced by the codex text. However, variant readings continued until well into tenth century when Islamic scholars, led by Ibn Mujahid, canonized one system of consonants and placed limits on the vowels that could be incorporated into the text. The creation of these clerical rules eventually led to the development of the "systems of the seven," seven accepted variant readings of the Qur'anic text.

The number of hadith in existence proliferated during this period as well. This matters because there are several fundamental differences between the Bible and the Qur'an. Within the Qur'an there is no sense of chronology or history. Instead the sura are arranged from longest to shortest. As many of the longer sura were written during Muhammad's time in Medina, many of them appear early in the Qur'an. In addition, there are abrupt shifts of subject matter within the sura themselves. The sirat (biographies) and hadith (sayings) help provide context to the Qur'an's written text.

From Warraq again, "During the early years of the Umayyad dynasty, many Muslims were totally ignorant in regard to ritual and doctrine. The rulers themselves had little enthusiasm for religion and generally despised the pious and the ascetic. The result was that there arose a group of pious men who shamelessly fabricated traditions for the good of the community."[3] However, "the ruling power itself was not idle. If it wished an opinion to be generally recognized and the opposition of pious circles silenced, it too had to know how to discover a hadith to suit its purpose. They had to do what their opponents did: invent, and have invented, hadiths in their turn. And that is in effect what they did."[4]

Also from Ignaz Goldziher, "Not a few pious persons admitted, as the end of life neared, how great their contribution to the body of fictive hadiths had been. To fabricate hadith was hardly considered dishonorable if the resulting fictions served the cause of good."[5] These fraudulent hadith were not rejected by society, but rather, "The pious fraud of the inventors of hadith was treated with universal indulgence as long as their fictions were ethical or devotional."[6] Just as happened with the Qur'an, the hadith underwent clerical review and categorization during the Abbasid dynasty to identify those that were true.

In summary, during this period there was a massive expansion in the Islamic state, conversion to Islam by both Arab and non-Arabs in an environment where little or no formal religious doctrines existed at a time when variant readings and fabricated hadith were being created by different groups in support of their goals within Islamic society. The instability created by the Umayyad's actions, some of which are mentioned later, led to their demise and the rising of the Abbasid dynasty by the middle of the eighth century.

Early History and Its Implications

Under the first four caliphs and the Umayyad dynasty, Islam advanced to the west through Palestine, Egypt, across North Africa, and into Spain. They were finally stopped in France at Tours in 734 by an army under Charles "The Hammer" Martel. In the east, it conquered modern day Syria, Persia (Iran), as far east as the Indus river in modern Pakistan and as far north as Armenia. The invading armies were often aided by Arabs who had previously settled in these areas as Monophysite and Nestorian Christians.

Bat Ye'or, in her book *The Decline of Eastern Christianity under Islam* provides the following example:

The attack on Babylonia took place on two fronts which corresponded precisely to the densest Arab settlements: in the south, around Ubulla; and slightly higher up the Euphrates, in the Hira region. Large numbers of Christian Arab tribes fought on the Persian side, but others, long settled in these regions and attracted by booty, went over to the Muslims. The chief of one of these tribes, the Banu Ijil, had even informed the caliph Umar, then in Medina, of deficiencies in the Persian defenses and had invited him to send an army there. Tribes from northern Arabia who pillaged villages along the Euphrates and took advantage of the Persian weakness were enrolled in the Islamic forces.[7]

Four thousand Jews, Christians, and Samaritans were executed in the area from Gaza up to Caesarea in the campaign of 634. The major towns, such as Jerusalem, were not taken at this time as they closed their gates. Towns were usually protected by walls and able to negotiate a treaty with the Islamic army; they became dhimmis. The rural areas were not so fortunate. The latter were devastated with crops being set on fire and peasants massacred or taken as slaves. In 642, the population of Dvin was annihilated, and the Islamic army returned later in the year, carrying off 35,000 captives.

The first caliphs were engrossed in conquest. They negotiated with town civic and religious leaders and left military governors to rule the new territories. Initially, Islam was simply viewed by the conquered people as another Jewish or Christian heresy. There were few copies of the Qur'an, and fewer outside of Arabia who could read it, and jihad did not appear to be any different than the razzias (raids) committed by Arab tribes during earlier centuries. As a result, the West never fully understood the change that had taken place with the coming of Islam. A mistake that we risk repeating today, because we are failing to study and learn history's lessons.

One example should provide insight. The prince of Nahavend (located in modern Iran) upon receiving Al-Mughira thought he was being driven to his door by hunger and poverty. He offered to "'supply you [Al-Mughira] with provisions and you can then go back whence you came.' In response, Al-Mughira replied that they were fighting in the cause of a prophet that had arose among their people, he had given them revelations that they would receive great victories where they saw such wealth and luxury 'that those who follow me will not wish to withdraw till it has become theirs.'"[8]

Dhimmis

It is during this period that the treatment and status of dhimmis began to be formalized. Dhimmi means "protected people." They were the defeated people of the book who did not convert to Islam and were required to pay several taxes in addition to a poll tax (jizya). Their protected status only lasted as long as they obeyed the terms of their treaty and did not offend the Muslims within the area in which they lived.

An early codification of dhimmitude can be found in the Pact of Umar, written by Umar al Khattab in the seventh century:

> We shall not build in our cities or in their vicinity any new monasteries, churches, hermitages, or monks' cells. We shall not restore, by night or by day, any of them that have fallen into ruin or which are located in the Muslims' quarters.
>
> We shall keep our gates wide open for the passerby and travelers. We shall provide three days' food and lodging to any Muslims who pass our way.
>
> We shall not shelter any spy in our churches or in our homes, nor shall we hide him from the Muslims.
>
> We shall not teach our children the Qur'an.

We shall not hold public religious ceremonies. We shall not seek to proselytize anyone. We shall not prevent any of our kin from embracing Islam if they so desire.

We shall show deference to the Muslims and shall rise from our seats whenever they sit down.

We shall not attempt to resemble the Muslims in any way.

We shall not ride on saddles.

We shall not wear swords or bear weapons of any kind, or ever carry them with us.

We shall not sell wines.

We shall clip the forelocks of our head.

We shall not display our crosses or our books anywhere in the Muslims' thoroughfares or in their marketplaces. We shall only beat our clappers in our churches very quietly. We shall not raise our voices when reciting the service in our churches, nor when in the presence of Muslims. Neither shall we raise our voices in our funeral processions.

We shall not build our homes higher than theirs....

Anyone who deliberately strikes a Muslim will forfeit the protection of this pact.[9]

The basis of dhimmitude is removing the salt and light from those who believe in Christianity. It is no different from the choice between freedom of religion we have had and the freedom of worship being offered by progressives in the U.S. today. Freedom of religion is the right to live according to your religion. Freedom to worship is merely the right to assemble in worship. In the latter case, the state's rights go right up to the church's threshold, as they did in the days of King John and Henry VIII. It is the difference between our founding principles and what the world's elites offer today, and one of the common connections between the modern Left and Islam.

Other Implications and Outcomes

Five different taxes were enforced upon the conquered peoples. These included (1) a land tax (*kharaj*); (2) provisions in kind, proportionate to harvests; (3) poll tax (*jizya*); (4) a tax covering the maintenance and expenses of the tax collectors; and (5) "a general sum devoted to requisitions, extraordinary taxes, and the upkeep and clothing of Muslims."[10] The taxation and pillaging by the Arabs forced many of these people to flee Islamic lands or go into hiding in the mountains. This deprived the caliph of much of the revenue necessary to support the large army used to continue Islam's conquests. To protect that revenue, he attached the taxes to the property. At this time, churches were also being converted into mosques.

During the first wave conquests, many towns were able to keep most of their religious and political autonomy by simply paying tribute to Medina instead of to Byzantine or Persia, as Islam's followers were the minority population. Local Christians or Jews were often left in administrative positions and the church took on the administration of collecting the taxes. Over time, Islam moved whole Arab tribes into these areas, a form of colonialization. Eventually, the Arabs were in a position to assume local power, and the administrative positions were filled by Muslims instead of Jews or Christians.

Several outcomes were precipitated by the changes occurring in the early caliphate. One, land was seized on the military authority of a tribe that had originated from Mecca and who exercised that military authority through nomadic Arab tribes. Two, the massive Arab emigration created anarchy in the areas where they settled. Three, the method for allocating property and booty between the tribes and Arab state created a perpetual state of bloody conflict, turning previously cultivated areas into wastelands. And four, the resulting destruction of the local labor force, the only means of taxation, resulted in drastically diminished revenues for the Umayyad. These led to inter-Arab religious conflicts and a destabilization of the Umayyad. The conflict in goals between different groups also led to the fabrication of the hadith we've discussed and the rise of the Abbasid dynasty that will be the subject of the next section.

The map below shows the rapid expansion of the caliphate during the first 120 years after Muhammad's death. During this time it conquered an area about the size of the Roman Empire at the height of its power. by way of contrast, it took the Romans a period of four or five centuries to effect their conquests.

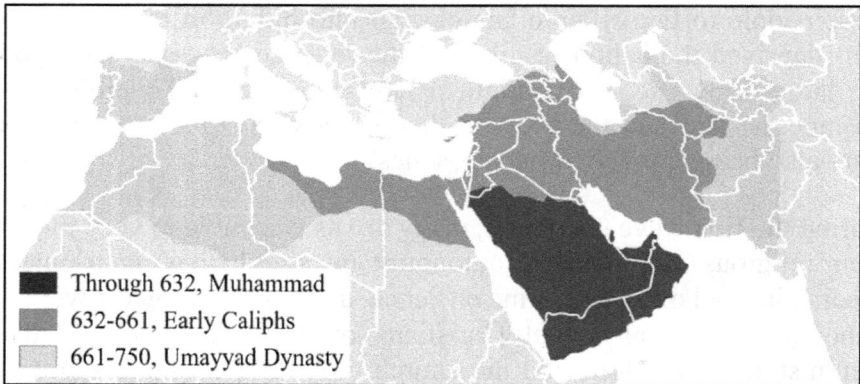

Figure 6-1: Expansion of Early Caliphate[11]

The Abbasid Dynasty

The Abbasid Dynasty lasted from 750 until 1258. It was during this period that many of Islam's structures began to transform into those we know today. The Qur'an, hadith, traditions (sunna), and schools of legal jurisprudence (shari'a) all reached their modern form during this time. Governance structures also solidified during this period. These changes had significant impacts on the various peoples conquered by the early caliphs and the Umayyad. This section will focus on the history from this period, and the next on the conquered peoples within the caliphate (the dhimmis).

Although this is often thought of as Islam's Golden Age, it should be noted that there was much upheaval and infighting that occurred during this period. The changes occurring were significant in terms of Islam's development. We will specifically look at the rise and fall of both the Fatimid and Seljuk Turk kingdoms within the caliphate that occurred during this period, and conclude with the crusades and Mongol invasion that ultimately ended Abbasid rule.

This is a good time to remind the reader once again that the intent of these materials is not to tell you what to think, but instead to simply present you with the facts and provide you with references where you can find more information if you want it. It is also time to reiterate that the subject of this book is Islam and not Muslims. It covers the development of Islam's tenets and not its people. We are each defined by the choices that we make.

A Shift in Power

The Abbasid overthrew the Umayyad in 750. They moved the capital to Baghdad and the caliphate came under greater Persian influence. This was not just a political revolution, but a religious one as well. The Abbasid viewed themselves not only as the rulers of the caliphate, but as princes and kings of Islam. They were much more rigorous in applying Islam's principles, and were much more intolerant of other religions. They set about creating a theocratic state, based upon the Persian model "in which church and state are conjoined."[12]

For Sunni Islam (which the Abbasid represent),

> the caliph is there to guarantee the carrying out of Islamic obligations, to represent and embody in his person the duties of the Islamic community. "At the head of the Muslims ... There must necessarily stand someone who sees to it that their laws are carried out, their statutes

maintained, their borders defended, and their armies equipped, who makes sure that their obligatory taxes are collected, that men of violence, thieves, and highwaymen are suppressed, that services are held on Fridays and feast days, that minors (in need of a guardian) can be married, that the spoils of war are justly divided, and that similar legal obligations, which no single member of the community can take care of, are performed."[13]

This dynasty traced its roots back to one of Muhammad's uncles, Al-Abbas. It went out of its way to show respect for the Umayyad they replaced. However, they viewed the followers of Muhammad's cousin Ali (the Shi'a) as rivals as they also had a bloodline claim to rule within the caliphate. During their rule the Shi'a were persecuted by the Abbasid. In the words of Goldziher, "Having plucked for themselves the fruit of Shi'a propaganda, the Abbasid had all the more reason to be on their guard against continued subversion by those who would not regard them, any more than the Umayyad, as the rightful successors of the Prophet. They strove therefore to deflect people from the veneration of Ali. Al-Mutawakkil razed the tomb of Husayn. People were not to recall at that sacred place that it was a son of Ali, and not a descendant of Abbas, who had shed his blood for the rights of the Prophet's house ... During Abbasid rule, some [Shi'a] ended their lives in prison, some on the scaffold, some by secretly administered poison."[14]

Under the Abbasid, the administration of the empire was delegated to bureaucrats. Viziers created decrees to be signed by the caliph. The Arab army was replaced by hired provincials, including Turkish mercenaries (the Mamluks). Persecution of non-Muslims within the empire increased during this time. In 772, the hands of Jews and Christians were ordered stamped. Monasteries were sacked and burned, and many of the monks were killed. The persecution became so severe that by the ninth century many Christians fled to Constantinople and other Christian cities outside of the reach of Islam.

The Fatimid Dynasty

But the Abbasid rule was not readily accepted by all. From about 909–1171, there arose a Fatimid Dynasty within the caliphate. They took their name from one of Muhammad's daughters Fatima, from whom they claimed descent (along with her husband Ali), providing justification for the Abbasid concern that rivals would also claim descent from Muhammad. The Fatimid were Shi'a and their rise was in part a response to the Abbasid persecution of their sect. They viewed the Abbasid caliphs as usurpers and dedicated themselves to overthrowing the religious and political order they created. The Fatimid rulers viewed themselves as spiritual leaders (imams). They were initially able to establish a firm base within Yemen. By 909, they were strong enough for their imam to come out of hiding and declare himself al-Mahdi (Divinely Guided One).

They established a base in modern Tunisia and spread through North Africa and into Sicily during the first half of the 10th century. During this time, they added the third branch of missions (religion) to the military and political branches of governance. While still keeping up the wars with Europe and internal divisions with the Berbers, the Fatimid turned eastward and toward the Abbasid. Finally, after several years of unsuccessful campaigns, the Fatimid broke through the Abbasid defenses in 969 and took portions of the Nile valley, Sinai Peninsula, Palestine, and southern Syria. Shortly after the conquest of Egypt, they founded the city of Cairo. At their height, they moved as far east as the Hijaz on the Arabian Peninsula and up to Anatolia. They briefly occupied Baghdad in about 1057 when a dissident general in Iraq joined the Fatimid. However, they were driven back by the Seljuq Turks a few years later. The map below shows the Fatimid Dynasty at its height.

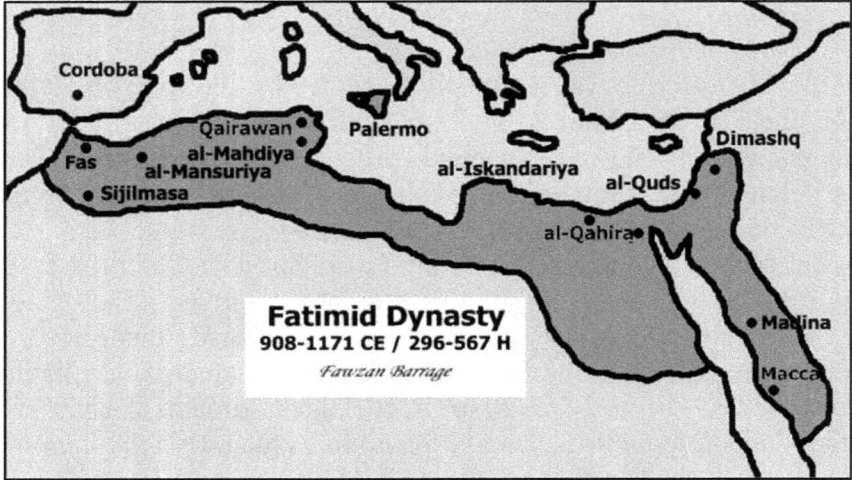

Figure 6-2: Fatimid Dynasty at its Height[15]

Their rule collapsed and they were gone a little over a century after taking Baghdad. There are several events that contributed to their demise. These included their religious doctrine being unacceptable to the Sunni majority—a Sunni revival in the 11th and 12th centuries made that rejection a certainty. The occurrence of the Crusades beginning in the 11th century also contributed to their defeat as there was no room for infighting amongst the Muslim sects during that time. Finally, the later years of the Fatimid were marked by infighting amongst Berber, Turkish, Sudanese, and Nubian troops. These were exacerbated by plagues and famines during the final years. The Fatimid reign ended in 1171 when Saladin became the ruler of Egypt and once again established Sunni Islam there.

Seljuk Turks

The Seljuk Turks were driven into southwestern Asia as a result of the Mongol sweep across Asia. The Seljuk were a warrior race and accepted Sunni Islam when they came in contact with the Abbasid.

> The Islamization of the Turks within the Muslim empire integrated new and unlimited forces. Uncouth and hardy,

they had, since the ninth century, supplied contingents of slaves exclusively reserved for the Abbasid caliph's guard and for military service. Thus, quite naturally, the ideology and tactics of *jihad* inflamed the warlike tendencies of the tribes, already roaming the Asiatic borders of the Greek and Armenian lands. They joined its ranks with the enthusiasm of neophytes and their ravages facilitated the Islamization and Turkification of Armenia, the Greek territories of Anatolia and the Balkans. Yet, it is also true that their depredations could not be controlled by the Muslim state and often harmed its economic interests.[16]

The Turks swept westward and eventually took control of the empire, effectively controlling it with the Persians after about 945. The Seljuk adopted the culture and language of their Persian instructors as they had no Islamic heritage or strong literary heritage of their own. This led to the adoption of the Persian language throughout the area that is now Iran.

As mentioned above, the Seljuk drove the forces allied with the Fatimid from Baghdad and were seen as restorers of Sunni unity within Islam. They continued to push westward until they reached the frontier of Egypt. In the east in 1071, the Seljuk defeated the Byzantine army at Manzikert (in Anatolia) and captured its emperor Romanus IV Diogenes. This opened the way for the Turkish settlement of Anatolia. After settling into Anatolia, they became mercenaries and found employment among rival Byzantine factions that were all vying for the throne in Constantinople. After the start of the Crusades, the Seljuk found themselves hemmed in by the Byzantine on the west and the crusaders on the east. Their practice of dividing provinces among all of a ruler's sons led to internal power struggles and instability. They continued to weaken and by the time of the Mongol invasion, they were unable to defend themselves and disappeared as an autonomous power early in the 13th century.

The Seljuk Empire left a significant imprint on Islam from both a religious and political perspective. They created a series of madrasahs to provide uniform training for both administrators and religious scholars. Below is a map of the Seljuk Empire at its height (the inset) and the area under its control toward the end of its reign.

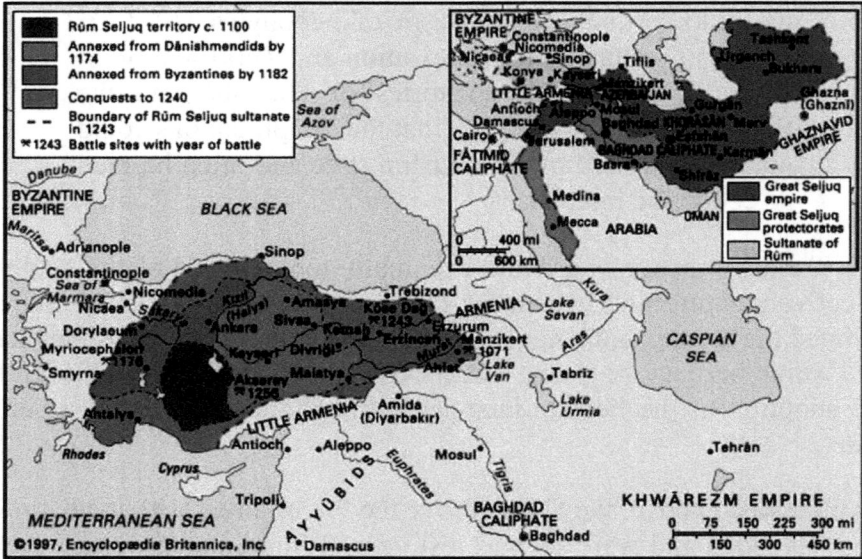

Figure 6-3: Seljuk Empire[17]

Byzantine Response

The advances by the Abbasid put the Byzantines into a defensive posture. However, in response to the persecution of non-Muslims within the caliphate, the Byzantines switched from a defensive posture to an offensive one against the caliphate. Beginning in 960, the Byzantine Emperor Nicephorus Phocas began retaking some territory from the Abbasid, reclaiming Crete, Cyprus, Cilicia, and portions of Syria, including Antioch. Islam was obliged to wage war to reclaim a part of dar al-Islam (the lands of Islam). Forces were brought from all parts of the caliphate, but the efforts were hampered by the split between Shia and Sunni. A ten-year treaty was signed in 1001 by Basil II. However, the truce was short-lived. In 1004, the sixth Abbasid caliph, Abu 'Ali al-Mansur, rebelled violently against the faith of his Christian mother and uncles (two of whom were patriarchs). He ordered churches destroyed, crosses burned, and all church properties to be confiscated. It is estimated that over 30,000 churches were destroyed over the next ten years, including the rebuilt Church of the Sepulcher in Jerusalem. He also implemented decrees intended to humiliate Jews and Christians, such as the wearing of extremely heavy crosses, and idols in the shape of calves for Jews. In 1021, the caliph mysteriously disappeared.

The End of the Abbasid: The Crusades, Mongols, and Mamluks

As noted above, the Seljuk Turks moved west into Persia and Asia Minor in the 11th century, fleeing the advance of the Mongols under Genghis Khan. Beginning in 1070, they took portions of Asia Minor and retook Syria. Jerusalem was sacked, and a sultanate established in Nicaea. The Byzantine Empire had been reduced to an area a little larger than Greece. At this time, the emperor Alexius I Comnenus appealed to Rome for help.

The Crusades (1095–1250)

During the Middle Ages, the practice of going on pilgrimages to religious shrines housing various artifacts of the saints developed. There were many shrines throughout Europe and the Middle East, but three cities stood out in importance. These were Rome, Santiago de Compostela (Spain), and Jerusalem. To support and protect travelers on their journeys to and from a shrine, numerous charitable organizations developed throughout Europe, including hospitals, hospices, and bridge brotherhoods. By the time of the High Middle Ages, every town and most villages came to have one or more of these charitable organizations. Military orders developed to provide these same services to areas under Islamic control, and the role of these organizations latter grew to include serving in the negotiation and ransoming of war captives during the crusades.[18]

Pope Urban II called for the First Crusade at the Council of Clermont in 1095. The crusades were a defensive war waged to

1. Stem Muslim aggression, as almost two thirds of what had been the lands of Christendom had at this time been conquered by the early caliphs, Umayyad, and Abbasid.

2. End the mistreatment of Christians living in Muslim lands (see the following section on the treatment of dhimmis).

3. End the harassment of Christian pilgrims traveling in the Holy Land.

Some short-lived success was achieved. The first crusade retook parts of Anatolia and Syria from the Seljuk, and Palestine, including Jerusalem, from the Fatimid. There were seven crusades in all, each with varying objectives and degrees of success. However, there was much mistrust between the East and their Western European allies, fueled in part by some Greek and Monophysite support being given to Islamic forces. Also, many of the participants in the later crusades were third and fourth sons of nobles without any wealth or land of their own. They looted and pillaged across both Europe and Arabia in search of wealth while travelling both to and from the crusades.

The Mongols and Mamluks

At the same time as the crusades were winding down, the Mongols were sweeping into western Asia. In 1253, Hulagu Khan, brother of Kublai Khan, was given the task of conquering what is now Iran, then under control of the Khwarezm, an independent Islamic dynasty that had wrested control of the area from the Seljuk Turks. He set out with an army of about 130,000 and founded the Il-Khanid dynasty in 1256. The Il-Khans reunited the area under the rule of a single political authority. At about this time, Hulagu Khan sent an emissary to the European powers offering help against the Muslims. However, after the crusades the Christians were too disorganized to come to any specific agreement.

The Mongols destroyed Baghdad in 1258 and ended the Abbasid dynasty. They next swept through Iraq and Syria and headed toward Egypt. They were defeated by the Mamluks in Palestine in 1260. The Mamluks (derived from the Arabic word for slave) handed the Mongols their first known defeat in open combat; however, they were neither Arab nor Egyptian. They were an imported force of Turkish and Circassian slave soldiers brought into Egypt with Saladin a century earlier. The Mamluk generals established their own sultanate upon the death of Al-Malik as-Salih Ayyub in 1249, and ruled Egypt and portions of Syria from about 1250 to 1517. They were Sunni, and their dynasty will be discussed further in conjunction with the Ottomans in the last section of this chapter.

As for the Mongols, by the end of the 13th century they lost all contact with the Mongol chieftains and embraced Islam. Their ruler Mahmud Ghazan embraced Sunni Islam, but his brother converted to Shia Islam early in the 14th century. This change gave rise to much internal conflict within the area ruled by the Il-Khans. The conflict was overted somewhat when a subsequent ruler converted back to Sunni Islam. Internal disputes continued, and the Il-Khanid dynasty disappeared by the middle of the 14th century.

Dhimmitude Under the Abbasid

This section covers both dhimmitude and the development of Islamic law related to this topic. This section examines the following: (1) definitions of some relevant terms, (2) the relationship between dhimmitude and jihad, (3) governance under dhimmitude, (4) taxation, (5) church complicity, and (6) outcomes.

Definitions

I am going to assume that the terms in these materials are unfamiliar to you. So we are going to start with defining a few of them.

Ata: A gift, in this case a gift of land given to someone who participated in jihad.

Dhimmi: Literally "protected people." These are the peoples of the book conquered through jihad. They belong to the umma and are administered by the state on the umma's behalf.

Iqta: Granting of land to army officials for a limited period of time, in lieu of wages.

Jihad: Warfare conducted to advance Islam. This warfare can be conducted either through arms or by peaceful means. The peaceful means recognized vary, but include jihad of the pen, mind, tongue, wealth, and hand. Jihad is required of all Muslims based upon the Qur'an.[19] While this term is sometimes used to refer to spiritual warfare, that is not the type of jihad that applies to this topic. Similarly, the word does not carry the spiritual connotation in most places where it occurs within the Qur'an.

The Maghreb: Region of North Africa between Libya and Morocco, incorporating the Atlas Mountains.

Mawalis: Non-Arabs who convert to Islam.

People of the Book: Christians, Jews, and Zoroastrians.

Qadi: Judge within a Muslim community who renders decisions based upon Islamic law.

Razzia: Bedouin raids conducted to obtain wealth and goods from others. These raids were a normal part of Arab culture long before Muhammad's birth.

Umma: The brotherhood of Islamic believers.

Jihad and Dhimmitude

This chapter's earlier portions discussed the rapid expansion of Islam after Muhammad's death. "After the Abbasid revolt, the caliphs ... contented themselves with sending their troops to pillage, sack, and carry off booty from across their frontiers with Anatolia and Armenia. But in the West, Islamic expansion continued by maritime warfare. In the ninth and tenth centuries, Berbers and Arabs from Spain and the Maghreb raided the coasts of France, Italy, Sicily, and the Greek Islands."[20] These attacks extended up the Italian peninsula as far as Rome in 846 and Naples just ten years later. Bat Ye'or has written extensively about this period of Islamic history and dhimmitude. Her book *The Decline of Eastern Christianity under Islam* provides a good historical overview of this period and aspect of Islam's history. Her work contains many references to original source material for those who want to learn more,[21] and is used extensively for this section.

The Islamization of this conquered area took place in two phases. "The first phase consists of a military conflict defined by specific rules, the *jihad*. The second phase represents *dhimma*, or the government of the conquered peoples. While the *jihad* stipulated the modalities of dividing the booty (land, property, conquered peoples) between the belligerents, the *dhimma* assigns a long-term economy function to the *dhimmis*, which consists of supplying the needs of the Muslim community."[22] While the events described in this section occurred across all the conquered areas, they unfolded differently across the towns and the rural areas. Later, we will consider the Ottomans who replaced the Abbasid in 1258. As mentioned earlier, the Turks in large part were the caliphate's ruling power by the middle of the tenth century. The biggest difference between dhimmitude within the two empires was that Islamic law was still being developed during the Abbasid dynasty, while it was mostly formed by the time the Ottoman ruled.

Drivers of jihad included Muslim adventurers who were "avid for booty, they, too, became soldiers of holy war (*ghazi*, from the word *ghazwa*: *razzia*). [Second] Arab judges (*qadis*), who knew the regulations of *jihad*, flocked toward the frontiers to instruct and lead them. Thus fanaticized by cohorts of theologians, these bands of ghazis, accompanied by regular armies composed of slaves, raided Armenia, Mesopotamia, and Anatolia, where gradually some Turkish emirates emerged."[23] This jihad lasted until the seventeenth century, with Islamic forces reaching as far as Vienna in 1683. The wars waged by these ghazis served to reconcile Islamic faith (as instructed by the Qur'an) with the lust for booty that was often satisfied by the capture of non-Muslims destined for either slavery or ransom.[24]

We should note that taking the spoils of war, captives as slaves, etc. was not an uncommon practice during this period. You will find many European nations, including the Byzantines, practicing the same things. What was unusual is the degree to which these actions were carried out and the period of time over which they extended. Moreover, their link to a religious ideology (Islam) was in and of itself unique. To say what is occurring in the Middle East today is a new form of extremism is simply wrong, and ignores historical facts. While one is free to form their own opinions, the facts speak for themselves. This period's events have been documented by both Islamic and non-Islamic sources. The information is there for those who wish to know the truth.

The following from Ye'or's book summarizes support for this position.

> The general picture of destruction, ruin, massacre, and deportation of urban and rural populations was common to all the conquered territories in Asia, Africa, and Europe. Well documented by contemporary Syriac, Greek, and Arabic chronicles, the few examples provided illustrate a general situation as it recurred regularly during the seasonal razzias, over the years, and for centuries. The chronicles, in great part translated and published, are well known to specialized historians and indicate clearly, beyond any shadow of doubt, that the rules of jihad concerning booty, the fifth part, the fay, levies on harvests, and the fate of populations

(conversion, massacre, slavery, or tribute) were not just vague principles laid down by a theoretical treatise on warfare, construed by some obscure theologian. The Arabs, stirred by their profound belief and the conviction of belonging to an elite nation, superior to all others (Koran 3:106), put them into practice, feeling that they were thereby fulfilling a religious duty and executing the will of Allah.

It must be stressed, however, that massacre or slavery of the vanquished peoples, burning, pillage, destruction, and the claiming of tribute were the common practices during the period under consideration of every army whether Greek, Latin, or Slav. Only the excess, the regular repetition and the systemization of the destruction, codified by theology, distinguishes the jihad from other wars of conquest or depredation.[25]

<u>Rural Areas</u>

Razzias were conducted on a seasonal basis. In rural areas these often eliminated the forthcoming harvest, the food supply of the local population, but the raiders also took livestock, people as slaves, and whatever other property was of value. All territory and slaves taken from non-Muslims became either *fay* (property belonging to the *umma* and administered by the state), or booty given to individuals who participated in the raid. This division of property between the state and the raiders was performed by the *qadi*, an Islamic judge. These judges normally accompanied the jihadi soldiers into new territory as it was conquered: "The nomadic tribes demanded that it [booty] be shared out immediately and the conquered peoples enslaved, as at the time of the Prophet. However, the redistribution of power within the Qurayshite clan where the caravan merchant bourgeoisie of Mecca was prominent replaced these practices by the concept of an Islamic state monopoly on the bulk of the war booty, which was then conceded in the form of domains (*iqta*) or allowances (*ata*) to the Arab tribes."[26] These lands could be granted for either a specific period of time or in perpetuity. One condition of receiving such a grant required the receiver to both equip an army and for it to participate in the fighting.

The basis for fay and dhimmis are both derived from Islam's sources. The basis for fay came from Muhammad's decision to keep the Banu Nadir's property in Medina when they were exiled, with the intent it be administered for the benefit of the *umma*. Dhimmi status came from the treatment of the Jews at Khaybar after they were defeated and their lands taken. They were made slaves and allowed to stay and farm the land, but had to give half of their crop to Muhammad. This dhimmi status was to be retained only so long as Islam allowed—it could be revoked at any time for any reason.

Some have compared this form of servitude to the feudal system in Europe that had already developed by this time, but these were not the same. The power of the European princes was normally limited and usually extended only over rural areas. To retain power, these local rulers needed some degree of cooperation from those they ruled. Normally a social contract outlining the responsibilities of the ruler and the subjects was created. Subjects typically provided labor for the ruler for a specific period of time over the year, and in return a ruler provided protection to their subjects. A violation by either party nullified the agreement, and if a ruler became too oppressive, some subjects would leave that kingdom. They could also move into cities or towns as feudalism did not normally extend over those areas; no one typically owned the buildings and the land upon which they set at times was often owned by a religious organization (church, abbey, convent, etc.). Often people who left feudal lands and remained within a town for a year and a day came to be recognized as free. None of this existed within dhimmitude where people were tied to a specific location; they were not free to leave, nor did they have the latitude to produce goods for themselves.

The effect of the razzias was to depopulate the rural areas as people either died, were enslaved, fled into the towns, or left the area altogether.

The struggles between the state and the tribes over the distribution of booty set up continued conflict and destruction across the land where war was being waged. This left much of the land uncultivated as the remaining native people again attempted to leave, and the invaders, being primarily soldiers, merchants and shepherds, would let the land lie fallow. As agriculture was the caliphate's primary income source, these events disrupted its revenue stream.

In response, the caliphate used censuses to forcibly repopulate the land with inhabitants who had previously cultivated it. This was complemented by the wholesale transfer and deportation of dhimmi populations from one area to another. These transfers fragmented the dhimmi populations further into groups that were often hostile toward each other, and contributed to yet further disintegration. However, the cycle of raids continued, each cycle resulting in more death and enslavement of smaller populations. Each time people tried to flee to non-Islamic countries, into the relatively remote mountainous regions, or to hide within the slave populations existing within the towns.

Several actions were undertaken by the caliphate in response. One was to create passports containing the individual's name, their parents' names, and their location. Individuals were not allowed to leave the area unless they had paid both their own taxes and their parents', even if the parents were deceased. Second, obligations were created requiring the wearing of distinctive clothing and markings to identify non-Muslims. Any violations were treated harshly.

Towns and Cities

The experiences of the towns were in some ways quite different. Towns normally had walls that served to protect the residents. Some, deprived of food, were conquered and the entire population was put to the sword or enslaved. Others were able to negotiate a treaty with the invaders. At times the towns would put up little to no resistance. Towns at this time were normally required to pay tribute to far-off rulers. From the town's perspective, it did not matter whether they paid tribute to a far-off ruler in Constantinople or one in Baghdad or Damascus. The local populations did not understand that the purpose driving the Arab razzias had changed. Islam at this time was thought to be just another religious heresy. The inhabitants did not understand the change that had taken place through the Arab conversion from paganism to Islam.

The agreements reached by the towns with the invaders largely left their civic and religious structures in place. This was important as initially the invaders were in the minority in the lands they had conquered. It is doubtful the jihad could have conquered such a large area so rapidly if the native populations had risen up in rebellion against the new rule. "All territory taken from infidels became the property (fay) of the state. It formed *dar al-Islam*, lands administered by Islamic law for the benefit of Muslims and their descendants. This principle, established by the Arab conquest, instituted a political and legal dogma rooted in theology."[27] Typically one-half of all churches and houses in a conquered area would become the property of Muslims, and the acquired churches would be converted into mosques.

The two pillars of early Islamic society were the army—formed of both Arab tribes and slaves taken in war—and the conquered peoples: tributaries, slaves, free men, and converts, a workforce used to feed the caliphate's economic engine. A third pillar, judicial power, was being developed, and it is to the governance formed under that power that we now turn. It should be noted that before this last pillar's development, force alone was used to resolve disputes and retain order.

Governance

As mentioned above, the Islamic conquerors were initially the minority population within lands they had acquired. When the Abbasids came to power, Muslims were still "the minority among the Monophysite Christian population (Egypt, Syria, Mesopotamia), or Nestorians (Iraq). Zoroastrians populated the towns and villages of Iran and a numerous Jewish population still survived, principally in Palestine, Syria and Iraq, but also in Persia, Egypt, North Africa and Spain."[28] Therefore, they typically left the existing civil and religious structures in place and installed a military governor who ruled on the caliph's behalf. The national languages were left intact, as the Muslims had to rely on the native population for a society's day-to-day functioning. As mentioned above, most of the Arabic population were either merchants or shepherds. What governance experience they had was based upon the tribes and clans. The societies they had conquered were both more complex and sophisticated.

The caliphs reasoned that this situation could not last. They needed to consolidate power in order to retain the lands they had conquered. They undertook a two-pronged approach to achieve that end. One was to increase the Muslim population within the newly acquired lands. "Caliphs, sultans, emirs, or provincial governors—whether Arab or Turkish—encouraged the emigration and settlement of their tribes on the conquered lands in order to consolidate their power against their rivals. The nomads, whose numbers increased incessantly, could only maintain their essential needs by pillaging villages and towns, confiscating goods, extorting money under torture, and ransoming and abducting the youth who were a marketable commodity and a source of wealth as slaves."[29]

The second approach has already been discussed: the native people taken as slaves within a conquered area were normally sent to other locations. The focuses here were to (1) develop rules for the division and administration of the conquered areas, and (2) both keep the dhimmis on the land and defend them in order to protect the revenue stream the caliph needed to maintain the army. In short, the population left to work the land simply became economic producers.

The rights of non-Muslims were extremely limited. "Islamic law forbade non-Muslims the ownership of landed property and transferred it to the Muslim public treasury administered by the caliph. Military districts were given as fiefs by the caliph to members of his family and to tribes or military chiefs for a limited period of time or in perpetuity-in exchange for the equipping of a military unit and its participation in expeditions. This military administrative hierarchy survived in the

Ottoman Empire till the nineteenth century."[30] In addition, other legal restrictions developed and included the following:

1. Forbidding either a Christian or Jew from exerting authority over a Muslim as they had received God's word but turned away from it, so dhimmis were excluded from public office.[31] (Also see S18.26 and S5.57)

2. "All litigation between a Muslim and a dhimmi was under the jurisdiction of Islamic legislation, which did not recognize the validity of the oath of a dhimmi against that of a Muslim."[32]

3. "Construction of new churches, convents, and synagogues was forbidden, but restoration of pre-Islamic places of worship was permitted, subject to certain restrictions and on condition that they were neither enlarged nor altered."[33]

4. "The Koran forbids forced conversions ... [but] the alternatives forced on the Peoples of the Book—namely payment of tribute and submission to Islamic law or the massacre and enslavement of survivors—is, in its very terms, a contravention of the principle of religious freedom ... After the Arab conquest, a number of Christianized Arab tribes suffered defeat, enslavement, and forced conversions."[34] At times these forced conversions included the use of torture.[35]

5. Non-Muslims were required to provide clothing, along with three days of shelter and provisions, to any Muslim traveler in need.

6. "The dhimma required the humiliation of the dhimmis, who were accused of falsifying the Bible by deletions, distortions, and omissions of the prophecies heralding Muhammad's mission."[36]

a. Houses had to be inferior and smaller than those of Muslims.

b. Arab honorific titles were forbidden to non-Muslims.

c. Marriage and sexual relationships between dhimmis and Muslim women were punishable by death.

d. Dhimmis could not ride upon a noble animal, such as a horse or camel.

e. Dhimmis were normally struck by the tax collector as they paid their taxes as a sign of the dhimmis' inferior position.[37]

Many more examples could be cited, but the above suffice to demonstrate the second-class status of the dhimmi under Islamic rule. Many of these provisions remained in effect until the eighteenth century, and in some areas they were retained until the middle of the twentieth century.

Taxation

Just as with other aspects of society, Islam absorbed what was around it and made the foreign structure, concept, or idea its own. This is also true of taxation. "The components of Byzantine and Persian taxation absorbed into Islamic institutions were specified by the concepts of jizya (poll tax on non-Muslims), kharaj (tax in kind or in money on their land), fay (state property), which were integrated into a theological conception of a war of conquest: jihad."[38]

Under the Umayyad, five types of taxes were levied. These included a land tax (*kharaj*), provisions in kind (related to harvests), a poll tax (*jizya*), a tax covering the expenses and maintenance of the tax collectors, and a general tax levied to provide for the upkeep and clothing of Muslims.[39] As noted earlier, the treatment of dhimmis through continued *razzias* and the devastation that resulted, even after the initial conquest, forced many to flee to comparative safety elsewhere. The administration resorted to brutal measures to prevent dhimmis from leaving, and taxes were often extorted using torture and death, particularly crucifixion.[40] When taxes could not be paid, children were often taken as payment. While Islamic works justifying fair treatment of dhimmis in the collection of taxes exist, such as those of Abu Yusuf Ya'qub (731-798), chronicles written by witnesses to the tax collection processes in place indicate that these practices were seldom, if ever, carried out.

Land was divided into two types. The first were Arab lands. These were tithe lands where tribute was paid by the Muslim tribes to the caliph. The second were the lands taken from non-Muslims. These were referred to as the kharaj lands and were owned by the state to be administered for the benefit of all Muslims. The conversion of conquered peoples to Islam and the resettlement of these areas by Arab emigrants resulted in the gradual transfer of these lands from those subject to the kharaj to those paying tithes.

Conflict arose between the caliph and those who participated in jihad as their interests were contradictory. The jihadi participants demanded payment in terms of land, slaves, and possessions as had occurred under Muhammad. This wealth was largely necessary as the Arab people had been principally merchants and shepherds; they generally did not know how to farm and were unable to create incomes sufficient to meet their own needs in the new lands. On the other hand, the caliph's taking of fay increased his wealth and power, and provided the resources that were needed to support the Muslims who had been relocated to the conquered lands. It is a classic example of the struggle between individuals trying to find a way to meet their own needs and an elite group claiming to have a higher authority who should be the one that provides those needs. The means used in this case are in no way comparable to those that unfolded in Europe or North America. More information on the struggle between individuals and elitists, or individualism and collectivism, can be found in *Do You Want to be Free*.[41]

The *jizya* was a wealth tax that initially had three rates, depending on the assessed wealth of the tax payer. The rates and number of tiers increased after their initial imposition. While dhimmis were subject to the *jizya*, Muslims were subject only to paying the *zakat*, the alms required by Islam. Extortion was used to collect the *jizya*, and tax collectors demanded gifts in addition to the taxes.[42] In theory those who could not pay—such as women, paupers, the sick and feeble—were exempt from this tax. However, chronicles from this period indicate that the *jizya* was extracted from widows, orphans, and even the dead.[43] When traveling, it was typical for a dhimmi to display a proof that they had paid the *jizya*, either around the neck, wrist, or chest. To travel without this proof was to risk death.[44]

The caliphate's need for funding increased as the size of the empire increased and war continued. "Economic problems, fragmentation of the empire, and the wars against Byzantium caused a tougher systemization of religious persecution which was integrated into Muslim government institutions."[45] The oppression was so great that rebellions sometimes resulted. Of special note were the rebellions by the Copts in Egypt in 725, 739, and again in 832. Ninth century writers indicate that the situation was similar in Islamic Spain.

In addition to taxes, ransoms were also often extracted from either wealthy non-Muslims (notables) or communities as a whole. This taking of ransom was a part of Arab culture that predated Muhammad and was extracted not only by the state but by the tribes and clans within an area as well. Its existence was the product of life in a difficult environment where there were often not enough resources to meet a tribe's needs. In order to survive, they took what they needed. This relates to the concept called *muruwa* that was described in the first chapter. We are shaped by our culture and often changes to such basic beliefs require a very long time to establish themselves.

If the ransoms (*avanias* or *awarid*) were not paid, an entire community could be subject to the sword, torture, or the women and children could be taken as slaves in payment. Again, these events occurred over an extremely long period of time. The Abbasid began their rule in the mid-eighth century, but these practices were still written about in areas such as Morocco until the eighteenth century, and in parts of Syria, Palestine, and Iraq until the nineteenth century. That is a period of over a thousand years. But as stated earlier in this chapter, all of this was unlikely to happen without the complicity of the church, and it is to that topic that we turn next.

Church Complicity

The initial approach of leaving the civic and religious powers in place ensured their complicity in the subjection of the dhimmi peoples they led. The civic and religious leaders retained local power over the people and wealth the city or town possessed. Their continued leadership being subject to the will of the caliph also ensured their allegiance in ways that could not be obtained by using Arab tribal leaders.

> In the first centuries of the Arab conquest, mainly Christian and Zoroastrian notables, but also Jewish—as well as innumerable *mawalis* and Christian and Jewish slaves originating from the spoils of war—held important positions, not only close to the caliphs but also in the administration and the army....
>
> Scribes, secretaries, treasurers, accountants, architects, craftsmen, peasants, doctors, scholars, diplomats, translators, and politicians, the Christians formed the base, the texture, the elite, and the sinews of the Muslim empire. It is probable that without their collaboration the creation and expansion of this empire would not have been possible. The conquered Christian masses placed all the resources—all the proficiency, the accumulation of technical skills, and sciences built up by earlier civilizations—at the service of nomad chiefs or semi nomad Arabs and, later, of Turks.[46]

There arose a powerful class of dhimmi merchants, bankers, and traders. Their presence in the caliph's courts belied the destruction that was occurring in the rural areas where jihad continued to be waged at the same time. Although the composition of this group changed over time, the group itself lasted for centuries until well into the nineteenth century under the Ottomans. Resistance in the form of peasant revolts were generally local in nature and, lacking leadership, they were usually doomed to failure before they began.

So why did this collaboration happen? There are at least four reasons. First, in the short-term it allowed the church to retain its rights, and exercise the fiscal, legal, and spiritual control of its communities. At the same time it provided great wealth for a privileged minority of its members. The church became an arm of the caliph and was initially often responsible for collecting the tribute. Second, there were many small kingdoms, particularly in Eastern Europe, where powers often went from being antagonists of Islam to collaborators in order to put to rest old scores with surrounding kingdoms to exact revenge for previous perceived wrongs. The disaffected also migrated toward Islam to settle old scores.

> One may discern a self-perpetuating Christian Islamophile current running consistently through history, even swelling the ranks of the Islamic armies, which strengthened and guided them toward the conquest of their former homelands. Princes, adventurers, and frustrated ambitious men flowed in a continuous wave toward the sultans, whom they advised and to whom they gave precise information on the state of the Christian provinces.[47]

Third, the Byzantine Church was often very repressive itself, particularly with those who varied from its religious doctrines. These disaffected groups welcomed Islam as liberators. In the words of Michael the Syrian, a cleric who chronicled events in the ninth century, "The God of vengeance ... seeing the evilness of the Romans

[Byzantines] who, wherever they ruled, cruelly pillaged our churches and monasteries and mercilessly condemned us, led the sons of Ishmael from the region of the south in order to deliver us from Roman hands."[48] Fourth, the Eastern Orthodox hierarchy found collaborating with Islam useful in deterring the advance of Catholic proselytizing within the areas of its influence.

What is interesting here is that the above all represent a form of corruption between the church and state within many of the local kingdoms where Christianity was present. This corruption was also present in kingdoms in various parts of Europe at this time as well. It would be one of the conditions that Pope Gregory VII would work to reform beginning in the eleventh century. It was also during this time that freedom, as we understand it today, began to develop within the Northern Italian states of Venice, Milan, Genoa, and Florence. While the events in Europe ended with the signing of the Magna Charta by King John early in the thirteenth century, the events within the area controlled by the caliphate ended with the rise of the Ottomans in the middle of the same century. The merging of the spheres of the state and church throughout history has always led to the corruption of both.[49]

Make no mistake, there was a definite division of power that accompanied the Islamic conquest. While economic and administrative power initially remained with the local civic and religious structures, all executive, political, and military power became exclusively Islamic. Again, this probably did not seem to be that signifanct a change for kingdoms that had been under Roman/Byzantine rule for centuries. It demonstrates how these groups did not understand the nature of the change that was occurring with the rise of Islam among the Arabic people.

> The collection of different forms of tribute was delegated to the religious leaders of the vanquished peoples. They divided the total amount due among their communities and paid the Islamic treasury the fixed sum, having deducted their part. The disappearance of the Byzantine

state thus transferred to the patriarchates the temporal, judicial, and fiscal duties which the Christian state no longer assumed."[50]

This corruption not only led to greater tribute being extracted from the dhimmi population by their own leaders, but also gave rise to a number of Islamic converts as well.

To summarize, a wave of Christian defectors from both the church and civic leaders, attracted by power and wealth, "set in motion the decline and destruction of that Christendom which they deserted."[51] The caliphs were able to win the hearts "at Serbian, Bosnian, Bulgarian, and Greek courts from among the Slav and Greek clergy by financing a Turcophile party which nourished pessimism, preached the inevitability of the triumph of Islam, and spoke highly of the economic advantages that Muslim markets offered."[52] Finally, they used the element of fear in furthering Islam within the conquered lands. In looking at current events, one should ask the following: How different is the situation today?

Outcomes

The number of dhimmis, as well as their place in Islamic society, deteriorated during the Abbasid and Ottoman Empires and continues today. This population's decline is due to a number of factors.

1. The Arab culture that existed before Muhammad.

    a. The harsh environment created an outcome based society, where right and wrong were viewed by what improved the status and/or economic condition of the tribe.

    b. The conducting of raids in order to obtain resources, and the payment of protection to create alliances to prevent raids from occurring.

2. The creation of an ideology that infused theology into the state, military, civic, and legal aspects of society.

    a. The systemization of jihad to expand the area ruled by Islam.

    b. The conflict in interests between the state and the tribes and clans.

    c. The elitism inherent in Islam's tenets. There is no freedom as we know it, only the freedom of a slave.

    d. The development of a legal code, shari'a, which only recognized the rights of Muslims. These all in turn resulted in the conversion of some dhimmis in order to survive.

    e. The corruption of both the state and religious spheres by combining both into a single sphere of influence and power.

    f. Supplanting the tribal ties with those of Islam (*umma*).

3. The cooperation of non-Muslims in supporting the caliphate's growth.

    a. The church in order to retain its structures and influence.

    b. The wealthy and powerful in order to retain some of their wealth and influence.

    c. Non-Muslim rulers who allied themselves with the caliphate in order to further their own aims.

    d. The disaffected, who saw a chance to gain wealth and power in the service of the caliphate against their homelands.

    e. All of this influence among non-Muslims disappeared over time, and also resulted in some of them converting to Islam.

A final observation: "Over the centuries, paying for their security and survival became the characteristic of the *dhimmi* communities and the prime condition of their tolerated existence in their own countries."[53] The dhimmi were valued only for what they could produce to support the Islamic community. Once they no longer had anything left to contribute, they no longer held any value. As recently as ten or twenty years ago, some Middle Eastern and North African countries had non-Muslim populations that approached ten percent. In general, that is no longer the case. Some have fled, some have converted, and many others have died.

We will finish out this chapter by looking at the Ottoman Empire.

The Ottoman Empire

Previous sections discussed some of the events occurring at the end of the Abbasid dynasty that included a Mongol invasion, the rise of the Mamluks, and the development of the Seljuk Turk kingdom that would eventually give birth to the Ottoman Empire. This section will look at the development of each of these events after the Abbasid's fall, and then look briefly at the issues of governance and dhimmitude as Ottoman rule is largely referred to as a more tolerant period within Islam. It will then close with some words from our sixth president, John Quincy Adams, on the differences, as he saw them, between Christianity and Islam and some implications arising from those differences.

But first a timeline is presented below to help understand the timing of some significant events occurring during the period of Ottoman expansion. It should be noted that the Ottoman Empire continued to exist until the early 20th century, about 300 years beyond the period presented below.

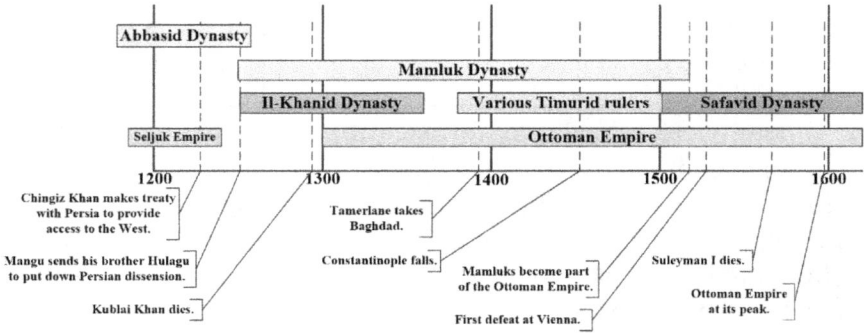

Figure 6-4: Events Related to the Ottoman Empire

History

The Abbasid decline did not result in the direct rise of the Ottoman Empire. Instead a vacuum was created by its defeat in which several powers rose. There were many smaller areas that exercised significant degrees of autonomy, and to some degree this occurred throughout the Ottoman Empire's existence. We will look at the three largest domains to arise within the territory that had been a part of the Abbasid Dynasty: (1) the Mamluks (Egypt and Syria), (2) the Il-Khanid (Persia), and (3) the Ottoman Empire (Anatolia). A part of that discussion will also outline some events that set in place the division between East and West within Islam.

The Il-Khanid

Early in the thirteenth century, Chingiz Khan (Genghis Khan) created an empire that stretched from parts of China toward the Dnieper River in the west. In 1222, he made a treaty with the Shah of Persia to allow his people access to the west. A short time later, a party of Mongol merchants were murdered by one of the Shah's governors, their goods were confiscated, and the envoy Chingiz Khan sent to obtain reparations was tortured and killed. Chingiz Khan and his four sons led a Mongol army west in retaliation. The Mongols were met by an Islamic army in modern Kazakhstan, where the Mongols are reported to have slain 160,000 of the 400,000 man army sent east to meet them. They invaded

Georgia in 1222 and also defeated the Russian army. Chingiz Khan died in 1227.[54]

He was succeeded by Ogdai who pushed further into China in the east and by 1241 in the west had destroyed Moscow and Kiev in Russia and marched as far as Poland and Hungary. In addition to the Mongols traveling west, Nestorian monks travelled to the east where they began evangelizing. By the time Ogdai's successor, Kuyuk, became Emperor in about 1243, Christianity had made significant inroads into the Mongol nation. It is said that Kuyuk's physicians and chief officials were Christians, and that he had a church-tent close to the royal pavilion.[55] A byproduct of these, and earlier, Mongol expansions was to force large numbers of Seljuk Turks into Anatolia and Syria, where they settled after decisively defeating the Byzantines at Manzikert in 1071.

Kuyuk was succeeded by Mangu, a nephew of Ogdai in 1251. He had two brothers, Hulagu and Kublai. While Mangu and Kublai focused their conquest efforts in the east, Mangu sent Hulagu west. Mangu made no distinction between Christians, Jews, Muslims, Buddhists, or believers in Lamaism. However, Hulagu was a Christian and a fanatical adversary of Islam. In 1256, he invaded the Kohistan district within Pakistan where 800,000 subjects were massacred and their king killed. He took control of Persia and reached Baghdad in 1258. He besieged the city and when it fell he spared the Christians but massacred thousands of others.

Hulagu's goal was to "gain possession of Jerusalem because they [the Mongols] wanted to destroy the Arabs who were in Syria and in Palestine, and to massacre their Seljuk supporters."[56] He sacked Aleppo and Damascus surrendered to him in 1260. But while preparing to take Jerusalem, he learned of Mangu's death and returned to Mongolia. He was empowered to take control over all the lands he had conquered, but instead he declared himself to be an independent king, an Il-Khan.[57] He was defeated by a Mamluk army in 1260 and continued to reign until 1265.

Initially the Mongols tried to form treaties and alliances with the Christian kings of Europe and the Pope in Rome. However, these rulers did not understand that Hulagu's goal was simply the destruction of Islam's followers, and no agreements were ever reached. When the Mongols saw "that there was no military assistance to be gained from Europe, their Christian zeal began to abate, and Western Mongols began to fraternize with Syrian and Egyptian Muslims, and Islam began to make progress among them."[58]

A larger degree of tolerance towards Christians within Islamic lands was exhibited at this time. Not only did Hulagu support Christianity, but his brother Kublai did as well, despite the latter's personal belief in Lamaism. Kublai did much to support the development of Christianity within his kingdom, which by this time stretched from the Yellow Sea in the east to the Black Sea in the west and from Mongolia in the north to Tonquin in the south. Muslims did not make any overt effort against other religions so long as Kublai Khan lived. He died in 1294.

With Kublai Khan's death, the Muslims began to rebel against the Mongols and rose again against the Christians. "The Arabs hated the Mongols both as men and as Christians, and their memories of the atrocities committed at Baghdad by Hulagu, nerved them to fight to the death, sparing no one."[59] Hulagu's son Abga, who reigned from 1265–1281, continued to correspond with the Pope and kings of Europe. It was during his reign that Marco Polo travelled to the east.

After Abga's reign, his successors initially vacillated between Christianity and Islam and became too weak to prevent attacks by local Islamic forces. By the fourteenth century, "the Nestorians were cruelly persecuted; the goods of their merchants were confiscated, their churches were destroyed, and those who refused to accept Islam and could not escape were slain. It is probable that large numbers became Muslims and excused themselves for so doing by saying that it was better to accept a religion which proclaimed God and His Unity, than to revert to paganism and idolatry."[60]

By the end of the fourteenth century, Nestorianism practically ceased to exist in Persia, Central Asia, or China. The last of the Il-Khans continued to rule until 1335. *The Monks of Kublai Khan Emperor of China* chronicles the persecution and massacres of Christians in the villages of Maraghah near Azerbaijan and Arbil northwest of Baghdad in Kurdish Iraq late in the thirteenth century. Other works chronicle similar events around Mosul,[61] Baghdad,[62] the Mardin region in Turkey, and a Nestorian village along the Tigris during this same period.[63]

The Mamluks

As noted above, the Mamluks defeated the Mongols in 1260. This is the first documented defeat of the Mongol army in open combat. *Mamluk* literally means *slave*, and the Mamluks were a slave army of Seljuk Turks and Circassians, created and employed by the Islamic rulers during the Abbasid dynasty. The Mamluks frequently used their military power to overthrow the local political authority. These usurpations of power often did not last long, but in Egypt they were able to become the power behind a caliph who was maintained as a symbol to legitimize their authority. Any caliph who did not acquiesce soon found themselves dispatched by the Mamluk generals. By the middle of the thirteenth century, they were strong enough to establish dynasties in both Egypt and India.

> Historians have traditionally broken the era of Mamluk rule into two periods—one covering 1250-1382, the other, 1382-1517. Western historians call the former the "Bahr'I" period and the latter the "Burji," because of the political dominance of the regiments known by these names during the respective times. The contemporary Muslim historians referred to the same divisions as the "Turkish" and "Circassian" periods, in order to call attention to the change in ethnic origin of the majority of Mamluks, which occurred and persisted after the accession of Barquq in 1382.[64]

The following is a map of the Mamluk Dynasty at its peak.

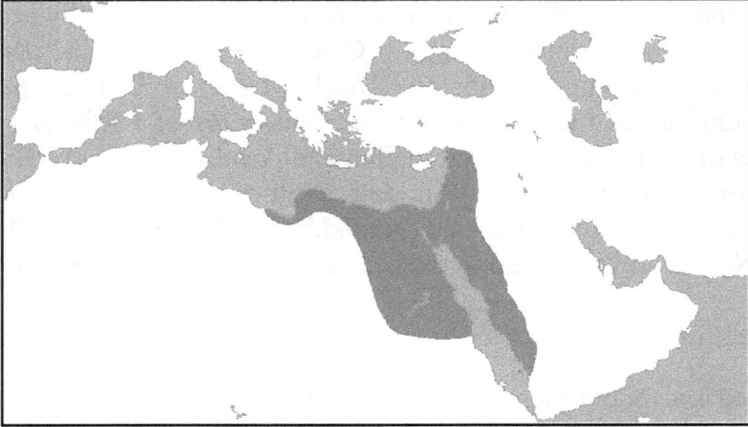

Figure 6-5: Mamluk Dynasty at its peak in 1317[65]

There is general agreement that the Mamluks declined during their Circassian period. They drove the last of the Crusaders out of the Holy Lands and turned back the Mongols, both of which occurred during the Turkish period. Advancement during the Turkish period was also based upon ability. Under the Circassians, advancement became based upon race (i.e., Circassian). Another factor weakening the Mamluks was their inability to unite against Bedouin raiding parties, thus creating economic disorder from trade disruptions and agricultural losses. These were further compounded by several plagues that occurred within Egypt and the East. This left the Mamluks unable to prevent Tamerlane from taking Baghdad temporarily in 1395. The final economic blow came with the Portuguese discovery of a sea route to the East at the beginning of the sixteenth century.

A declining economy weakened the army as the taxes needed to support it could not easily be raised. The Mamluks were defeated by the Ottomans in both Syria and Egypt. Another reason for their defeat was the adoption of field artillery by the Ottomans, while the Mamluks still used artillery only when conducting sieges. Mamluk territory became a part of the Ottoman Empire in 1517, when much of the general population rose up against the Mamluks and the corruption they represented.

The Mamluks continued to be a presence within the Ottoman Empire. They became part of the Ottoman army and over time once again achieved positions of significant power and influence over the Empire. The Ottomans removed the Mamluk requirement of excluding their sons from serving only in non-slave regiments. This resulted in changing the dynamics of loyalty from one based upon their regiment to one based upon family ties, and created additional factions that made it difficult to hold the Empire together. As we will see shortly, by the end of the seventeenth century, the Mamluks once again controlled the armies, tax revenue, and government. Napoleon faced a Mamluk army when he entered Egypt in 1798, but Mamluk power ended when they were massacred by Muhammad Ali Pasha in 1811.[66]

The Ottomans

As noted previously, the Turks had been driven into Anatolia and Syria by the advance of the Mongols. During Hulagu's reign, the Mongols took portions of eastern Anatolia from the Turks, but their primary objectives were Syria and the city of Jerusalem. It was from northwestern Anatolia that the Ottoman Empire rose. Osman was from the Kayi tribe, the prince of a territory on the border frontier with the Byzantines. After the last defeat of the Seljuk Turks by the Mongols in 1293, Osman was able to take additional territory from the Byzantines who were in a state of decline. He ruled until 1324 and it is during his reign that the Ottoman Empire began.

Osman was succeeded by Orhan and his son Murad I. They continued taking territory from the Byzantines, eventually moving into southeastern Europe, but bypassing the major cities like Constantinople and Belgrade as they did not yet have the means to conquer the more heavily fortified cities. They continued the Abbasid tactic of destroying the sources of food and tax revenue in order to weaken their adversaries.

The wealth generated by taking of Byzantine territory attracted many nomads to fight for the Ottomans, but Orhan began a tradition of employing Christian mercenaries to lessen the Empire's reliance on nomads. Orhan's annexation of Karasi (in southern Anatolia) also made the Ottoman Empire the primary ally of the Byzantines. This alliance provided the Ottomans with the opportunity to gain direct knowledge of the Byzantine territory and its weaknesses. The early Ottoman rulers also strengthened their alliances by marriage, to both Christian courts and Islamic principalities. Orhan ruled until 1360. A map of the Ottoman and Byzantine Empires around 1350 is shown below.

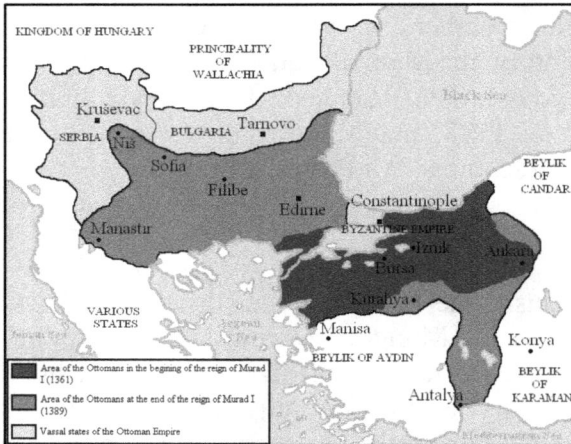

Figure 6-6: Byzantine and Ottoman Empires about 1350[67]

Murad I died in one of the battles for Kosovo and was succeeded by his son Bayezid I. Bayezid turned his attention to Anatolia to eliminate a threat from the Karaman Turkish territory to the east. His accomplishments were so significant that "he was given the title of sultan by the shadow Abbasid caliph of Cairo, despite the opposition of the caliph's Mamluk masters."[68] Tamerlane attacked the Turks in 1397 in order to protect his flank as he drove into India and Persia. Bayezid then attacked Tamerlane, but his followers deserted him—all except his Christian mercenaries—and he was captured at the battle of Ankara and died a short time later. Tamerlane broke up the Ottoman territory in order to remove the threat they posed to his ambitions.

Murad II was made ruler by Turkish notables in 1421 and ruled until 1451. Murad began to resent the power that had been gained by the notables and created the *devsirme* system as a counter-balance. This system formalized the practice begun by Orhan of levying, as tribute, one fifth of the Christian children from the Balkan region.[69] The children of non-Muslims were viewed as fay, property belonging to the state, and under Murad the levies began to be collected annually. The youngsters were generally 14-20 years of age when drafted, taken in contingents of a thousand at a time, and taken from the families of the aristocracy and priests. They converted to Islam and served the sultan for life in his *janissary* corps, an infantry used against Christian kingdoms in the Ottoman wars. A parallel system of *ichoghlani* was also created that took children six to ten years of age into the sultan's service as administrators, after a training period of fourteen years.[70]

To increase the sultan's power further, the concept of using a military slave force for the benefit of the Empire (*kapikulu*) was enlarged to include the Turkish nobility as well. With this change only persons accepting the status of slave, whether Muslim or non-Muslim, could hold positions in the Ottoman army or government.[71] Anyone could achieve this status as long as they accepted "absolute obedience to their master [the sultan] and the devotion of their lives, properties, and families to his service."[72]

Sultans later continued to play the notables against the janissaries in order to retain power and control the Empire. With the fall of Constantinople in 1453, Turkish notable power significantly decreased, and many were executed or exiled to Anatolia. However, the power between the janissaries and notables continued to fluctuate within the Empire. The Ottomans continued to fight against the kingdoms of Europe, the Mamluks in Syria and Egypt, and the Safavid in Persia.

The Safavids were Turkish tribes who emigrated from eastern Anatolia into Persia in reaction to the Ottoman return to a strictly orthodox form of Sunni Islam. They embraced Shia and Sufi doctrines, and spread dissension leading to several revolts within Ottoman provinces. The Ottomans were unable to conquer the Safavids, as the latter generally chose not to engage in direct conflict. The Safavid dynasty lasted from about 1501 through the early part of the 18th century. This rift left the Islamic world divided as we see it today. As was mentioned earlier, the Mamluk Dynasty was defeated and became part of the Ottoman Empire in 1517. It advanced as far as Vienna, where it was defeated a second time in 1683.

The map below shows the Ottoman Empire's expansion from its inception to its peak in about 1599.

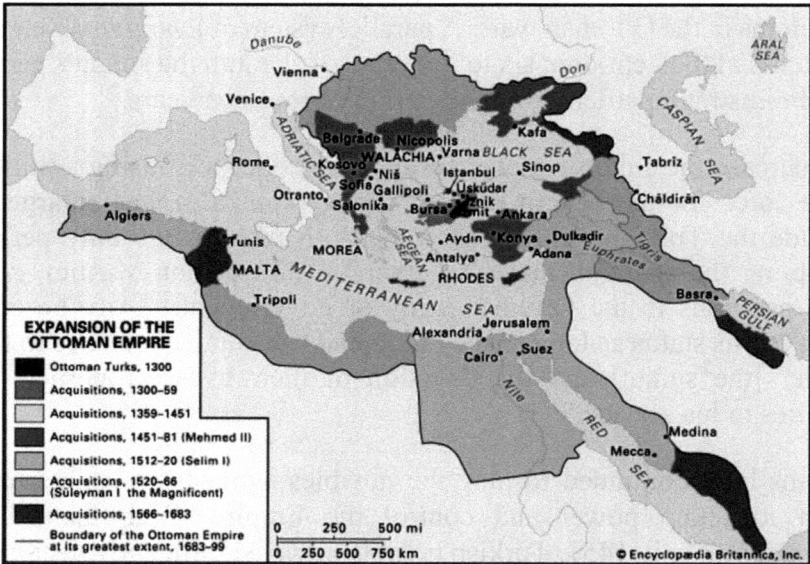

Figure 6-7: Rise of the Ottoman Empire 1300–1599[73]

Governance

Religion was added to the state and military functions as a third functional institution of the ruling class during the Abbasid Dynasty. The Ottomans added a fourth functional institution of administration. This new function was responsible for collecting all the Empire's revenue and its expenditures. During Ottoman rule all members of the army and government were required to submit in complete obedience to the sultan. Increasingly this required administrators to be followers of

Islam, and the employment of the *janissaries* and *ichoghlani* over time ensured that shift occurred.

The attributes needed to enter the Ottoman ruling class included the following:

1. Professing complete loyalty to the state.

2. Acceptance of orthodox (Sunni) Islam.

3. Knowing and practicing the Ottoman Way, a complicated system of customs, behaviors, and language.[74]

The function of this ruling class was to preserve the Islamic state. *Its main duty was to enlarge, protect, and exploit the Empire's wealth for the state's benefit.*

The Empire increased its territory through war. The janissaries and mercenaries used by the Empire were paid with salaries instead of booty. While this provided more control over the Empire's wealth, it also resulted in much larger fixed expenses that had to be met. The size of the army that needed to be maintained proved to be a great weight on the Empire's economy. Large debts accumulated to finance its continuing wars. Several sultans took some of the following actions to try and maintain economic order:

1. Devaluation of coins by reducing the amount of precious metal they contained. This led to inflation and individuals hiding more valuable coins from the Empire's tax collectors, which then led to policies forcing remittance of older coins or their confiscation by the Empire.

2. Creation of government sanctioned monopolies. Monopoly sales provided a temporary increase in government revenues, but was offset by weak economic conditions created by the inferior goods produced and sold for much higher prices than were available outside the Empire.

3. All revenue producing property was determined to belong to the state and therefore confiscated, reducing the incentive to effectively manage the land's production.

4. As the army grew, land was given as timars and tax farms in lieu of wages, a structure that still allowed revenue to be produced for the Empire, but set up conflict between local ruler's and sultan interests.

The weakened economic conditions led to shortages and increased social unrest. The rise of nationalism in the eighteenth and nineteenth centuries led to many rebellions, particularly in the Balkan region. While the government was able to play rebel factions against each other, this often disrupted the food supply, leading to widespread famines, and a further increase in social unrest.

Society's fabric was exemplified by shari'a. Shari'a became the core of political, social, and moral regulations and principles. It was intended to cover all aspects of Muslim life. Sultans were left to create civil law where it did not conflict with shari'a. While civil law could be invalidated where it conflicted with shari'a, as we saw earlier, such conflicting rules were often co-opted and over time incorporated into Islamic law. (Also see the next section on dhimmitude in the Ottoman Empire.)

Sultans were able to exercise great authority as they had the army to back them up. But in reality they were more like tribal chiefs. They received the extra fifth of booty advocated by Islamic law but retaining notable loyalty depended on conquering new territory and providing booty to those who followed. The decline of Turkish notable power left the sultans with no counter-weight against the janissaries. The army (including the Mamluks) began exercising greater control over the sultans and using the government for their own benefit.

The increase in military power led to the creation of innumerable factions within the ruling class, and these worked to reduce the sultan's power by keeping them uneducated and out of any situation where they could learn how to exercise their power. Several attempts at reform were undertaken by some of the later sultans, but these were hampered by (1) the factions themselves, (2) a decrease in centralized authority as power had devolved to the various factions, and (3) a sense of Ottoman superiority leading it to reject many of the changes that had occurred in the rest of the world. From the Ottoman's view, their failure was not that the changes occurring elsewhere were superior, but rather that they were somehow failing to apply the techniques that had worked so well for them in the past.

As Islam is orthopraxic (concerned primarily with correct practice), it tends to look backward, whereas Christianity relies on orthodoxy (concern with correct belief) and tends to be forward looking.

The final blow came with the Ottoman's alliance with the Central Powers in World War I. The surrender of Bulgaria in 1918 severed the direct links between the Ottoman Empire and Germany, and the Ottoman Empire signed an armistice later that year. The map below shows the disintegration of the Ottoman Empire.

Figure 6-8: Ottoman Empire, 1800–1924[75]

Dhimmitude Under the Ottomans

As noted earlier, the Abbasid dhimma's policies continued under the Ottomans, and the harsh treatment of conquered peoples under jihad continued until the seventeenth century. This corresponds with the period leading to the Ottomans peak territorial expansion. In addition, large forced relocations of both Muslim and non-Muslim populations occurred as they had during the Abbasid period. In regards to jihad and its aftermath,

> The holy war being the cornerstone of the Ottomans state and the source of its expansion, strength, and wealth, the government and administration of the empire was entirely dominated by militaristic imperatives. When resistance from the Habsburgs in central Europe and from Persia in the East halted Ottoman expansion in the sixteenth and seventeenth centuries, the war machine lost its external combat zones and imploded, devastating the territory of the empire itself. As in the Arab period when an anarchical phase followed a period of conquests, so the immigration of semi-nomadic tribes engendered uncontrollable disorders in Anatolia, Armenia, and the Balkans. Turkish immigrants, adventurers, fleeing slaves, and peasants, driven from their lands or deported, formed a floating, rootless population living from banditry, rebel chiefs recruited their troops and their liege men from such groups.[76]

The Ottoman sultans at times tried to help the conquered peoples, but the actions of local chiefs often undermined the sultan's policies. Several actions are pointed to as being indicative of more humane treatment of non-Islamic populations under the Ottomans. One is the conquest of Constantinople. The city was spared devastation during the siege. It had to be repopulated after its fall, as "fifty to sixty thousand people were enslaved and deported."[77] Mehmed II had a goal of restoring the city's industry and trade. To do this he brought in people from all ethnicities and religions from the Empire to the renamed

Istanbul. An invitation was extended to Jews living outside the Empire to come to Istanbul in particular and the Empire in general. Later under Suleyman I, France was given special dispensations in trade and commerce in return for coordinating its efforts against their mutual enemy, the Hapsburgs. The French privileges later grew to allowing the Catholic Church to create schools and missions within the Empire to convert non-Muslims to Catholicism.

We also noted earlier that the Islamic Empire was sometimes welcomed as a religious liberator. With the Christianization of the Roman Empire the mixing of state and religion had institutionalized persecution within Byzantine's government and administration. These policies and laws,

> based on religious dogma, were henceforth integrated into Islamic legislation, [and] now justified by other theological principles. In an ironic twist of history, Islam found—in the countries which had come under its domination—an outstanding instrument of oppression for the destruction of Christians, already formulated and perfected by the Church itself.[78]

> Similarity exists in the two sets of legislation [Byzantine and Islamic] concerning the possession of slaves, proselytism, blasphemy, apostasy, religious buildings, conversions, exclusion from public office, prohibition of mixed marriage, social segregation, and the refusal to accept testimony in court.[79]

Although there was great similarity between both sets of laws, it must be remembered that Islamic law developed within an entirely different ideological structure. Within Islam, these laws were placed within the concept of religious war where the rights of non-Muslims depended on a relationship of protection borrowed from Arabic culture.

To this set of regulations the Muslims added the *jizya*: "the blood ransom in exchange for the right to life. Later, additional degrading legislation brought persecution to a level of refinement rarely attained.

It decreed the form and color of the dhimmi's clothing and shoes, their haircut and headgear. It specified the type of mounts and saddles permitted and the way in which they could be ridden, as well as greetings and behavior in the street."[80]

Monophysites, Copts, Jacobites, Armenians, and Nestorians had all been persecuted and tortured at various times under the Byzantines. And all these different groups at times persecuted the Jews. The Persians had welcomed many of these groups, and the Nestorians were the largest non-Zoroastrian group within Persia before its fall to the early caliphs. This religious persecution was a primary cause for many groups deserting the Byzantines and welcoming Islam during the early jihad.

Third, under the Ottomans many non-Muslims were allowed to live in self-governing communities called millets under their own religious laws, traditions, and language. A millet's leader was both a religious and government leader, again a mixing of state and religion into a single function. With the institutionalized persecution noted above, religious intolerance was exacerbated within the millet system. The Ottomans at times exploited these religious hostilities to maintain order. These schisms reignited again during the rebellions related to the nationalism movements of the nineteenth and twentieth centuries at the end of the Ottoman Empire.

The dhimmis rebelled in order to restore their basic freedoms and recognize their nationality, culture, and languages. These actions brought reprisals from the umma. A few significant persecutions include the following:

1. The 1822 taking of the Greek island of Chios where all but 1,800 of the 113,000 inhabitants were either massacred or sold into slavery.[81]

2. The execution of 100,000–200,000 Armenians in eastern Anatolia during 1894–1896 that encouraged many Armenians to become Orthodox in order to seek the protection of Russia.[82]

3. The execution of as many as 600,000 Armenians in eastern Anatolia during World War I, with others being deported.[83]

Observations of John Quincy Adams

In closing this chapter, John Quincy Adams wrote some observations about the Ottoman Empire and Islam over one hundred and eighty-five years ago. In addition to being the sixth President of the United States, he had a long experienced career serving on diplomatic missions that started with accompanying his father, John Adams, to France and the Netherlands when he was only twelve years old. Beginning at the age of fourteen, he spent time in Russia, Finland, Sweden, and Denmark. He was appointed minister to the Netherlands in 1793 at the age of 26, and the first minister to Russia in 1809 where he served until 1814. At that time, he was recalled to help negotiate the treaty ending the War of 1812 between the US and Great Britain. He served as Secretary of State from 1817–1825 and was selected by the House of Representatives to be President in 1825 when the candidates running all failed to receive the necessary number of electoral votes to win the election.

He was one of the chief architects of the Monroe Doctrine as Secretary of State and a witness to the wars against the Barbary Pirates and the Greek War for Independence from the Ottomans. While he opposed intervening in European affairs, he was very well acquainted with both the Ottoman Empire and Islam, and was a long-time opponent of slavery. The following is an extract from the 1830 *The American Annual Register* where he compared Christianity with Islam.

> The Christian was taught, that the end of his being on earth, was the salvation of his soul hereafter.... THE ESSENCE OF THIS DOCTRINE IS, TO READY THE SPIRITUAL PART OF HIS NATURE....
>
> In the seventh century of the Christian era, a wandering Arab of the lineage of Hagar, the Egyptian, combining the powers of transcendent genius, with the preternatural

energy of a fanatic, and the fraudulent spirit of an imposter, proclaimed himself as a messenger from Heaven, and spread desolation and delusion over an extensive portion of the earth.

Adopting from the sublime conception of the Mosaic law, the doctrine of one omnipotent God; he connected indissolubly with it, the audacious falsehood that he was himself his prophet and apostle. Adopting from the new Revelation of Jesus, the faith and hope of immortal life, and of future retribution, he humbled it to the dust, by adapting all the rewards and sanctions of his religion to the gratification of the sexual passion.

He poisoned the sources of human felicity at the fountain, by degrading the condition of the female sex, and the allowance of polygamy; and he declared undistinguishing and exterminating war, as a part of his religion, against all the rest of mankind. THE ESSENCE OF HIS DOCTRINE WAS VIOLENCE AND LUST: TO EXALT THE BRUTAL OVER THE SPIRITUAL PART OF HUMAN NATURE.

Between these two religions, thus contrasted in their characters, a war of twelve hundred years has already raged. That war is yet flagrant; nor can it cease but by the extinction of that imposture, which has been permitted by Providence to prolong the degeneracy of man. While the merciless and dissolute dogmas of the false prophet shall furnish motives to human action, there can never be peace upon earth, and good will towards men. The hand of Ishmael will be against every man, and every man's hand against him....

It [Islam] is the dominion of matter over mind; of darkness over light; of brutal force over righteousness and truth. But divine justice finds not its consummation upon earth. Individual virtue or vice, receives much of its retribution after its mortal career has closed; and the rewards and punishments of nations are adapted to measures of time, extending over numerous successive generations, and many centuries of years.[84] (Emphasis in the original)

Adams contrasts the engine of commerce to that of war, and uses the examples of the American War for Independence with the role of the East India Company in India.

In the half century that has elapsed since the publication of that work [Gibbon's *Decline and Fall of the Roman Empire*], this truth, which a philosophical historian ought then to have discerned and traced to its causes, has been manifested in broader light from year to year. While the whole power of the British empire has been signally baffled by inglorious defeat in the attempt to retain in subjugation three millions of their own countrymen and fellow Christians in North America; a company of London merchants, under the patronage, though with little aid, of their government, have subdued in the far more distant regions of Hindustan, ten times as many millions of the disciples of Mahomet, or their subjects, and, as if Providence had specially intended to mark the contrast of glory and shame between the crescent and the cross, the same Christian chieftain who surrendered his sword to Washington at Yorktown, afterwards received as captive hostages the sons of Tippoo Saib, seven years before the extinction of his life and empire at the storm of Seringapatam.[85]

Adams also cites Christianity's obligations and contrasts those with Islam.

The infidel [follower of Islam] denies it in vain—This system of ethics, and of religion, promulgated by "the

Galilean," has raised the standard of human power, as
well as of human virtue, higher than that of any other
portion of the inhabitants of the globe....

The first of his [Christian] obligations is to himself: to
persevere in the program of self-improvement. ... His
next duties are to his fellow men: to those whom he only,
of all the tribes and nations of the earth, is bound by the
law of his God to consider as his brethren; as children of
the same parent, doomed like him to a pilgrimage of
probation here, but entitled, like himself, to look forward
to a more joyful and glorious hereafter.

His superior acquirements have vested him with the
privilege, and imposed upon him the obligation of
becoming the teacher of his less enlightened fellow
creatures; to make them acquainted with the blessings
within their reach; and to lead them in the path of their
own felicity....

The precept of the koran is, perpetual war against all who
deny, that Mahomet is the prophet of God. The
vanquished may purchase their lives, by the payment of
tribute; the victorious may be appeased by a false and
delusive promise of peace; and the faithful follower of
the prophet, may submit to the imperious necessities of
defeat: but the command to propagate the Moslem creed
by the sword is always obligatory, when it can be made
effective. The commands of the prophet may be
performed alike, by fraud, or by force.[86]

He goes on to describe an incident after the Barbary pirates were
defeated by Decatur. Treaties were drawn up in both English and Arabic
where the Dey renounced all claims of tribute from the United States.
Both treaties were signed, but unbeknownst to Decatur, an additional
clause was inserted into the Arabic copy of the treaty that had not been
a part of the negotiations. "Within a year the Dey demands, under

penalty of the renewal of the war, an indemnity in money for the frigate taken by Decatur ... The arrival of Chauncey, with a squadron before Algiers, silenced the fraudulent claim of the Dey, and he signed a new treaty in which it was abandoned; but he disdained to conceal his intentions; my power, said he, has been wrested from my hands; draw ye the treaty at your pleasure, and I will sign it; but beware of the moment, when I shall recover my power, for with that moment, your treaty shall be waste paper. He avowed what they always practiced, and would without scruple have practiced himself."[87]

One trend seen repeatedly throughout this material is the mixing of religion and government into a single power corrupts both, leading to society's detriment, regardless of the religion. This is one reason why our Constitution includes the protection of religion from government. But while religion is to be protected from government, religion is to have an indirect influence on government through the virtue and morality it instills in a people. For that virtue and morality to exist, there must be an ethical moral basis in a religion's underlying beliefs and philosophy that teaches and promotes these values, and they must always be taught to the next generation. This topic is no longer taught in our public schools today and is discussed in *Do You Want To Be Free*[88] and *Charity and Society*.[89]

The objective of this material has been to provide you with information about Islam's basic tenets, their development, and some implications arising from its doctrines by stating the facts using original source material wherever possible. While the material on Islam's history ends here, I hope that your journey to learn more will continue. Truth can only be found in our Creator, and it is in the search for truth alone that we find our freedom as we come to know Him. May we all find and live in the truth. We now move on to the topic of Islamic attitudes.

Chapter 7

Attitudes and Beliefs

What is Extremism?

We hear repeatedly from the media, and also from some of our leaders, that extremists are a very small part of Islam. A figure normally put at about 1%. We also hear that there are about 1.6 billion Muslims in the world today. Even 1% of that population is about 16 million people. While that is a lot, it is still less than 5% of the entire U.S. population.

But there are a couple of things missing from this conversation. First, what exactly is meant by extremist? Is it action or belief? Attitude or thought? Second, what is the 1% figure based upon? Is that assertion supported? Toward the first question, being an extremist is a relative term. There are likely some issues where I could view you as an extremist, and there are undoubtedly others where you could view me as an extremist. This label really doesn't help very much in even determining what is extreme, let alone a solution. So let's start with a definition. According to the dictionary an extremist is someone who carries something to excess. From a Westerner's perspective, and given Islam's history and doctrines outlined earlier, extremism could be interpreted as adhering to a very literal meaning of Islam.

The Pew Research Center asked Muslims 'What is Islamic extremism?' and obtained the following responses.

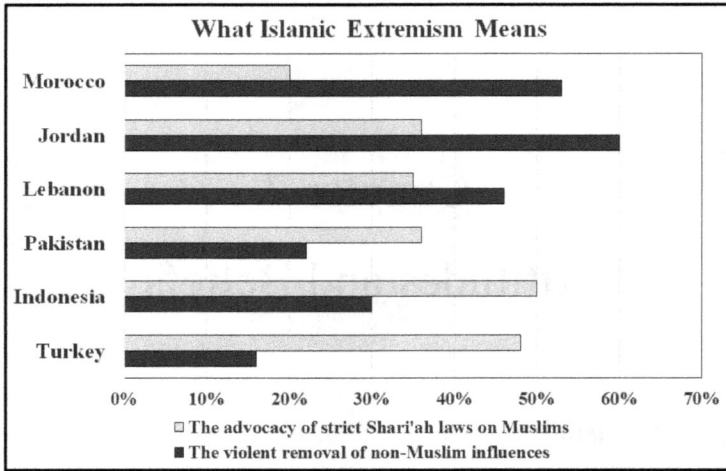

Figure 7-1: What Extremism Means to Muslims[1]

Muslims themselves interpret this term differently. In the Middle East and North African countries, it generally meant the violent removal of non-Muslim influences, but within non-Arabic countries, it generally meant the imposition of shari'a law upon other Muslims. In addition, a significant percentage in all of the countries above, except Jordan, declined to even respond to this question. From a Western perspective, both of these responses would likely be interpreted as Islamic extremism.

This chapter provides some information relevant to both questions posed above. My hope is that it will spark conversations for you with your friends, your families, and your co-workers. It is, after all, okay to disagree, but at least you should understand the nature of your disagreement. Otherwise, how can we effectively ever solve a problem?

Pew Research Center (Center) surveys measured the responses of Muslims from several parts of the world, are used and extrapolated to Islamic populations in several regions. The specific topics covered are the following:

1. General Attitudes

2. Politics

3. Law

4. Culture, with a focus on women's rights

The Center has been surveying Muslim populations across the globe for over fifteen years. It has the experience to ask relevant questions and has done so long enough to have meaningful trend information.

Before we begin, there is one point that is critical to this discussion. As mentioned before, this material is not intended to label Muslims as good or bad. The decisions each of us makes determines our character and who we are. This chapter's purpose is to examine Muslim opinion relevant to the above topics; it is Islam's tenets that matter. Muslim opinion is shaped by Islam, so how consistent are those opinions with our society's foundations? This is a discussion we need to have. In the end, these discussions should determine what is extreme and what is not, and therefore how many people make up what is called the "1%." It is only after relevant discussion that we can effectively determine our response as a people. Currently, it is a discussion we have yet to take up, and many of our leaders do not even want us to start.

We only need to examine a couple of our foundational principles to create a baseline for these discussions and to begin to understand the gulf that exists. These include the following:

- We have a common ancestry, a common nature, and therefore the same rights. We are not equal in all ways, but as concerns our nature and rights, we are all unequivocally the same.

- The institutions of the church and state, along with the family, were implemented by our Creator. The Church and State have separate domains, but both—just like the family—are to be oriented toward our Creator. This does not mean the State should be directly connected to any religion, but rather the belief and morality that underlie religion should carry over as an influence on those who govern. If not, man is only accountable to himself, and that approach throughout history *has always failed.*

Let's start by looking at the general Muslim population. We often assume that it is primarily Arabic, but that is not the case. If we look at the top ten countries in terms of population, they are the following:

Country	% of Total	% Muslim Population
Indonesia	12.6%	86%
Pakistan	10.9%	97%
India	10.9%	13%
Bangladesh	9.1%	83%
Egypt	4.9%	90%
Nigeria	4.6%	75%
Iran	4.6%	99%
Turkey	4.6%	99%
Ethiopia	2.7%	33%
Algeria	2.1%	99%
Total	67.0%	

The top five countries in this list account for about 48% of the world's Muslim population, and only one of them is in North Africa or the Middle East. Further, only two of those ten are countries whose primary language is Arabic (Egypt and Algeria). In all, only about 22% of the world's Muslim population lives in countries within the Middle East or North Africa. Finally, with the exceptions of India and Ethiopia, the non-Muslim populations are the minority in these countries.

The surveys were all conducted in the Eastern Hemisphere and were broken into the following six regions:

1. Southern-Eastern Europe, including Albania, Bosnia-Herzegovina, Kosovo, and Russia.

2. Middle East–North Africa: the countries of the Arabian Peninsula and on the African continent along the Mediterranean Sea. These include Egypt, Morocco, and Tunisia.

3. Sub-Saharan Africa: all countries on the African continent, except those bordering the Mediterranean Sea. These include Cameroon, Ethiopia, Mozambique, Nigeria, Senegal, and Tanzania.

4. Central Asia, including Azerbaijan, Kazakhstan, Tajikistan, and Turkey.

5. South Asia, including Afghanistan, Bangladesh, and Pakistan.

6. Southeast Asia, including Indonesia, Malaysia, and Thailand.

The countries with the largest Muslim populations within each region were included in the surveys, with the exceptions of Iran and India. The surveys used are *The World's Muslim Population: Religion, and Politics, and Society*[2] and *Muslim Publics Divided on Hamas and Hezbollah.*[3] The percentages are the median from a region or the individual countries within a region. These percentages are applied to the Muslim population within the region, using 2010 Pew Research Center Muslim population estimates. Pew's population estimates were compared to the 2008 *CIA Handbook* figures. Where significant population differences existed, the Pew Research Center population figures were consistently lower. The numbers are in millions. Dashes indicate a particular question was not asked in a region. Remember that 1% of the current Muslim population is about 16 million.

General Attitudes

The relevant questions asked in the surveys were the following:

1. Is it necessary to believe in God to be a moral person?

2. How many faiths lead to heaven?

3. Converting others is a religious duty.

Region	Belief in God		Islam Alone		Conversion a Duty	
	Pct	Number	Pct	Number	Pct	Number
Southern-Eastern Europe	61	14	50	12	35	9
Middle East – North Africa	91	333	91	341	76	284
Sub-Saharan Africa	70	202	76	228	85	246
Central Asia	69	94	66	94	40	53
South Asia	87	466	90	483	78	417
Southeast Asia	94	219	88	204	43	82
Totals		1,329		1,362		1,090

The above results should not be a surprise. Most Muslims believe that (1) you need to believe in God to be moral, (2) that Islam is the only way of being obedient to God, and (3) you have a responsibility to reach out to others. These thoughts are typically held by any religion.

These next survey questions concern Islam and things outside it. These are the following:

1. Percentage of Muslims who say Islam and Christianity are very different.

2. Percentage of Muslims who say all or most of their close friends are Muslims.

3. Percentage of Muslims who say Western music, movies, and TV hurt morality in their country.

Region	Islam Different		Muslim Friends		Western Culture	
	Pct	Number	Pct	Number	Pct	Number
Southern-Eastern Europe	38	9	80	19	35	8
Middle East – North Africa	46	169	91	333	51	187
Sub-Saharan Africa	46	132	-	-	65	188
Central Asia	53	73	96	132	38	52
South Asia	75	402	98	523	59	316
Southeast Asia	83	201	95	221	51	119
Totals		986		1,228		869

It is interesting that the regions with the largest percentages saying that Islam and Christianity are different are those where a significant non-Muslim segment still exists (Indonesia in Southeast Asia and South Asia). Those who see much less difference between the two religions are places where either (1) there are almost no Christians (or any other minority religion), or (2) a communist state has controlled the church for most of the last one hundred years.

It is not surprising that people living in areas where there are few non-Muslims have Muslims for most of their close friends. What is more interesting is that this trend continues in places where there are other religions (Southern-Eastern Europe, South Asia, and Southeast Asia). A fair number of Muslims also view Western culture as a moral threat. Using the responses to estimate numbers within the Islamic population for all three questions yield results approaching 1 billion people (out of 1.6 billion).

The final panel in this section looks at Muslim support for institutions and actions that are generally looked upon as terrorism in the West.

1. Percentage that view Hezbollah favorably.

2. Percentage that view Hamas favorably.

3. Percentage that say support for suicide bombing is often/sometimes justified.

Region	Hezbollah Favorable		Hamas Favorable		Suicide Bombings	
	Pct	Number	Pct	Number	Pct	Number
Southern-Eastern Europe	-	-	-	-	-	-
Middle East – North Africa	34	119	50	182	21	75
Sub-Saharan Africa	45	130	49	141	34	98
Central Asia	5	7	9	12	6	8
South Asia	19	102	18	96	8	43
Southeast Asia	43	100	39	91	15	35
Totals		457		523		259

While the support for these items is less, they still approach a half billion people for supporting Hezbollah and Hamas, and a quarter billion people for suicide bombings, considerably more than 1%. I think that there is a common thread through these three items. Within the Muslim world, Hezbollah and Hamas are viewed as charitable organizations. Islamic charitable organizations are not like their Western counterparts in some respects. Islamic charities can only expend funds in the support of Muslims, and then only in a few areas that include (1) supporting the person collecting the funds; (2) supporting travelers, particularly those on the hajj; (3) supporting those in need: the poor, widows, and orphans; (4) payment of individual's debts; and (5) the spread of Islam through jihad.

Jihad is much broader than we typically think of it in the West. It does include warfare (jihad of the sword), but also the more non-violent means of the hand (piety), mind (teaching), pen (writing), tongue (speaking), and wealth (resource use). Wealth in many Muslim majority countries is relatively concentrated in the hands of an elite few. Witness the building of mosques in the U.S. financed by Saudi Arabian money through the North American Islamic Trust (see Chapter 8). This is no different than in any other collectivist society. It is just within Muslim majority countries that the elite are defined a little differently.

It is interesting to note that those places expressing the greatest support for Hezbollah and Hamas also express the largest support for suicide bombings. These are regions where there is generally a high concentration of Muslims in the general population, or where there is civil unrest or open warfare. Examples include Afghanistan, Iraq, Syria, Nigeria, Cameroon, Niger, Somalia, Kenya, Libya, Pakistan, Yemen, Egypt, and the Sudan.

The next section will pick up with looking at politics.

Politics

In the previous section, we started to look at what extremism means and some general attitudes within the Islamic world. This section will turn that discussion to the issue of politics. We will use the same information source as before. But first we are going to look at another general question asked of Muslims, which is "Do you consider yourself a national citizen first or a Muslim first?" Responses from six countries representing most of the regions in the survey are shown below.

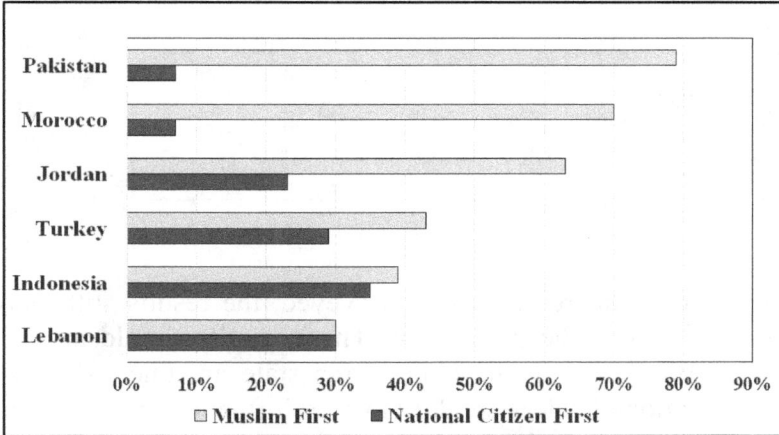

Figure 7-2: Percentage of Muslims who consider themselves ...[4]

Not a single country in this survey put national citizenship ahead of being a Muslim. This should not be surprising. Muhammad's teachings put the ties of religion above those of blood in tribal Arabia. Muslims are called to be followers of Islam first, and that is why Islam's tenets matter. Within an Islamic country, there is little if any difference between being a Muslim or a national citizen as governance is based on Islamic principles. These matter, however, if you extrapolate this position to non-Muslim countries as Islamic governance is not only contrary to, but incompatible with, all other governance forms.[5]

Relevant survey questions related to politics include the following:

1. Median percent of Muslims who believe religious leaders should have a political influence.

2. Percent of Muslims who say religious leaders should have a large or some influence.

3. Median percent of Muslims who prefer democracy over a strong leader.

The results are shown in the table below.

Region	Political Role		Political Influence		Prefer Democracy	
	Pct	Number	Pct	Number	Pct	Number
Southern-Eastern Europe	22	5	-	-	58	14
Middle East – North Africa	65	238	84	307	55	201
Sub-Saharan Africa	-	-	82	237	72	208
Central Asia	28	38	38	51	52	71
South Asia	69	370	69	370	45	241
Southeast Asia	79	184	91	212	64	149
Totals		835		1,176		884

Even though not all regions were surveyed, the results still represent roughly 50–70% of the population. These results should also not be surprising. Within Islam the church and state are one. All is Islam, therefore religious leaders should have an influence over all society's aspects, including not only politics, but law, governance, civics, culture, the military, etc. as well. More about this later with culture.

The democracy result is interesting. Generally, when I have had a political discussion with a Muslim, the line of reasoning goes something like this: they do not have freedom in (*insert a country here*) because the leader at the top is corrupt. We need to replace the leader with someone who is not corrupt, then that country will have freedom. We use the same word, *freedom*, but it does not have the same meaning. It does not represent the same idea.

As previously discussed, within Judeo-Christian beliefs, freedom is a gift from God and necessary in fulfilling our purpose. We cannot be put into motion like inanimate objects and still fulfill our purpose of becoming good, like our God. Within Islam, the concept of Allah is built upon the works of Plotinus, particularly his *Enneads*. Allah has no being, no essence, no nature, but is instead only pure will. Within this framework, there is no relationship possible between man and his Creator as He is inscrutable—unknowable.

According to Plotinus, freedom is the negation of a negative. It is what you have when you are not being coerced. *Your natural state is not to be free but instead to be coerced* by your Creator and His representatives on earth (the state and church)—a slave. Verses from the Qur'an support this position, and two of those are shown below. This same notion of freedom is similar to all other forms of collectivism; the only difference is that with these other forms (communism, fascism, progressivism, or socialism), freedom comes solely from the state. In either case, within Islam (and collectivism) freedom comes from without, whereas within Christianity, it comes from within an individual.

> "I created the jinn and humankind only that they might worship Me." (S 52.56)

> "There is none in the heavens and the earth but comes unto the Beneficent as a slave." (S19.93)

Both of the above come from Meccan sura, indicating that this view was a part of Islam from early on.

In Western culture, in places like America which rely on a Judeo-Christian governance philosophy, our freedom comes from within—it does not come from the state. Within Islamic culture, freedom comes from without. This is one reason why creating a republic within an Islamic country will never work; its ideology is incompatible with freedom as we know it. It is also one reason why Western culture is viewed as a threat to Islam. Another is the morals expressed by much of today's music, television programming, etc. in the West. Those pose a threat to Islamic culture and to those of us living in the West, as these artistic expressions are often corruptions of what should reflect our core values.

Another example on this last point comes from the survey. The median percent of Muslims who say religious freedom is a good thing is shown in the table below.

	Religious Freedom	
Region	Pct	Number
Southern-Eastern Europe	95	22
Middle East – North Africa	85	311
Sub-Saharan Africa	94	271
Central Asia	92	126
South Asia	97	520
Southeast Asia	93	217
Totals		1,467

The survey goes further to say that "Medians (percentages) show Muslims who say non-Muslims in their country are very free to practice their religion and consider this a good thing."[6] The numbers are very high across all regions. But is this true? Consider, non-Muslims are not free to build new churches or synagogues, repair existing ones, ring bells, or perform other overt acts of worship within these countries. In some instances, it is even illegal to possess a Bible. Non-Muslim populations have dwindled to the point of non-existence in many of these countries. In addition, non-Muslims do not share the same legal status as Muslims in Islamic countries.

Instead, they are subjected to laws and cultural norms intended to humiliate them in an effort to force them to convert. Think this is not true? You might want to see the footnoted video from an Islamic cleric on Islamic conversions.[7] But the idea he expresses is not new: it comes from the dhimmitude practices that have been developed over the last thousand years that were outlined in the previous chapter. Non-Muslims who live in these countries must possess a level of devotion that greatly exceeds what we might consider possible.

What is more correct to say is that within Western culture, religious freedom means one is free to choose what religion one will follow, even if one's choice is no religion at all. Within Islamic countries, religious freedom is synonymous with any non-Muslim being free to choose Islam at any time they wish. This is consistent with the point made in Chapter 5 that all are born Muslim: some just do not know it yet, which is why conversion is viewed as a duty. It is a very small step from here to consider what assimilation means to Islam's followers who immigrate. In the West, this means others adapting to your ideas. Within Islamic culture, it means you are free to adapt their ideas whenever you wish.

To further support this point, we can look at one final result from the surveys. The table below contains the percent of Muslims who say they would be very/somewhat comfortable with a son or daughter marrying a Christian.

Region	Son		Daughter	
	Pct	Number	Pct	Number
Southern-Eastern Europe	52	12	42	10
Middle East – North Africa	19	69	5	17
Sub-Saharan Africa	-	-	-	-
Central Asia	23	31	17	23
South Asia	11	60	6	33
Southeast Asia	7	16	3	7
Totals		189		90

While over 90% of Muslims say religious freedom is a good thing, only a little over 10% would be comfortable with a son marrying someone from outside of Islam—specifically a Christian—and about half that figure would be comfortable if it were a daughter. In this case, freedom is not the freedom to choose from all things, but the freedom to choose one thing alone.

We will pick up law in the next section.

Islam and Law

Previous sections have touched upon some of Islam's general attitudes and how those are reflected in its views on extremism, politics, and freedom. This section will continue to use the same surveys[8] to look at some attitudes around law. Islamic law is encompassed within what is called shari'a and is derived from several of Islam's source documents as outlined in Chapter 4.

The table below shows the percentages of Muslims who agree with the following:

1. Shari'a is the revealed word of God.

2. Median percent of Muslims who favor enshrining shari'a as official law.

3. Among shari'a supporters, the median percent of Muslims who favor religious judges to oversee family law. All columns denoted with a "*: in this section reflect percentages of the shari'a as Official Law column results.

Region	Shari'a Revealed Law		Shari'a as Official Law		Religious Judges*	
	Pct	Number	Pct	Number	Pct	Number
Southern-Eastern Europe	51	12	18	4	41	10
Middle East – North Africa	71	261	74	271	78	285
Sub-Saharan Africa	-	-	64	185	-	-
Central Asia	51	69	12	16	62	85
South Asia	74	395	84	450	78	418
Southeast Asia	53	123	77	179	84	196
Totals		861		1,106		993

Even though sub-Saharan Africa was excluded from the survey questions, over 50% of Islam's followers in the remaining regions believe that shari'a is divinely revealed law, and almost 45% that religious judges should oversee family law within the courts. This climbs to two-thirds believing that shari'a should be official law. Note that there is a regional difference within this last result. The areas formerly under control of the Soviet Union (Southern-Eastern Europe and Central Asia) are once again much lower than the rest of the Islamic world. These results demonstrate again that all is Islam, provide another reason why Islam is not simply a religion but an ideology with a religious facet.

So what do shari'a supporters want? Some responses are shown in the following two tables.

1. Median percent of Muslims who favor severe corporal punishments for criminals. Remember these are punishments as sanctioned by Islam's tenets and embodied by shari'a, such as beheadings, amputations, stoning, and crucifixions.

2. Percent of Muslims who favor stoning as a punishment for adultery.

3. Percent of Muslims who favor whippings/cutting off of hands for theft and robbery.

Region	Corp. Punishment*		Stoning for Adultery*		Whipping & Cutting	
	Pct	Number	Pct	Number	Pct	Number
Southern-Eastern Europe	36	2	25	1	-	-
Middle East – North Africa	57	154	71	194	74	270
Sub-Saharan Africa	-	-	-	-	65	188
Central Asia	38	6	32	5	13	17
South Asia	81	365	74	331	82	440
Southeast Asia	46	82	49	88	36	84
Totals		609		619		999

1. Median percent of Muslims who favor executing those who leave Islam.

2. Are honor killings permissible? The percent of Muslims who say they are never justified when a male committed the offense.

3. Are honor killings permissible? The percent of Muslims who say they are never justified when a female committed the offense.

Region	Execute Apostates*		Never Male Honor Killings		Never Female Honor Killings	
	Pct	Number	Pct	Number	Pct	Number
Southern-Eastern Europe	13	3	68	16	62	15
Middle East – North Africa	56	205	47	172	38	140
Sub-Saharan Africa	-	-	-	-	-	-
Central Asia	16	22	64	88	67	92
South Asia	76	407	42	224	40	214
Southeast Asia	27	63	80	186	80	186
Totals		700		686		645

The numbers speak for themselves. Again we see a general trend of lower acceptance within the former Soviet-bloc countries. It should be noted that most of these results did not include sub-Saharan Africa (about 289 million followers of Islam). When adjusting for that exclusion, support for various forms of corporal punishment range between 40–60% in the surveyed regions. In addition, roughly 50% of surveyed Muslims believe honor killings are never justified, indicating that about half believe there are circumstances where honor killings are permissible.

Culture

In this final section, we'll turn to some cultural behaviors, specifically Islamic views on some moral issues and the role/rights of women within society. Things that are considered morally wrong are likely to be subject to the harsh corporal punishment under shari'a as noted in the previous section.

The following tables show the median percent of Muslims who say each of the following behaviors is morally wrong:

1. Prostitution

2. Sex outside marriage

3. Homosexuality

4. Drinking alcohol

5. Abortion

The final column in the second table contains the percent of Muslims who say polygamy is morally acceptable.

	Prostitution		Sex Outside Marriage		Homosexuality	
Region	Pct	Number	Pct	Number	Pct	Number
Southern-Eastern Europe	90	21	67	16	83	19
Middle East – North Africa	95	348	94	344	93	340
Sub-Saharan Africa	91	263	78	225	91	263
Central Asia	89	122	85	116	85	116
South Asia	84	450	87	466	79	423
Southeast Asia	94	219	94	219	95	221
Totals		1,422		1,386		1,383

	Drinking Alcohol		Abortion		Polygamy	
Region	Pct	Number	Pct	Number	Pct	Number
Southern-Eastern Europe	62	14	71	17	31	7
Middle East – North Africa	84	307	72	263	42	152
Sub-Saharan Africa	82	237	88	254	59	172
Central Asia	66	90	61	83	14	19
South Asia	82	440	64	343	35	186
Southeast Asia	93	217	93	217	32	75
Totals		1,305		1,177		610

Results to questions regarding suicide and euthanasia being morally wrong were similar to those shown above. The data across all regions strongly support these behaviors as being morally wrong (a minimum of 61% in any region). Even if a person agrees that these behaviors are morally wrong, should the types of punishment advocated under shari'a and supported by Islam's followers be sanctioned?

Polygamy is interesting as it is allowed by Islam's doctrines, yet its support sits below 40% overall and again is lowest in Central Asia and Southern-Eastern Europe. Polygamy also has different interpretations within Islam. Some define it as having no more than four wives in one's lifetime. Others view the numbers one, two, three, and four as simply the beginning of a numerical sequence. Under this view, it does not matter how many wives you have over time, only whether or not you are limited to four at a time.

I recently heard a missionary who has performed Muslim outreach for over twenty years speak. His observations included what life was like in many Middle East Muslim families. Certainly not all families are like those he described, but they are not atypical. You would likely grow up in a household where your mother is beaten. For those who think otherwise, you should see one of the many videos on how to properly beat your wife.[9] In many cases, your father is looking for his next wife. Divorce is very easy for the male, so you may grow up without your mother's presence for a significant part of your childhood. Women within Islam are property. They are always owned by a male, either a family member or their husband.

The following results related to women were presented within the surveys.

1. Median percent of Muslims who completely or mostly agree that a wife must obey her husband.

2. Median percent of Muslims who say that women have a right to divorce.

3. Median percent of Muslims who say that sons and daughters should have equal inheritance rights.

Region	Women Obey		Women Divorce		Equal Property Rights	
	Pct	Number	Pct	Number	Pct	Number
Southern-Eastern Europe	43	10	86	20	69	16
Middle East – North Africa	87	318	33	121	25	91
Sub-Saharan Africa	-	-	-	-	-	-
Central Asia	70	96	70	96	60	82
South Asia	88	472	44	236	46	247
Southeast Asia	93	217	32	75	61	142
Totals		1,112		547		578

Over 80% of those in the regions surveyed say they agree that a women should obey her husband, but less than 45% think that women have the right to divorce or should have equal inheritance rights. Again, these results were supported less in the former Soviet-bloc countries. It is difficult to justify giving a group such rights when they are viewed as being property themselves. It is no different for non-Muslims in these countries as they are dhimmis who are owned by the state. Such treatment is sanctioned by Islam's ideology and supported by its doctrines.

None of the survey items included in these articles represent a fringe element within Islam, instead they represent its mainstream beliefs. Are these beliefs consistent with our values, or are they contrary to them?

Islam presents a tortured form of dualistic thought about life that is grounded in fatalism. Take the sanctioned forms of wife beating that are permitted. One does not have to perform these actions, but if they are done, it is because another is at fault. Their decisions forced me to do it. There is no accountability from within, as expediency and obedience become morality. Your actions are driven from outside behaviors, as is your freedom. How is this different from the "I was only following orders" defense offered by some accused of committing crimes against humanity?

It is not my intent to denigrate Muslims, but instead to educate about some of Islam's prevailing attitudes so that they can be understood by those of us in the West. The framework for the notions supported in these surveys is as foreign to us in the West as our values are to those who follow Islam. As I have said before, it is not Muslims who are the issue, but Islam's tenets. Can anyone doubt that the Islamic values cited within this material are both contradictory and incompatible with our most basic founding values and beliefs—beliefs that have their basis in living according to God's commands. Beliefs that include the separation of church and state and the protection of the church from the state, equality under the law, and the primary role of government being to protect our Creator given rights, to promote the virtue of justice? These two contradictory viewpoints cannot have come from the same source.

Here are several points in closing. First, those within the Muslim world who claim our Constitution is of human origin and therefore transitory do not possess any understanding of it or its source. The discussion in the last section about freedom is just one example. We should welcome those fleeing from this ideology, but should we accept those as immigrants who cling to it? Would we have accepted as immigrants avowed communists during the height of the Cold War, or active Nazi supporters during World War II? Why is this ideology any different? Present and support your arguments if you believe otherwise.

The proof of what I say is in this: consider what America has been able to achieve while it has been turned toward God (a period of maybe two hundred years). Sadly today, and over the last fifty years, many have chosen to turn away from Him. But that choice is one we each make every single day, the gift of our freedom. As we make this choice daily, we can also change our direction at any time. Our past choices do have repercussions, but our future choices are ours to make.

Second, we need a national conversation and response to Islam's ideas. To do that we need to have an honest understanding of both their ideology and our own founding principles. Sadly, both are lacking in our society today. These materials are intended to get you started in removing those deficiencies. Third, we need to reassert our national sovereignty and once again take control of our immigration process. While immigration is one of the few powers constitutionally granted to the federal government, it has abdicated much of its responsibility and acted irresponsibly through the laws and regulations it has enacted, and those it has failed to enforce. This puts us at risk as a people and a nation. But the answer is surprisingly simple. Governments power comes from us. All we have to do is say no more; witness the reason for the 2016 election results at both the national and state levels.

Our government seems to be taking the approach that if you cannot change a people's heart or mind, then change the people. To set things right, we need to return to our founding values of faith, reason, virtue, and morality. To do that, we first need to understand what they truly are. They are not the form of social justice advocated by today's political left. Nor are they grounded in the moral relativism that is today expressed as an absolute—those ideas are an inane form of pretzel logic that is shared by all forms of collectivism.

In the next and final chapter, we'll discuss some responses to the challenges posed by Islam. Compare America and the West's progress against that of the Middle East or North Africa over the last fourteen hundred years, as outlined in the previous chapter. If you do not yet think a response is necessary, then consider the gulf between the ideologies underlying both societies. In the following passage *Jahiliyyah* refers to those in ignorance of divine guidance and refers to all non-Muslims: infidels.

> Islam cannot accept any mixing with Jahiliyyah, either in its concept or in the modes of living which are derived from this concept. Either Islam will remain, or Jahiliyyah: Islam cannot accept or agree to a situation which is half-Islam and half-Jahiliyyah. In this respect Islam's stand is very clear. It says that the truth is one and co-existence of the truth and falsehood is impossible. Command belongs to God, or otherwise to Jahiliyyah; God's Shari'ah will prevail, or else people's desires.[10]

Chapter 8

Responding to Islam

Like it or not, believe it or not, we are in a war. A war that has been declared upon us simply because of what we believe. We did not ask for it, nor did we start it. It has been going on for almost 1,400 years, and there are only two choices. One can submit or resist. There are no other options because Islam does not allow for them.

Again, the problem is not Muslims, they are as much our brothers and sisters as anyone else. Created by God, just as we have been. They have the same God-given nature that we have been blessed with. You will find good Muslims and bad Muslims, just like you will find good Christians and bad Christians. However, if your father is a Muslim, you are a Muslim by birth. There is no choice. From Islam's perspective, even if you grow up with another religion, all are born as Muslim—some just don't realize it yet.

Islam is a fatalistic ideology that contains no hope, and I believe this is one basis for the number of suicide bombers that we see. If you have nothing to hope for in this life, then maybe the next will offer something better. No, the problem is not Muslims, but is instead Islam's tenets. We need to understand this, because this notion underlies everything discussed in this chapter.

As we are in a war, this chapter will focus on three items. The first relates to understanding our adversary, for without that understanding you cannot communicate effectively, develop a sound strategy, or select the correct tactics to defeat them. Words matter for this first item and the next. We've already seen that while we often use the same words, they do not necessarily mean the same thing. The second item is a brief comparison with who we are to be as a people. All war must be defined and described in moral terms, and God is the source of all morality. We need to understand who we are and the differences between the opposing forces in order to make good decisions, regardless of the outcome. These lead to the third item: What should we do?

All three items are relevant regardless of the decision you make. If you choose to submit, then you should understand what you are voluntarily submitting to. If you chose to resist, then you must understand what you are fighting in order to be effective. We've covered a lot of ground already. We'll start with pulling together some of the main points outlined in earlier chapters about Islam related to culture, ideology, history, and attitudes. We'll follow that with a brief look at jihad, slavery, refugees, and the implications we can draw from these items.

Putting It All Together

Islam did not add any new theological ideas, but instead borrowed from all the religions it contacted. This borrowing was not limited to theology, but also took place in the areas of law, governance, and philosophical thought regarding society and its people's role. These were all absorbed into the Arab culture, which is where we begin.

Culture

Some relevant cultural concepts incorporated into Islam include the following:

1. A culture where the ends matter most, and actions are evaluated by whether an outcome is considered to be good or not.

2. Tribal loyalty and the concept of muruwa, where one is responsible for the wellbeing of their tribe or clan. Their honor depends upon it. Defending that honor is expected. Not acting results in a loss of prestige.

    We can see this present in the Middle East today. In discussing the general population's desire to fight during the war in Iraq, General Flynn notes the following: "First and foremost, the population does not want to get dragged into the fighting at all. They will stay out as long as they can, until *they decide* which side is destined to win. Only then are their battle lines drawn."[1] This is consistent with the principles of being responsible for a tribe's welfare and a focus on the ends alone as just indicated.

3. Couple both of the above with a harsh environment where survival is difficult and there are often not enough resources to support everyone and the result is competition and conflict for scarce resources. In the West, peace is the normal state, one that is interrupted by war. In the Islamic culture, conflict is the typical state and peace the interlude in between periods of conflict. As we saw earlier, the Arab word for peace is derived from a word meaning the path of security, and within this culture that path is submission. Submission generally occurs after surrender to another, whether conflict is present or not.

4. In Chapter 1 we discussed the idea of peace within the Arabic culture being arrived at through submission. Further, that within Western culture peace is considered to be man's normal state, interrupted by war when he turns away from God. This stands in contrast to Arabic culture where conflict is normal and peace occurs only after submission of one party to another.

    Sayyid Qutb takes these ideas further:

God has informed the Believers that the life of this world is such that checking one group of people by another is the law of God, so that the earth may be cleansed of corruption.[2]

When Islam strives for peace, its objective is not that superficial peace which requires that only that part of the earth where the followers of Islam are residing remain secure. The peace which Islam desires is that the religion (i.e. the Law of the society) be purified for God, that the obedience of all people be for God alone.[3]

His conclusion is:

It may happen that the enemies of Islam may consider it expedient not to take any action against Islam, if Islam leaves them alone in their geographical boundaries to continue the lordship of some men over others and does not extend its message and its declaration of universal freedom within their domain. But Islam cannot agree to this unless they submit to its authority by paying Jiziyah, which will be a guarantee that they have opened their doors for the preaching of Islam and will not put any obstacle in its way through the power of the state.[4]

Islam did not create any of these conditions, but instead sanctioned them and increased their legitimacy, while at the same time replacing loyalty to the tribe with loyalty to Islam.

Ideology

Islam's ideology is not only contradictory, but incompatible with our founding principles, principles that have their basis in the Bible and God's divine law. Relevant aspects of this dimension include the following:

1. Islam is another form of collectivism, or statism, if you prefer.

    a. The church and state are one. The sole existence for the state is to ensure that Islam's requirements are carried out.

    b. Everyone does not possess the same nature, and therefore does not have the same rights. Some are meant to rule and others to serve. These are reflected in the status of women and dhimmitude within Islamic societies.

    c. Citizens exist to serve their government. They are to be molded to suit the state's needs. Persuasion and compulsion are acceptable for those who do not submit. These are the concepts of sunna and shari'a. The first defines the standards of conduct, and the second the punishment for their violation.

    d. War is permissible and just against those who will not submit. This is jihad, which will be covered further below.

A table summarizing some collectivism principles and their Islamic counterparts follows. The collectivism principles come from the writings of Aristotle and Plato.

Collectivism Principles	Islamic Counterparts
All are not equal, rather some are more equal than others.	Dhimmitude
Those most fit should rule.	Superiority of Islam's followers to other people
Some are marked for subjection and for those who do not submit, war is proper.	Jihad
Citizenship is only for the elite—some are by nature free and others slaves.	Umma
Good of the State and not the individual is the proper subject of political thought.	The State's sole purpose is to see Islam's requirements are carried out.
Citizens should be molded to suit the form of government under which they live.	Sunna
Citizens do not belong to themselves, but to the State.	All are Allah's slaves.
Persuasion and compulsion to be used to bring harmony to citizens.	Shari'a

2. Within Christianity, freedom is God's gift. It is necessary in fulfilling our purpose of becoming good. Freedom is a positive attribute of our nature. Within Islam, freedom is the negation of a negative. It is what you have when you are not coerced, as one's natural state is that of a slave. All that is required is obedience and submission.

History

We have fourteen hundred years of history to assess Islam's ability to co-exist with other ideologies and religions. The results are instructive.

1. Islam absorbed ideas, laws, governance structures, etc. from those cultures it encountered during its expansion. In many ways it did not behave differently from those kingdoms it encountered. What was different is the extent to which it carried out those actions and the length of time over which they occurred. These actions are once again being carried out today. A resurgence is visible after having been lost in the Ottoman Empire's fall after the First World War.

2. Islam's documents and doctrines were not formed at Muhammad's death, but instead evolved over about a three-hundred-year period. These included the collection and selection of the codex for the Qur'an and the interpretation of that text, the review and determination of trustworthy hadith necessary for understanding and providing context to the Qur'an, the integration of these ideas into the existing sunna, and their codification into shari'a.

3. The death toll from the spread of Islam is unknown, but is likely several hundred million or more. Remember that during Muhammad's life, outside of pagan Arabia, the rest of the known world was largely dominated by several already established religions. These included Christianity in Europe, North Africa, and portions of the Middle East; Zoroastrianism in Persia; Hinduism and Buddhism in India; and a large number of Jewish settlements throughout much of this region.

    Within one hundred years, Islam had violently advanced from its base on the Arabian Peninsula to include an area from Spain and Morocco in the west to India in the east. Several have attempted to estimate the number of deaths during the last fourteen hundred years. These estimates go as high as 80 million Hindus in the Indian subcontinent, 10 million Buddhists in Afghanistan, 120 million in Africa, and 60 million in the former Roman territories. Missing from these figures is the number of deaths that occurred in Persia.[5]

4. During Islam's early expansion, Muslims were the minority population in the areas they conquered. They could not have succeeded without the cooperation of the existing civic and religious powers in the conquered areas. These were referred to as the notables, and included members of both the government and church. Our political correctness is taking us down the same path that the notables followed.

5.   The collapse of the church and state into a single power leads to the corruption of both. One can look at the wealth of resources in countries like Iran and the poverty of its people. The exception are a few leaders who line their pockets with some of the country's wealth. This is what occurs when elitism is present and *all forms of collectivism are elitist.*

Attitudes

Attitudes within Muslim majority areas support the above behaviors.

1.   While we use the same words, they do not share the same meaning. Even within Islamic countries, extremism has different meanings. Further, allegiance is to Islam and its principles first over everything else.

2.   The above should not be surprising as belief in God is considered necessary to be a moral person. Couple this with the views that Islam alone leads to heaven and the belief that all are Muslims. As a result, conversion becomes a religious duty. Conversion occurs peacefully, if possible, but by persuasion or intimidation, if necessary. Warfare is reserved for those who will not willingly submit. Once again, there is a connection to collectivism.

3.   Church and state are one; therefore, religious leaders should have a significant political influence. While many of Islam's followers prefer democracy, it does not take the form that we recognize in the West as freedom does not have the same meaning within this culture.

4.   The mixing of church and state also allows for religious influence on the law and should include the use of religious judges and implementation of shari'a. The negative effects of these structures on families and societies is discussed by Nonie Darwish and others.[6]

Jihad and Slavery

Jihad is a religious war. Slavery was a part of Arab culture before Muhammad. The taking of slaves and ransoming of captives were carried over into early Islam, sanctioned by Muhammad's actions. They continue today. It is estimated that there are between thirty and forty million slaves in the world today. Of the twenty countries with the largest slave populations, thirteen of them are either Islamic or places where war is occurring against Islamic supporters. These thirteen countries represent about 25% of the world's slave population. To put this into context, it must be remembered that about one half of the entire world's slave population (17.5 million) reside in just two countries, China and India.

War breaks down society. The rule of law often does not apply during periods of war. This leaves populations in areas where war occurs more vulnerable to slavery. Coupled with Islam's disposition toward slavery, this provides both a means and justification for slavery. Having a means of taking in new slaves is important, as they live relatively shorter lives and generally produce few children.

There are three primary areas where slaves are used. These are the drug trade, forced labor, and sex trafficking. Forced labor and sex trafficking occur in many Islamic countries, but there are also some where the drug trade creates a demand for slaves. In support of these assertions, we are going to look at a couple of maps.

The first is the distribution of slaves by both raw numbers and as a percentage of a countries population. The slavery estimates come from *Wall Street 24/7* and the *Global Slavery Index* sites.[7] Country populations come from the *CIA Handbook*.

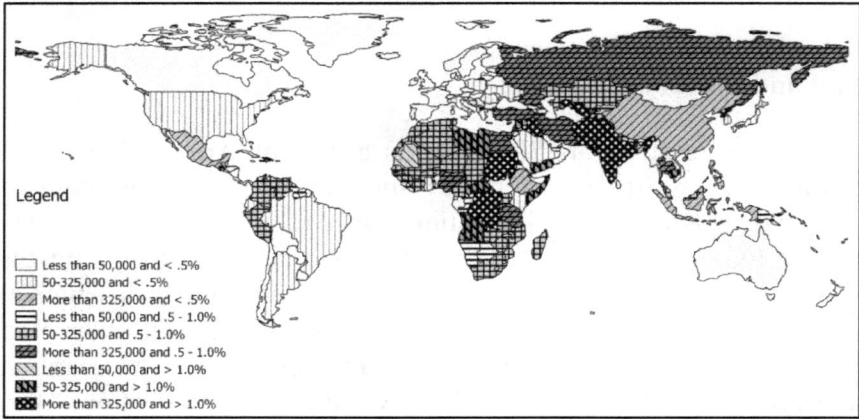

Legend

☐ Less than 50,000 and < .5%
▦ 50-325,000 and < .5%
▨ More than 325,000 and < .5%
▤ Less than 50,000 and .5 - 1.0%
▦ 50-325,000 and .5 - 1.0%
▨ More than 325,000 and .5 - 1.0%
▨ Less than 50,000 and > 1.0%
▨ 50-325,000 and > 1.0%
▨ More than 325,000 and > 1.0%

Figure 8-1: Slavery by Number and Percentage

Slavery occurs to a greater extent within Africa and South Asia, particularly in an arc from The Democratic Republic of the Congo in central Africa, through Egypt, and on into India. This also corresponds with the part of the world with both the oldest Islamic conquests and most concentrated Muslim populations, and where most conflict currently exists.

The breakdown of the 177 countries into the categories indicated in the legend above are the following:

Low		High	
5	7	8	High
16	27	10	
58	25	2	Low

Jihad represents an institutionalized form of war within Islam, and war leaves people more vulnerable to being taken into slavery. The map below shows conflict areas overlaid by the degree to which a country is Islamic (as measured by the percentage of its population that follows Islam). The war figures come from Wikipedia[8] and represent the countries involved in various conflicts classified by the number of deaths occurring annually.

- Major War: 10,000 or more deaths within the past year

- War: 1,000 to 9,999 deaths within that same period

- Minor Conflict: 100 to 999 deaths within the past year

- Skirmishes: less than 100 deaths within the past year

The Islamic population figures come from the *CIA Handbook* and Pew Research Forum.

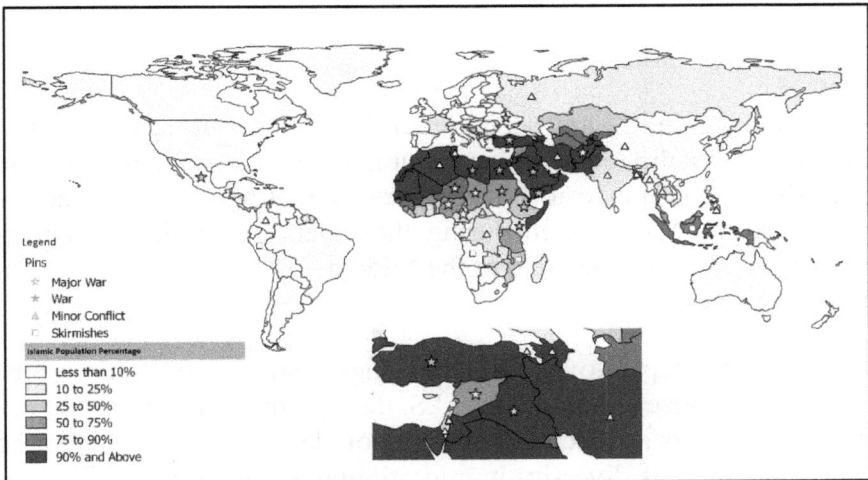

Figure 8-2: Degree Country is Islamic and Conflict

There is a high degree of correlation between the extent to which a country is Islamic and level of conflict that is present. This is consistent with the results in the last section as most countries across North Africa and the Middle East have a relatively higher percentage of their population as slaves, and their number is relatively greater.

The conflict within this area generally takes one of two forms.

- Spread of Islam to non-Islamic countries. This includes the fighting within (1) Nigeria that has spread into Cameroon,

Niger, and Chad; (2) Sudan, (3) South Sudan and Ethiopia; (4) Kenya and Somalia; and (5) Israel and the West Bank/Gaza.

- The attempt to implement more fundamentalist Islamic principles within existing Islamic societies. These include (1) insurrections within Algeria, Tunisia, Libya, Egypt, Afghanistan, and Pakistan; (2) fighting between Saudi Arabia and Iran backed groups in Yemen; and (3) fighting against ISIS by Syrian and Iraqi factions backed by Iran, Russia, and the U.S.

Refugees and Violence

The breakdown in law and social order that occurs during war not only increases the likelihood of slavery, but many civilians attempt to leave the conflict area. This results in refugees attempting to flee to places of relative safety. We've seen during the Obama administration many individuals leaving large areas of the Middle East and Africa for Europe and other places.

The U.S. has accepted over 730,000 refugees since 2003. This number includes only those coming to the U.S. through the refugee resettlement program and does not include immigration data from any other source or program such as diversity immigration and student visas. The data for the map below comes from the government's Refugee Reprocessing Centers.[9]

A key follows the map. As the number of refugees increase the fill lines become thicker, and as the percentage of refugees from Islamic countries increases the shading becomes darker.

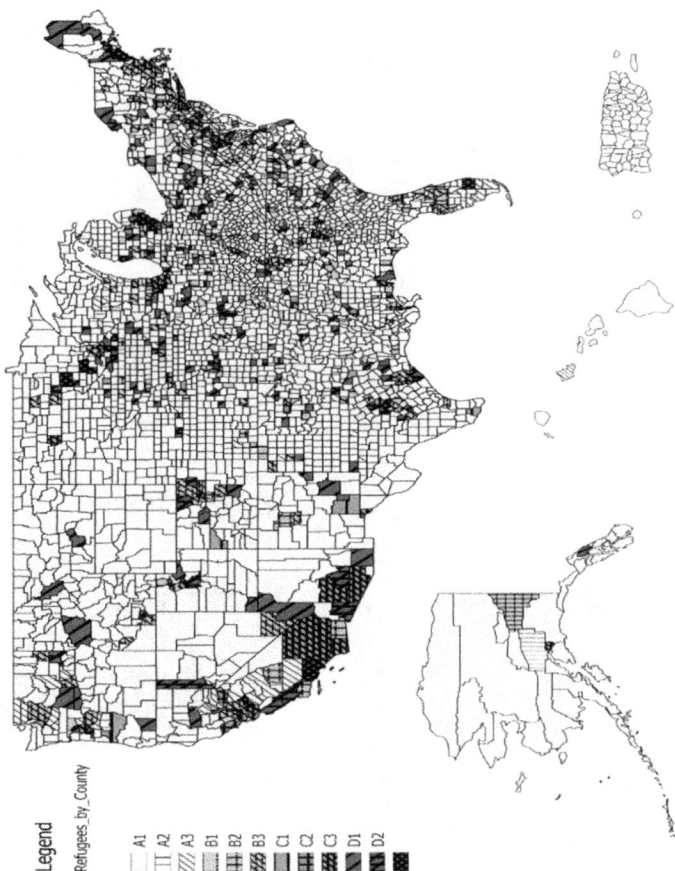

Figure 8-3: Refugee Resettlement by County

% Islamic Majority Countries			
Over 85%	D1	D2	D3
50 to 85%	C1	C2	C3
15 to 50%	B1	B2	B3
< 15%	A1	A2	A3
# of Refugees	< 10	10 to 100	>100

Resettlement by County			
D	149	55	24
C	21	56	44
B	34	80	136
A	172	93	64
	1	2	3

2,292	# Counties Not Receiving Refugees

The top twenty-five counties receiving refugees and the percentage of Islamic refugees within that number through 2015 are shown in the table below.

State	County	Non-Islamic Refugees	Islamic Refugees	Total Refugees	Pct Islamic Refugees
AZ	Maricopa	11,606	12,718	24,324	52.3%
TX	Harris	12,407	9,179	21,586	42.5%
WA	King	10,856	8,374	19,230	43.6%
CA	Los Angeles	1,593	17,170	18,763	91.5%
GA	DeKalb	12,070	6,001	18,071	33.2%
CA	San Diego	4,622	12,402	17,024	72.9%
TX	Dallas	9,728	5,931	15,659	37.9%
IL	Cook	6,672	8,676	15,348	56.5%
MN	Hennepin	7,715	5,352	13,067	41.0%
NY	Erie	8,238	4,627	12,865	36.0%
CA	Sacramento	9,755	3,086	12,841	24.0%
CO	Denver	8,158	4,633	12,791	36.2%
FL	Miami-Dade	12,580	113	12,693	0.9%
UT	Salt Lake	5,791	6,171	11,962	51.6%
TX	Tarrant	6,965	4,021	10,986	36.6%
MN	Ramsey	8,650	2,292	10,942	21.0%
OH	Franklin	3,840	7,077	10,917	64.8%
KY	Jefferson	6,021	4,352	10,373	42.0%
OR	Multnomah	6,726	3,519	10,245	34.4%
NY	Onondaga	6,301	3,395	9,696	35.0%
GA	Fulton	6,229	3,320	9,549	34.8%
TN	Davidson	5,336	4,142	9,478	43.7%
AZ	Pima	4,097	4,770	8,867	53.8%
FL	Duval	6,027	2,030	8,057	25.2%
MI	Oakland	292	7,414	7,706	96.2%

Accepting refugees is in itself not bad, but when one comes to America, they are giving themselves to a specific idea, one that we've seen is incompatible with Islam's ideology. We should be having a discussion as a people whether this is acceptable or not, but it has not yet happened. This is true because, in large part, the Obama administration in the name of compassion took actions to prevent that discussion from occurring. It is a morally bankrupt argument.

Recently, I've seen a number of Islamic oriented articles discussing America's founding, noting that a primary driver of early immigration to the American Colonies was flight from religious persecution. This is correct as far as it goes, but they generally then go on to make a comparison that today's Muslim immigrants are also fleeing religious persecution. However, this argument is false for a number of reasons. First, settlers like the Pilgrims were fleeing religious persecution within their own country. By contrast, much of the persecution in Islamic countries is against their dwindling non-Muslim populations. Sadly, we are taking almost none of these brothers and sisters (many of whom are Christians) into our country.

Second, Muslim immigrants often do not assimilate into their host society and often do not even integrate. Instead, they form isolated communities that when they get large enough begin to push for adherence to Islamic law and doctrine. Look at what is happening in many European countries. Or ask the group of Christians who had stones thrown at them by Islam's followers at a festival in Dearborn, Michigan for simply holding signs about Christianity.[10] While many of the early immigrants to the colonies were fleeing religious persecution, Islamic migrants often bring the same religious persecution with them that exists within the country they left, as required by their doctrines. This is why understanding Islam's tenets is crucial for us today, and it will only come about by educating ourselves.

Relatively large numbers of Islamic refugees have been resettled in:

- much of California

- southern Arizona

- Minnesota (in the Minneapolis/St. Paul, Rochester, and St. Cloud areas)

- Michigan (in the Detroit, Lansing, and Ann Arbor areas)

- Texas (in the Houston, Dallas/Fort Worth, Austin, and San Antonio areas)

- Virginia (in the Northern Virginia, Richmond, Harrisonburg, and Charlottesville areas)

- Ohio (in the Columbus and Cleveland areas)

- Florida (in the Tampa Bay and Jacksonville areas)

- New York (in the Buffalo, Syracuse, and Rochester areas)

- southeastern Maine

The full impact of taking in large numbers of Islamic migrants has yet to be determined. We can look at the events in Europe, however, and the terrorist attacks occurring in the U.S. over the last several years to get an indication. We have attacks in Columbus (OH), New York City, St. Cloud (MN), Orlando, San Bernadino, Philadelphia, Chattanooga, Garland (TX), and the Virginia Beltway sniper—just to name a few. We can look at the treatment of women and the number of rapes in Germany, Sweden, Austria, France, and other places in Europe. The list could go on. Some will say that these are not representative of all Muslims. This is true. However the problem, as has been stated several times, is not Muslims but Islam's tenets. These attacks are representative of its ideology, and supported by over fourteen hundred years of history.

We will compare that ideology's principles with some of our underlying principles before closing with some ideas for a response.

A Comparison of Gods

Chapter 5 discussed the differences in God, man, and the relationship between both that exist between Islam and Christianity. The table below lists some of these differences.[11]

Topic	Allah	God
Creator's Nature	First cause and cannot be known except by His names which are extrinsic based upon His actions.	First cause, but is personal-infinite. As intrinsic can be known by His actions, the Logos, and a personal relationship based upon His image that we possess.
Good and Evil	Source of good and evil	Source of good. Man is the source of evil by his turning away from God.
Man's Nature	All men are not created equal. Men are above women. Some are favored more than others. A form of elitism.	All men have an equal nature. We all have different gifts and abilities.
Man's Purpose	Worship Creator. Man is his Creator's slave. Man cannot know his Creator.	Love our Creator and man. Man was created in His image, an inward image and not a physical image. Man's purpose is to know His Creator.
Free Will - Freedom	None. A person's fate is determined before they are born.	Man has free will to make his own choices. Free will is essential to man's fulfilling his purpose.
Divine Providence	Creator's will changes. Revelations change as a result.	Creator's foreknowledge takes into consideration even our bad choices and turns them to good within His plan (Providence). Creator's will does not change. He keeps His promises.
Salvation	Outwardly focused based upon one's works.	Inwardly focused based upon one's heart. If one's heart is focused upon man's purpose, then he will be transformed and do good works.
Source of Determination	Fatalistic as outcomes are predestined and therefore unalterable. Based on external deeds and obedience alone.	Hopeful as outcomes are based on our individual free choices. Based on internal changes within one's heart which in turn are reflected in external deeds.
Virtue	The ends justify the means. That which furthers Islam is good.	The means and ends both matter as man is intended to acquire virtue.

The idea that is America comes from the individualism that has its basis in Biblical principles. While not religion per se, these principles are derived from a divine source. The following diagram compares the relationships inherent in individualism with Islam and collectivism.

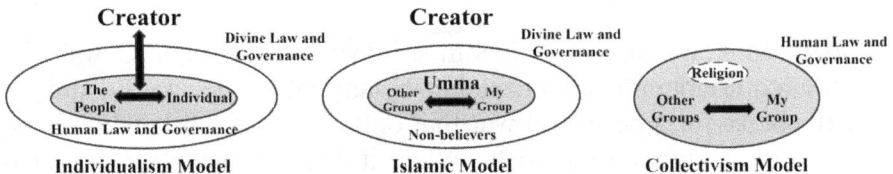

Individualism Model   **Islamic Model**   **Collectivism Model**

The individualism model includes the following components:

1. We have a relationship with God. This relationship is at two levels, one as an individual and a second as a people of God. Note that there is one people as there is only one Creator.

2. Our Creator has divine law and governance. Human law and governance is to lie within and align with our Creator's.

The counterparts within the Islamic model include the following:

1. Allah is inscrutable—unknowable. There can be no relationship between humanity and its Creator. Allah has divine law and governance that have been given through the Qur'an. While man can tinker at the edges, Allah's law is absolute.

2. Rights are based upon the group to which you belong. Non-believers are simply another group, as are women. *There is no equality based on our nature as those differ.*

3. There is only divine law and governance. Islam is all. *The church and state are one.*

Finally, the following compares the above with collectivism:

1. There is only human law and governance. Rights and law are derived by man, and subject to change by man.

2. Rights are based upon the group to which you belong, and driven by the degree to which that group is useful to society.

3. Religion, if it is to be present, is subject to man. Any god(s) are the creation of man and exist to suit the state's purpose and goals.

These world views are simply incompatible with each other. Couple that with the requirement to advance Islam by any means necessary, and you have the basis for a perpetual war that only subsides when Islam is not in a position to pursue its tenets. When it does not have the power or money to exercise its collective will. So how should we respond? That is where we will close this book.

Responding to Islam

We've looked at Islam. We've also looked at who we are called to be as a people and some of the relevant underlying principles associated with that calling. It is now time to begin discussing a response to the problem. There are two final topics that must be discussed as they must be incorporated into any response. First, not all Muslims are the same in regards to the extent that they hold to Islam's tenets. Second, through the Muslim Brotherhood we have a roadmap of their plans for America. Both of these follow next.

Islamic Groups

Contrary to what it may appear, Islam is not made up of a single group. By this I do not mean the religious differences that have resulted in the various sects present within Islam. Instead, my research and experience indicate that there are at least three groups who follow Islam. It is their relationship with Islam that is different. These groups include the following:

- One that is largely secular (and may even include atheists) and associates Islam with part of their cultural identity.

- A second that views Islam as a religion, largely focusing on the more peaceful Meccan verses of the Qur'an. There are some within this group that are attempting to reform Islam. Dr. Jasser is one such individual. I pray that they will be successful, but it will not be easy. Islam as a religion rests solely on Muhammad's claim to be a prophet. For him to be a prophet, all of his revelations must be true. Disconnecting the more violent and political Medinan revelations risks negating his prophethood, thereby removing the basis for Islam's religion.

- The third group are the so-called extremists. They simply follow all of the Qur'an's teachings. They are only radical in that they attempt to follow all of Islam's tenets. These encompass those who believe in the ideas of ISIS, Al-Qaeda, Boko Haram, the Muslim Brotherhood, and other such groups. Whereas most of those in the groups above do not adhere to implementing shari'a, this group believes in its full implementation.

This raises a serious issue that must be considered in any response. We do not wish to dictate to, or alienate, those in the first two groups who do not believe in recognizing shari'a. Remember from the last chapter that roughly 50% of the Islamic population does not believe that shari'a is the revealed word of God. Those who do not adhere to the implementation of shari'a are considered apostates. Their view is punishable by death. The Muslims not wanting to follow shari'a are simply pursuing what they believe to be important in living their lives.

However, *each individual determines to what extent they will follow Islam's tenets. This decision can change at any point in their life, and each new generation must in turn make its own decision in this regard. If we do not address the threat that Islam's tenets pose outside of religion, we will only address the effects and not the cause. By taking this approach, no solution will be found.*

The Muslim Brotherhood in America

The Muslim Brotherhood (MB) has sworn to remove Israel and the U.S. from the Earth. Yet it has not been deemed to be a terrorist organization by our own government, despite its own documents. This section's information comes from papers entered into the 2007-08 Holy Land Foundation trial. It shows the growth in MB affiliates in the U.S. from the early 1960s through 1991. It has grown significantly since that time.

The diagram below includes organizations contained in its documents. The rectangles outlined with dashes represent the unindicted co-conspirators in the trial. The Obama administration Department of Justice shelved these investigations in 2008.

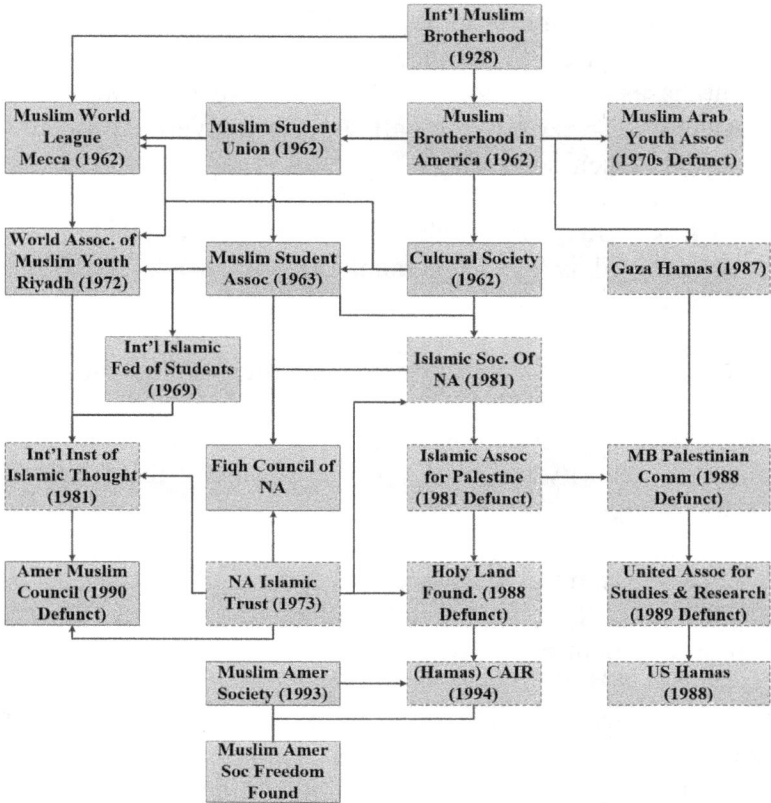

```
                          Int'l Muslim
                          Brotherhood
                            (1928)

Muslim World        Muslim Student        Muslim              Muslim Arab
  League              Union (1962)    Brotherhood in          Youth Assoc
Mecca (1962)                          America (1962)        (1970s Defunct)

World Assoc. of     Muslim Student     Cultural Society
 Muslim Youth        Assoc (1963)         (1962)           Gaza Hamas (1987)
Riyadh (1972)

                     Int'l Islamic
                    Fed of Students    Islamic Soc. Of
                        (1969)            NA (1981)

Int'l Inst of       Fiqh Council of    Islamic Assoc         MB Palestinian
Islamic Thought          NA            for Palestine          Comm (1988
   (1981)                            (1981 Defunct)            Defunct)

Amer Muslim                           Holy Land             United Assoc for
Council (1990        NA Islamic      Found. (1988          Studies & Research
  Defunct)          Trust (1973)        Defunct)           (1989 Defunct)

                    Muslim Amer       (Hamas) CAIR            US Hamas
                    Society (1993)       (1994)               (1988)

                    Muslim Amer
                    Soc Freedom
                      Found
```

Holyland Found Trial Unindicted Co-Conspirator, halted by Obama Admin.

Figure 8-4: Muslim Brotherhood in America

There are several key organizations to note:

The Muslim Brotherhood: It has an American chapter founded in 1962.

The Muslim Student Associations (MSAs): There are more chapters on college campuses than Young Republican and Young Democrat groups combined. It is now starting to form chapters in high schools. The goal of these groups is to inculcate the Muslim Brotherhood's brand of Islam. It too was created in 1962.

The North American Islamic Trust: Includes Saudi money to used to finance mosques, imams, property purchases, and support Islamic organizations in America. These activities all support the various forms of jihad discussed earlier.

Fiqh Council of North America: An organization whose goal is the implementation of shari'a in U.S. Courts

Fortunately, we know their tactics because they documented them and they were discovered during the Holy Land Foundation trial. Anyone interested can still obtain some of this trial's primary documents from the Center for Security Policy's website.[12] Some of their stated tactics include the following:

- Expand Islam's presence in terms of people, mosques, businesses, etc. This touches upon the refugee resettlement program mentioned earlier.

While a full review of this program is beyond the scope of this discussion, an excellent presentation is available at the Virginia Free Citizen website.[13] They document the organizations (VOLAGs) involved in refugee resettlement program, the number of individuals being brought to the U.S., and the costs associated with these programs. More importantly they outline specific steps that can be taken to blunt this effort, some of which we'll mention in in the response.

- Silence other Islamic groups who disagree with their objectives or methods.

- Create misinformation and control the narrative about Islam through a variety of means. This includes creating and supporting organizations such as the Council on American-Islamic Relations (CAIR), a group affiliated with Hamas, the latter a declared foreign terrorist organization.

- Hampering law enforcement.

- Incorporating shari'a into the U.S. court system.

- Subverting Christian organizations. This includes coopting where possible, and intimidation where needed. This is no different from the implementation of dhimmitude that occurred under the Abbasid. Over time, as Islam became more prevalent, those threats turned to violence against those who would not comply.

- Infiltrate the education system. This is already being done through both textbook materials and course curriculums

- Infiltrate government. Muslim Brotherhood members are our government's primary advisors in the war on terror and the Middle East. We can see the results in Egypt, Libya, Syria, Iran, and Iraq under the Obama administration. However, it did not start there, but started with the Bush administration after 9/11.

One example is Huma Abedin. She has been one of Hillary Clinton's closest advisors, and served as a national officer for the Muslim Student Association. Her family are principals of the pro-shari'a *Journal of Muslim Minority Affairs*, where Huma Abedin also worked for thirteen years, up until the beginning of the Obama Administration in 2008.

The Responses to Islam

So what can we do? First, Islam is an ideology, in many respects similar to the fascism and communism that were beaten in the twentieth century. So some of the same approaches and tactics should be effective against Islam as well. This is where most solutions that I have seen focus. While this is a good start, such an approach ignores the religious component that Islam has but these other ideologies do not. Without incorporating this second aspect into a response we will simply not address the cause, but only some of the effects. This will at best lock us into a stalemate that is never fully resolved. We should attempt to formulate something better.

These responses are predicated on the fact that there are both spiritual and temporal aspects to this war. In addition, there are things that can be done at the individual level, and others that must be done by organizations that support our society (such as government, military, and first responders). But even then, in the end it is our responsibility. We are ultimately responsible for holding our elected leaders and supporting organizations accountable for the actions they take—or choose not to take.

Individual Responses

These first responses are for each of us as individuals and are broken into spiritual and temporal aspects. One can reasonably argue that these are the most important, as they will exert pressure on our leaders to simply do the right things. We'll start with the spiritual actions. If we fail to get those right, little of the rest will matter.

Spiritual Actions

Most of the recommendations I've read deal only with the worldly conflict, but if we do not also engage this spiritually, we will not win because the ideology will remain. One of the greatest tools we have is the Qur'an itself. Many who leave Islam do so after reading it. The problems are having them read it, if they have not, and to question its contents. Islam does not permit its followers to question any of its tenets. High illiteracy rates, the availability of few books if one can read, and the fact that only about 20% of the worlds Muslim population's native language is Arabic contribute to the difficulty. What many Muslims understand about Islam comes from what the imams teach.

- Pray for our nation, our leaders, our people. But also pray for Muslims, that they will truly find Christ and come to understand who He is. There are many conversions going on in Iran and other parts of the Middle East today. These are largely driven by individuals who have had visions of Christ.

- Demand accountability from the leaders of our religious organizations, churches, and synagogues. Simply ask that they fully teach the truth—God's word—and act upon it. Those seeking to build 'inter-faith" relations risk building a one-way bridge away from their own faith if they do not seek first to fully understand Islam. There is a direct connection between faith and governance, one that the preachers of the First and Second Great Awakenings understood and voiced. We need to restore that truth to our pulpits and charitable organizations today.

- Live the life to which you are called. If you have Muslim neighbors or co-workers, reach out to them and befriend them. They are people like us and share many of the same concerns that we do about the economy, our children's future, healthcare, schooling, etc.

  o Have a basic understanding of their culture, such as the following:

    ▪ No pork, shellfish, lard in baked goods, or alcohol at a meal.

    ▪ Never offer your left hand.

    ▪ Interact primarily with people of your own sex.

  o Don't be afraid to talk to them about religion, if they are willing.

    ▪ Know what you believe and why.

    ▪ Do not be afraid to voice your beliefs, otherwise you will appear as a hypocrite or someone not strong in their faith.

- "Faith cannot be proved by necessary reasons, because it exceeds the human mind, so because of its truth it cannot be refuted by any necessary reason."[14] Do not prove the faith, but defend it.

- Use your story to tell how your life has been transformed. No one can refute your experiences.

- You are not reaching out to someone with no faith, but a person who believes they already have some understanding of who their Creator is, and may think some of your beliefs are either ridiculous or blasphemy.

I heard the following story from a Christian missionary not too long ago. The missionary has spent most of their adult life in Muslim outreach and often walks in predominately Muslim areas to engage a person in conversation. One day while walking, the missionary stopped to ask a person sitting in a park about nearby places to eat. The two began to talk. The Muslim asked the missionary if they were a Christian. The missionary said yes. The Muslim's name was Achmed. He had been a farmer in Yemen. He had also been in America for over twenty years and had come here to find out more about Jesus. In all the time Achmed had been here, the missionary was the first Christian who had ever stopped and spoken to him.

Achmed continued to talk about his family's struggles to make a living in this country, and ended by saying that he was simply tired and now only cared about returning to Yemen to farm once again. How can we be the salt and light of the earth if we do not reach out to those who are searching for the truth within our midst?

Temporal Actions

These actions build on those above.

- Educate yourselves. This cannot be stressed enough. It must be an education in both reason and faith. Both are needed to truly be educated and in a position to accomplish what we have each been created to do. You will not get that type of education within our public schools today. This requires a big effort, but it is critical as we've seen how different the framework is between Eastern and Western culture. Just as we find it hard to understand Islam's followers, they have as much difficulty understanding us.

We not only need to better understand Islam, but our founding principles and their biblical roots as well. Those roots are why our approach works, when we follow it, and why as a country America has been successful. These principles were largely ignored during the Obama administration. The fact that he was elected a second time is an indication of how little we now understand of those core principles. We will not remain free without them. Faith and freedom are connected, and both must be learned by the current generation in order to be passed on to the next.

- Be willing to stand for our shared principles and act accordingly.

- Get to know your local, state, and federal representatives. They are there to serve you.

  - Most know nothing about the issues discussed in this book.

  - There is a weekly Arab-American Newsletter that goes to all representatives, delegates, and senators in all fifty states and likely goes to federal government officials as well. Sign-up to get the newsletter.

  - Muslims are making active outreach efforts to your representatives at the state and local level. Do the same. If they know you are knowledgeable, your representatives will reach out to you.

    o   Write, call, or visit them. Share your concerns.

    o   Get to know your law enforcement members. If you see something that doesn't look right, let them know. There is also an initiative called SHIELD in which law enforcement agencies at all levels can participate. Urge your state and local agencies to join, if they have not already done so. It allows information to be shared, and facilitates the discussion of tactics and policies which work, and those that do not.

    o   The Department of Justice for the last eight years has been trying to silence opposition to the building of mosques in the U.S. We have one county in my community where some officials were required to take "sensitivity training" when they initially opposed the building of a mosque. Laws have now been set aside and ignored in order to allow the mosque to be built. Our elected officials must be held accountable, and if they do not uphold the law they must be voted out of office and replaced by people who will enforce it.

• State Department officials have stated that Refugee Relocation program meetings are open and the information is being shared with local officials.

    o   Find out who your state coordinator is for the Refugee Relocation program. Contact them and let them know your concerns and expectations to be informed.

    o   Demand that you and your local officials be notified of any and all meetings regarding refugee resettlement, and follow-up with your local officials to make sure someone attends.

o   Demand to know if refugees have already been settled within your community, and ask for the disclosure of any and all future resettlement plans for your area.

o   Demand that the voluntary agencies (VOLAGs) bringing refugees into your community make themselves available at public meetings to explain their program and how it fits into the overall process. The number of people being brought in has an impact on local service demand, and you and your local officials have a right to know what that impact is going to be. It's your money and your community.

- Sign the Center for Security Policy's petition to end refugee resettlement into a locality unless the locality approves the resettlement.

- Demand accountability of your elected officials.

o   Rep. Bob Goodlatte (VA) has a bill to designate the Muslim Brotherhood a foreign terrorist organization. It is H.R. 3892. Ask your representative to support and consider signing on as a cosponsor to the bill, or provide you with an explanation of why they will not do so.

o   Standard protocol for our elected representatives used to include a security background check before they were allowed to serve on committees where access to national security information is provided. That is no longer the case. There are estimates provided by knowledgeable security experts that a significant number of our current representatives and senators would not pass such a screening, but are being allowed to serve on these committees anyway. That is irresponsible. Demand that this policy be reimplemented.

- Collectivism destroys communities as it replaces self-sacrifice and virtue with self-interest and vice. Resist it. Get involved in your community.

  - We've each been given different skills, abilities, and gifts. Use them, and help others. While we all have different gifts, we all share the same purpose, and acts of charity are the way in which we fulfill that purpose. These apply to all in our communities.

  - Islam can only spread through deceit, deception, misinformation, and darkness. It only requies that the light of truth be focused upon it to defeat it. This is not without risk. Our lives have been threatened, but we are at war. We must each decide where we stand, and there are only two choices: submission or resistance. You must determine which one you will choose.

Organizational Responses

These items are all temporal and apply to all levels of governance, and directly address the Muslim Brotherhood tactics outlined earlier in this section. Some of these items will no doubt seem provocative and confrontational. Just like the recommendations above, they are not meant to be. They are not aimed at Muslims, but Islam's ideology. However, given the cultural nature that this ideology is rooted in, the ideas need to be clearly and strongly expressed so there is no misinterpretation and it is clear that we mean what we say. The actions in this section include the following:

- Expose the weaknesses that are inherent in Islam's ideology. There are several significant ones.

  - Lack of freedom. In looking at the Heritage Foundation's Economic Freedom Index, there is a significant negative correlation between the Islamic population percentage and the measure of freedom. The greater the percentage

Islamic population, the lower the freedom index composite score. This correlation exists despite the inclusion of such totalitarian countries as North Korea, Malaysia, Cuba, Venezuela, and Argentina in the non-Muslim countries. These should bias the analysis against finding such a negative correlation. Survey results indicate that most Muslims prefer freedom, but as mentioned earlier their definition is different from what we would normally use.

o Lack of scientific development. In his article "All European Life Died in Auschwitz,"[15] Sebastian Rodriguez effectively pointed out the lack of thought, creativity, and talent present within Islam. This makes sense in light of its directive of not questioning but merely accepting—submission. To do this he used the number of Nobel prizes that have been received by Jews and Islamic followers. Islam's followers number about 1.6 billion and make up about 20% of the world's population. As of 2008, when the article was written, Muslims had only received a total of seven total Nobel prizes, four of them for Peace. Of the remaining three, one was a European scientist and a second worked and spent much of his life in California. The Jewish population, on the other hand, makes up only about .2% of the world's population but have received a total of 291 Nobel prizes during the same period. Many of those came in the areas of physics, economics, and medicine.

o Money and criminality are principal drivers of the jihadi. Gen. Flynn points out the degree of collaboration between former Soviet agents and terrorists in the Middle East. The relationship is confirmed in the U.S. by law enforcement agencies such as the New York City Police Department: "Terrorists and criminals work together very closely." Further, "In Iraq at the beginning of this decade we found that fully three quarters of those involved in the terror network were in it for the money rather than religious convictions."[16]

- o Lack of economic opportunity. Of the forty-two countries having an Islamic population of 75% or more, thirty-five are included in the International Monetary Funds list of countries projected GDP per capita, a measure of earning power within a country. Only six of those thirty-five countries rank above the global GDP per capita figure in terms of nominal dollars, and only eleven of them rank above that global measure when adjusted for the differences in purchasing power (PPP).[17] This occurs despite the wealth of natural resources that exist within some of these countries. Power and money are concentrated within the hands of a relative few, a byproduct of all forms of collective governance.

- Define the enemy (the ideology), the threat, and why it is a threat.

- Confront our enemy's supporters. Let them know there is a price for continuing their support, and give them a single clear choice.

- In connection with Rep. Goodlatte's bill mentioned above, pass H.R. 3892. Once this measure is passed, all members of the Muslim Brotherhood should be identified and removed from any and all government positions. Those here and breaking the law should be tried, and those working subversively should be treated as terrorists.

- Mobilize our resources.

- o Military: Our military resources need to have both the tools and directives that enable them to pursue and destroy the enemy wherever they are. According to Gen. Flynn, "This authorization should be broad and agile, with clearer and more decisive language and unconstrained by unnecessary restrictions. ... If this is due to a lack of confidence in our military and intelligence leadership, get rid of these leaders and find new ones."[18]

o National Security: This is an ideological war that has a military component, and our enemy will "not hesitate to kill its own people, even its fighters, if they prove unworthy of the caliphate's mission."[19] There should be a single individual directing this war, reporting directly to the president. All resources need to inform the American people of the threat we face, why it is a threat, and what will change if we fail. We must also develop resources both within our borders and abroad to infiltrate the enemy and enable the military and law enforcement agencies to take them down. We've done this successfully before during World War II and the Cold War, but our leadership needs to have the will and commitment to our ideas to take the necessary actions.

o Law Enforcement: Create policies that enable national security and law enforcement agencies to share intelligence, and pursue not only those who mean to do us harm, but those who support them as well.

- Speak the truth. We do not need propaganda. The truth, and ideas consistent with it, are on our side. This needs to come from the top down and be consistent—as the truth should be. This message needs to come from our elected, religious, educational, and civic leaders.

- Fix our immigration process, one of the few powers actually delegated to the federal government. This includes both securing the border (including internal points of entry such as airports) and reforming the process so that people willing to commit to the idea that is America can successfully emigrate to this country. After they arrive, it is our responsibility to help them assimilate into our society. This is best done through private charitable organizations.[20] We should scrap the Refugee Act of 1980 which hands over our immigration sovereignty to the U.N. and unelected bureaucrats.

For these changes to be successful, individuals must understand freedom and what they are committing to uphold. Few immigrants today understand that when they arrive, and even many of our own citizens no longer understand those ideas.

- Absolutely no recognition of shari'a at any time in any place. Its underlying ideology is incompatible with our founding principles. Those who advocate for its use are demonstrating that they did not come here for the right reasons and should be returned from whence they came.

  Those within our government who allow shari'a to be recognized also show they either do not understand or support our founding principles and should be replaced.

- Remove the federal government from education. Return all control to state and local authorities. There is no constitutional basis for the Department of Education, and initially our country's educational institutions were the student's home. In addition, the Department of Education has failed its mission.[21]

  o State and local education should return to principles based education and abandon the schooling practices now in place. This requires education in both reason and faith in order to instill the virtue and morality necessary to be a successful people. Some will argue that this violates the separation of church and state. These have no idea what they are talking about. First, this barrier was intended to protect religion from the state, and not the other way around. Second, this does not mean teaching religion, but teaching the biblically-based principles supporting our founding, and derived from religious sources as God alone is the source of all morality. Third, all education is religious: it is just a matter of whether God's or man's is used.

- o Create policies giving parents and students control over education dollars and how they are spent for their students.[22]

- Restore our founding principles. Multiculturalism is a failure and should be thrown on the trash heap where it belongs.

- Be willing to change and adapt when things do not work.

We've reached the end. My goal was to help you become informed about Islam, understand some of the significant ways in which it differs from Christianity—and thereby differs from some of our basic underlying governance principles—and what we can do as a people to address the threat this ideology poses. Further, to provide all of that in one resource, with information on where you can go to find out more if your wish. There is an additional reading list in a few more pages to get you started. These include both resources to learn more about Islam and our founding principles.

It is only with truth and knowledge that we will be able to acquire wisdom and make good decisions, and to have the capacity to make changes when needed as things will change. It will not be easy. The last eight years have dug us a deep hole, but we have received a reprieve with the 2016 election. We have what we need to accomplish the task, and we've done it before. All we need is the will to do the right things and the resolve to perservere.

Appendix A

Approx. Timeline of Muhammad's Life

570   Muhammad born in Mecca

595   Muhammad marries Khadija

610   Muhammad receives his first revelation from Allah through Gabriel

613   Muhammad begins preaching publicly in Mecca

615   Escalation in treatment of Muslims results in some fleeing to Abyssinia

?   Muhammad's night journey

619   Khadija and Abu Talib die

622   Muhammad and the Muslims flee to Medina

622   Muhammad consummates his marriage to Aisha (about nine years old at the time)

624   The first raid by the Muslims at Nakhla

624   The Battle of Badr

624   Muhammad besieges the Banu Qaynuqa and they are exiled from Medina

625   The Battle of Uhud

625   The siege of the Banu Nadir and their exile from Medina

627   The Battle of the Trench: Massacre of the Banu Qurayzah and
       enslavement of their women and children

628   Treaty of Hudaybiyya signed with the Meccans

628   Khaybar besieged and the Jews are exiled. The Banu Nadir
       men are executed and their women and children taken into
       slavery

628   Muhammad poisoned at Khaybar

630   Muslims conquer Mecca

630   The Battle of Hunayn and conquest of Ta'if

631   Remaining Arab tribes accept Islam

631   War against Christians and Jews begins. Raid against Tabuk.

632   Muhammad dies in Medina

Suggestions for Further Reading

This list of readings includes works about aspects of Islam and the biblical based principles that our society is based upon. We must be educations in both to understand ourselves and our adversary.

Al-Misri, Ahmad ibn Naqib, *Reliance of the Traveller*, Amana Publications, 1991.

Aquinas, St. Thomas, *Summa contra Gentiles*, University of Notre Dame Press, 1975.

Aquinas, St. Thomas, *Reasons for the Faith Against Muslim Objections*, 2010, In St. Francis Magazine, Retrieved from http://www.stfrancismagazine.info/ja/images/stories/7_SFM%20August%202010.pdf. Accessed 01/2013.

Budge, Sir E. A. Wallis (translator), *The Monks of Kublai Khan emperor of China*, Assyrian Press, Http://www.aina.org/books/mokk/mokk.htm#c72.

Burke, Edmund, *Reflections on the Revolution in France*, Penguin Books, 1986.

Darwish, Nonie, *Cruel and Usual Punishment*, Thomas Nelson, 2008.

Dashti, 'Ali, *23 Years: A Study of the Prophetic Career of Mohammad*, Mazda Publishers, 1994.

Durie, Mark, *The Third Choice: Islam, Dhimmitude and Freedom*, Deror Books, 2014.

Geisler, Norman L. and Saleeb, Adbul, *Answering Islam: The Crescent in Light of the Cross*, Baker Books, 2008.

Goldziher, Ignaz, *Introduction to Islamic Theology and Law,* Princeton University Press, 1981.

Goldziher, Ignaz, *Muslim Studies, Vols. 1 and 2,* Transaction Publishers, 2006.

Guillaume, A., *The Life of Muhammad: A Translation of Ibn Ishaq's Sirat Rasul Allah,* Oxford University Press, 2006.

Hamilton, Alexander, Madison, James, and Jay, John, *The Federalist*, MetroBooks, 1961.

Harak, Amir (Translator), *The Chronicle of Zuqnin, Parts III and IV, A.D. 488-775,* Pontifical Institute of Mediaeval Studies, 1999.

Horowitz, David, *Unholy Alliance: Radical Islam and the American Left*, Regnery, 2004.

Houssney, Georges, *Engaging Islam,* Treeline Publishing, 2010.

Huff, Toby E., *The Rise of Early Modern Science: Islam, China and the West*, Cambridge University Press, 2003.

Ketcham, Ralph, *The Anti-Federalist Papers and the Constitutional Convention Debates*, Signet Classic, 1986.

Michael the Syrian, *The Chronicle of Michael the Great, Patriarch of the Syrians*, translated by Robert Bedrosian, Sources of the Armenian Tradition, 2013. Retrieved from: http://rbedrosian.com/Msyr/Chronicle_Michael_Syrian.pdf. Accessed 12/2016.

Pickthall, M. M., *The Meaning of the Glorious Qur'an*, amana publications, 1996.

Qutb, Sayyid, *Milestones*, Mother Mosque Foundation, n.d.

Schacht, Joseph, *An Introduction to Islamic Law,* Oxford: Clarendon Press, 1982.

Spencer, Robert, *The Politically Incorrect Guide to Islam (and the Crusades)*, Regnery, 2005.

Sperry, Paul, *Infiltration: How Muslim Spies and Subversives Have Penetrated Washington*, Nelson Current, 2005.

Stark, Rodney, *Discovering God*, Harper One, 2007.

Stark, Rodney, *The Victory of Reason: How Christianity Led to Freedom, Capitalism, and Western Success*, Random House, 2006.

Toqueville, Alexis de, *Democracy in America*, Bantam Classics, 2000.

Warraq, Ibn, *Why I am not a Muslim*, Prometheus Books, 2003.

Woods, Thomas E., *How the Catholic Church Built Western Civilization*, Regnery, 2005.

Ye'or, Bat, *The Dhimmi: Jews and Christians Under Islam*, Fairleigh Dickinson, 1985.

Ye'or, Bat, *The Decline of Eastern Christianity Under Islam: From Jihad to Dhimmitude,* 1996.

Ye'or Bat, *Islam and Dhimmitude: Where Civilizations Collide*, 2001.

Notes

CHAPTER 1:

[1] https://commons.wikimedia.org/wiki/File:Byzantine_and_Sassanid_Empires_in_600_CE.png.

[2] David, Ariel, *Before Islam: When Saudi Arabia Was a Jewish Kingdom*, Haaretz, March 15, 2016. http://www.haaretz.com/jewish/archaeology/.premium-1.709010.

[3] Wolf, Dan, *Collectivism and Charity: The Great Deception,* p. 3, Living Rightly Publications, 2016.

[4] Schaefer, Francis A., *Escape from Reason,* p. 26, InterVarsity Press, 1968.

[5] Ibid, p. 1.

[6] Ibid.

[7] Ibid, p. 2.

[8] Ibid.

[9] Goldziher, Ignaz, *Introduction to Islamic Theology and Law*, pp.4-5, University of Princeton Press, 1981.

[10] Schaff, Philip, *Nicene and Post-Nicene Fathers, Vol. 2, Augustin: City of God, Christian Doctrine*, p. 407, Wm. B. Eerdmans Publishing Company, Book XIX, Chapter XII.

[11] Ibid, p. 408.

[12] Houssney, Georges, *Engaging Islam*, p. 93, Treeline Publishing, 2010.

CHAPTER 2:

[1] Qutb, Sayyid, *Milestones*, SIME ePublishing, 2005.

[2] Jones, Lindsay, Ed., *The Encyclopedia of Religion, 2ⁿᵈ Edition,* Vol. 11, p. 7563, MacMillan Publishing Co., 2005. The full quote is "While Muslim tradition holds that some written works indeed existed from the mid-seventh century, the evidence of recent research indicates that they had begun to emerge at least by the early part of the eighth century … The earliest exegis … was primarily oral and depended on oral transmission."

[3] Eliade, Mircea, Ed., *The Encyclopedia of Religion*, Vol. 12, p. 164, MacMillan Publishing Co., 1987.

[4] Ibid.

[5] Goldziher, Ignaz, *Introduction to Islamic Theology and Law,* p. 50, Princeton University Press, 1981.

[6] Ibid, p. 51.

[7] Ibid, p. 52.

[8] Ibid.

[9] Also see *Of Allah and Man* at http://www.livingrightly.net/Blog/tabid/87/articleType/ArchiveView/month/12/year/2014/Default.aspx for more information on this topic.

[10] Warraq, Ibn, *Why I Am Not a Muslim*, pp. 109-110, Prometheus Books, 1995.

[11] Eliade, Mircea, Ed. *The Encyclopedia of Religion*, Vol. 12, p. 165, MacMillan Publishing Co., 1987.

[12] Ibid.

[13] Goldziher, Ignaz, *Introduction to Islamic Theology and Law,* p. 69, Princeton University Press, 1981.

[14] Ibid, pp. 43-44.

[15] Ibid, p. 40.

[16] Ibid, p. 37.

[17] Ibid, p. 43.

[18] Humphreys, R.S., *Islamic History, A Framework for Inquiry,* Princeton, 1991 as quoted in Warraq, Ibn, *Why I Am Not a Muslim*, p. 69, Prometheus Books, 1995.

[19] Warraq, Ibn, *Why I Am Not a Muslim*, p. 71, Prometheus Books, 1995.

[20] Ibid.

[21] Goldziher, Ignaz, *Introduction to Islamic Theology and Law,* p. 37, Princeton University Press, 1981.

[22] Ibid, p. 231.

[23] Ibid, pp. 46-47.

[24] Ibid, p. 210.

[25] Ibid, p. 47.

[26] Ibid, p. 44.

[27] Ibid.

[28] Wolf, Dan, *Collectivism and Charity,* pp. 19-57, Living Rightly Publications.

[29] Goldziher, Ignaz, *Introduction to Islamic Theology and Law,* p. 51, Princeton University Press, 1981.

[30] Ibid, p. 56.

[31] Ibid, p. 61.

[32] Guillaume, A., *The Life of Muhammad: A Translation of Ibn Ishaq's Sirat Rasul Allah*, Oxford University Press, 2006.

[33] Geisler, Norman L. and Nix, William E., *A General Introduction to the Bible*, p. 408, Moody Publishers, 1986.

[34] Schaff, Philip, *Companion to the Greek Testament and English Version*, p. 177, Harper, 1883.

CHAPTER 3:

[1] Pickthall, M.M., *The Meaning of the Glorious Qur'an*, amana publishing, 1999.

[2] Guillaume, A., *The Life of Muhammad: A Translation of Ibn Ishaq's Sirat Rasul Allah*, Oxford University Press, 2006.

[3] Ibid, pp. 165-166.

[4] Ibid, pp. 181-187.

[5] Ibid, pp. 211-212.

[6] Geisler, Norman L. and Saleeb, Abdul, *Answering Islam*, p. 77, Baker Books, 2002.

CHAPTER 4:

[1] Wolf, Dan, *Do You Want To Be Free?*, pp. 262-282, Telemachus Press, 2013.

[2] Osborn, E.F., *The Philosophy of Clement of Alexandria*, pp. 17-24, Cambridge University Press. 1957.

[3] Cooper, John M., Ed., *Plato Complete Works*, pp. 372-387, Hackett Publishing Company. 1997. This and the other quotes in this section come from *Parmenides*.

[4] Osborn, E.F., *The Philosophy of Clement of Alexandria*, p. 18, Cambridge University Press. 1957.

[5] Geisler, Norman L. and Saleeb, Abdul, *Answering Islam*, pp. 135-138, Baker Books, 2002.

[6] Pickthall, M.M., *The Meaning of the Glorious Qur'an*, amana publishing, 1999.

[7] Plotinus, *Enneads*, Translated by Armstrong, A.H., Vol. VII, pp. 311-313, Harvard Press, 1984. Vol. VI, Book 9, Chap. 3.

[8] Osborn, E.F., *The Philosophy of Clement of Alexandria*, pp. 35-37, Cambridge University Press, 1957.

[9] Geisler, Norman L. and Saleeb, Abdul, *Answering Islam*, p. 102, Baker Books, 2002.

[10] Rev. Alexander Roberts and James Donaldson, *Vol. 2, The Ante-Nicene Fathers, Fathers of the Second Century: Hermas, Tatian, Athenagora, Theophilus, and Clement of Alexandria (Entire)*, p. 524, Wm. B Eerdmans Publishing Co., 1989. *Stromata*, VII, II.

[11] Wolf, Dan, *Collectivism and Charity,* pp. 11-4, Living Rightly Publications, 2016.

[12] Guillaume, A., *The Life of Muhammad, A Translation of Ishaq's Sirat Rasul Allah,* p. 367, Oxford Press, 1955.

[13] Ibid, p. 676.

[14] Ibid, p. 458.

[15] Rodinson, Maxime, *Muhammad, Translated from the French by Anne Carter,* p. 205, The New Press, 1971.

[16] Ibid, p. 207.

CHAPTER 5:

[1] Houssney, Georges, *Engaging Islam,* p. 77, Treeline Publishing, 2010.

[2] This section comes from Chapter 3 of *Do You Want To Be Free?*.

[3] Rev. Alexander Roberts and James Donaldson, *The Ante-Nicene Fathers, Fathers of the Second Century: Hermas, Tatian, Athenagora, Theophilus, and Clement of Alexandria (Entire),* Vol. 2, p. 348, Wm. B Eerdmans Publishing Co., 1989. *Strom,* II, II.

[4] Rev. Alexander Roberts and James Donaldson, *The Ante-Nicene Fathers, Fathers of the Second Century: Hermas, Tatian, Athenagora, Theophilus, and Clement of Alexandria (Entire),* Vol. 2, p. 192, Wm. B Eerdmans Publishing Co., 1989. *Protrepticus,* Chapter VI. Further references to this work with use *Prot.* followed by the Chapter.

[5] Ibid, p. 449, *Strom,* V, IV. "All then, in a word, who have spoken of divine things, both Barbarian and Greeks, have veiled the first principles of things, and delivered the truth in enigmas, and symbols, and allegories, and metaphors, and such like tropes."

[6] Ibid, p. 460, *Strom,* V, XI. "But the most of men, clothed with what is perishable, like cockles, and rolled all round in a ball in their excesses, like hedgehogs, entertain the same ideas of the blessed and incorruptible God as themselves. But it has escaped their notice, though they be near us, that God has bestowed on us ten thousand things in which he does not share: birth, being Himself unborn; food, He wanting nothing; and growth, He being always equal; and long life and immortality, He being immortal and incapable of growing old. Wherefore let no one imagine that hands, and feet, and mouth, and eyes, and going in and coming out, and resentments and threats, are said by the Hebrews to be attributes of God. By no means; but that certain of these appellations are used more sacredly in an allegorical sense."

[7] Ibid, p. 461, *Strom,* V, XI. "We shall understand the mode of purification by confession, and that of contemplation by analysis, advancing by analysis to the first notion, beginning with the properties underlying it; abstracting from the body

its physical properties, taking away the dimension of depth, then that of breadth, and then that of length. For the point which remains is a unit, so to speak, having position; from which if we abstract position, there is the conception of unity.

If, then, abstracting all that belongs to bodies and things called incorporeal, we cast ourselves into the greatness of Christ, and thence advance into immensity by holiness, we may reach somehow to the conception for the Almighty, knowing not what He is but what He is not. And form and motion, or standing, or a throne, or place, or right hand or left, are not at all to be conceived as belonging to the Father of the universe, although it is so written."

[8] Ibid, p. 461, *Strom*, V, XI.

[9] Ibid, p. 462, *Strom*, V, XI. "In reasoning, it is possible to divine respecting God, if one attempt without any of the senses, by reason, to reach what is individual; and do not quit the sphere of existences, till, rising up to the things which transcend it, he apprehends by the intellect itself that which is good, moving in the very confines of the world of thought."

[10] Ibid, p. 350, *Strom,* II, IV.

[11] Ibid, p. 461, *Strom,* V, XI.

[12] Ibid, p. 463-464, *Strom,* V, XII. "This discourse respecting God is most difficult to handle. For since the first principle of everything is difficult to find out, the absolutely first and oldest principle, which is the cause of all other things being and having been, is difficult to exhibit. For how can that be expressed which is neither genus, nor difference, nor species, nor individual, nor number; nay more, is neither an event, nor that to which an event happens? No one can rightly express Him wholly. For on account of His greatness he is ranked as the All, and is the Father of the universe. Nor are any parts to be predicated of Him.

For the One is indivisible; wherefore also it is infinite, not considered with reference to inscrutability, but with reference to its being without dimensions, and not having a limit. And therefore it is without form and name."

[13] Ibid, p. 464, *Strom,* V, XII. "And if we name it, we do not do so properly, terming it either the One, or the Good, or Mind, or Absolute Being, or Father, or God, or Creator, or Lord. We speak not as supplying His name; but for want, we use good names, in order that the mind may have these as points of support, so as not to err in other respects. For each one by itself does not express God; but all together are indicative of the power of the Omnipotent. For predicates are expressed either from what belongs to things themselves, or from their mutual relation. But none of these are admissible in reference to God. Nor any more is He apprehended by the science of demonstration. For it depends on primary and better known principles. But there is nothing antecedent to the Unbegotten."

[14] Ibid, p. 460, *Strom,* V, X.

[15] Rev. Alexander Roberts and James Donaldson, *The Ante-Nicene Fathers, Fathers of the Second Century: Hermas, Tatian, Athenagora, Theophilus, and Clement of*

Alexandria (Entire), Vol. 2, p. 215, Wm. B Erdmans Publishing Co., 1989. *Paed,*
I, V.

[16] Ibid, pp. 209-210, *Paed,* I, II.

[17] Ibid, p. 225, *Paed,* I, VIII.

[18] Ibid, p. 232, *Paed,* I, IX.

[19] Ibid, p. 257, *Paed,* II, VIII.

[20] Ibid, p. 438, *Strom,* IV, XXV.

[21] Ibid, p. 524, *Strom,* VII, II.

[22] Ibid, p. 525, *Strom,* VII, II.

[23] Ibid, p. 453, *Strom,* V, VI.

[24] Ibid, p. 493, *Strom,* VI, VII.

[25] Ibid, p. 354, *Strom,* II, VI.

[26] Ibid, p. 174, *Prot,* I.

[27] Barnes, Jonathan, Ed., *The Complete Works of Aristotle: The Revised Oxford Translation, Vol. II,* p. 1600, Princeton University Press, 1995. *Metaphysics*, Book 5, 1013a.

[28] Rev. Alexander Roberts and James Donaldson, *The Ante-Nicene Fathers, Fathers of the Second Century: Hermas, Tatian, Athenagora, Theophilus, and Clement of Alexandria (Entire),* Vol. 2, p. 438, Wm. B Eerdmans Publishing Co., 1989. *Strom,* IV, XXV.

[29] Ibid, p. 523, *Strom,* VII, I.

[30] Ibid, p. 465, *Strom,* V, XIII.

[31] Ibid, p. 375, *Strom,* II, XXII.

[32] Ibid, p. 225, *Paed,* I, VIII.

[33] Ibid, p. 459, *Strom,* V, X.

[34] Ibid, p. 232, *Strom,* I, IX.

[35] Ibid, p. 516, *Strom,* VI, XVII.

[36] Ibid, p. 305, *Strom,* I, V.

[37] Ibid, p. 190, *Prot,* IV. "For if the heavenly bodies are not the works of men, they were certainly created for man. Let none of you worship the sun, but set his desires on the Maker of the sun; nor deify the universe, but seek after the Creator of the universe."

[38] Ibid, p. 440, *Strom,* IV, XXVI. "For all things are of one God. And no one is a stranger to the world by nature, their essence being one, and God one. But the elect man dwells as a sojourner, knowing all things to be possessed and disposed of ... having care of the things of the world ... but leaving his dwelling place and

property without excessive emotion ... and blessing [God] for his departure, embracing the mansion that is in heaven."

39 Ibid, pp. 210-211, *Paed,* I, III. "The other works of creation He made by the word of command alone, but man He framed by Himself, by His own hand, and breathed into him what was peculiar to Himself. What, then was fashioned by Him, and after He likeness, either was created by God Himself as being desirable on its own account, or was formed as being desirable on account of something else."

40 Ibid, p. 527, *Strom,* VII, III. "He is the true Only-begotten, the express image of the glory of the universal King and Almighty Father, who impresses on the Gnostic the seal of the perfect contemplation, according to His own image; so that there is now a third divine image, made as far as possible like the Second Cause, the Essential Life."

41 Ibid, p. 370, *Strom,* II, XIX.

42 Ibid, p. 199, *Prot,* X. "For the image of God is His Word, the genuine Son of Mind, the Divine Word, the archetypal light of light; the image of the Word is the true man, the mind which is in man, who is therefore said to have been made 'in the image and likeness of God.'"

43 Ibid, p. 495, *Strom,* VI, VIII.

44 Ibid, p. 271, *Paed,* III, I.

45 Ibid, p. 271, Paed, III, I.

46 Ibid, p. 506, *Strom,* VI, XIV.

47 Ibid, p. 534, *Strom,* VII, VII. "Prayer is, then, to speak more boldly, converse with God. Though whispering, consequently, and not opening the lips, we speak in silence, yet we cry inwardly. For God hears continually all the inward converse."

48 Ibid, p. 515, *Strom,* VI, XVII.

49 Ibid, p. 203, *Prot,* XI.

50 Ibid, p. 491, *Strom,* VI, VI. "One righteous man, then differs not, as righteous, from another righteous man, whether he be of the Law or Greek. For God is not only Lord of the Jews, but of all men."

51 Ibid, p. 211, *Paed,* I, IV.

52 Ibid, p. 420, *Strom,* IV, VIII. "We do not say that woman's nature is the same as man's as she is woman. For undoubtedly it stands to reason that some difference should exist between each of them, in virtue of which one is male and the other female. ... As then there is sameness, as far as respects the soul, she will attain to the same virtue (as man)."

53 Ibid, p. 524, *Strom,* VII, II.

54 Ibid, p. 460, *Strom,* V, XI.

55 Ibid, p. 460, *Strom,* V, XI.

[56] Ibid, p. 461, *Strom*, V, XI.

[57] Ibid, p. 461, *Strom*, V, XI.

[58] Ibid, p. 445, *Strom,* V, I. "He who communicated to us being and life, has communicated to us also reason, wishing us to live rationally and rightly. For the Word of the Father of the universe is not the uttered word, but the wisdom and the most manifest kindness of God, and His power too ... but since some are unbelieving, and some are disputations, all do not attain to the perfection of the good. For neither is it possible to attain it [faith] without the exercise of free choice."

[59] Ibid, p. 525, *Strom,* VII, II.

[60] Ibid, p. 321, *Strom,* I, XVIII.

[61] Ibid, p. 353, *Strom,* II, VI.

[62] Ibid, p. 363, *Strom,* II, XV.

[63] Ibid, p. 364, *Strom,* II, XVI.

[64] Ibid, p. 437, *Strom,* IV, XXIII.

[65] Ibid, p. 413, *Strom,* IV, V.

[66] Ibid, p. 361, *Strom,* II, XIV.

[67] Ibid, p. 195, *Prot,* IX.

[68] Ibid, p. 418, *Strom,* IV, VII.

[69] Houssney, Georges, *Engaging Islam*, p. 113, Treeline Publishing, 2010.

[70] Wolf, Dan, *Do You Want To Be Free,* p. 68, Telemachus Press, 2013.

[71] Ibid, p. 308, *Strom,* I, VII.

[72] Ibid, p. 305, *Strom,* I, V.

[73] Ibid, pp. 349-350, *Strom,* II, IV.

[74] Ibid, p. 223, *Paed,* I, VII.

[75] Ibid, p. 323, *Strom,* I, XX.

[76] Ibid, p. 350, *Strom,* II, IV.

[77] Ibid, p. 323, *Strom,* I, XX.

[78] Ibid, p. 502, *Strom,* VI, XI.

[79] Ibid, p. 323, *Strom,* I, XX.

[80] Ibid, p. 550, *Strom,* VII, XV.

[81] Ibid, p. 502, *Strom,* VI, XI.

[82] Ibid, p. 420, *Strom,* IV, VIII.

[83] Ibid, p. 369, *Strom,* II, XIX.

[84] Geisler, Norman L. and Saleeb, Abdul, *Answering Islam*, pp. 374-5, Baker Books, 2002.

[85] *An Explanatory Memorandum: On the General Strategic Goal for the Group In North America,* 5/22/1991, p.4, http://www.clarionproject.org/Muslim_Brotherhood_Explanatory_Memorandum, accessed 11/2016.

[86] Ibid, p. 7.

[87] Imani, Amil, *Islam's Useful Idiots*, American Thinker, August, 2006. http://www.americanthinker.com/2006/08/islams_useful_idiots_1.html#ixzz4Pi5z 3Qk1. Accessed 11/2016.

[88] Geisler, Norman L. and Saleeb, Abdul, *Answering Islam*, p. 139, Baker Books, 2002.

[89] Ibid, p. 142.

[90] Ibid, p. 145.

[91] Ibid.

[92] Ibid, p. 148.

[93] Ibid, p. 149.

[94] Qutb, Sayyid, *Milestones*, p. 38, SIME ePublishing, 2005.

[95] Ibid.

[96] Ibid.

[97] Ibid.

[98] Rev. Alexander Roberts and James Donaldson, *The Ante-Nicene Fathers, Fathers of the Second Century: Hermas, Tatian, Athenagora, Theophilus, and Clement of Alexandria (Entire),* Vol. 2, p. 423, Wm. B Erdmans Publishing Co., 1989. Strom, IV, XI.

[99] Ibid, p. 308, Strom, I, VII.

[100] Ibid, p. 305, Strom, I, V.

[101] Maritain, Jacques, *Christianity and Democracy,* pp.33-4, Ignatius Press, 1986.

CHAPTER 6:

[1] Guillaume, A., *The Life of Muhammad, A Translation of Ishaq's Sirat Rasul Allah,* p. 681, Oxford Press, 1955.

[2] Warraq, Ibn, *Why I Am Not a Muslim,* p. 108, Prometheus Books, 2003.

[3] Ibid, p. 70.

[4] Goldziher, Ignaz, *Muslim Studies, Volume 2,* p. 43, State University of New York Press Albany, 1971.

[5] Goldziher, Ignaz, *Introduction to Islamic Theology and Law,* p.43, Princeton University Press, 1981.

[6] Ibid, p. 44.

[7] Ye'or Bat, *The Decline of Eastern Christianity under Islam: From Jihad to Dhimmitude,* p. 46, Associated University Presses, 1996.

[8] Ibid, p. 57.

[9] Warraq, Ibn, *Why I Am Not a Muslim,* p. 230, Prometheus Books, 2003.

[10] Ye'or Bat, *The Decline of Eastern Christianity under Islam: From Jihad to Dhimmitude,* p. 72, Associated University Presses, 1996.

[11] Wikipedia, *Rashidun Caliphate,* 2015. Via Wikipedia Commons. https://en.wikipedia.org/wiki/Rashidun_Caliphate. Accessed 12/2016.

[12] Goldziher, Ignaz, *Introduction to Islamic Theology and Law,* p. 46, Princeton University Press, 1981.

[13] Ibid, pp.182-3.

[14] Ibid, p. 137.

[15] Medieval History Facebook, *Fatamids,* In Wikispaces. https://medievalhistoryfacebook.wikispaces.com/Fatimids. Accessed 01/2017.

[16] Ye'or, Bat, *The Decline of Eastern Christianity under Islam,* p. 52, Farleigh-Dickenson University Press, 2006.

[17] The Editors of the Encyclopaedia Britannica, 2012, *Seljuq Turkish Dynasty,* In *Encyclopaedia Brittanica,* retrieved from: https://www.britannica.com/topic/Seljuq. Accessed 9/2016.

[18] Wolf, Dan, *Collectivism and Charity,* p. 22-36 Living Rightly Publications, 2016.

[19] Pickthall, M. M., *The Meaning of the Glorious Qur'an,* p. 166, Amana Publications, 1999. One commonly cited verse is S9.29 which states, "Fight against such of those who have been given the Scripture as believe not in Allah nor the Last Day, and forbid not that which Allah has forbidden by His Messenger, and follow not the religion of truth, until they pay the tribute readily, being brought low." This verse is also cited as authority for the jizya – the poll tax.

[20] Ye'or, Bat, *The Decline of Eastern Christianity under Islam: From Jihad to Dhimmitude,* p.43, Farleigh Dickinson University Press, 2002.

[21] Ibid. Additional relevant works by this author include:
   - *The Dhimmi: Jews and Christians under Islam,* Farleigh Dickinson University Press, 1985.
   - *Islam and Dhimmitude: Where Civilizations Collide,* Farleigh Dickinson University Press, 2002.

[22] Ibid, p.100.

[23] Ibid, p.53.

[24] Ibid.

[25] Ibid, pp. 51-52.

[26] Ibid, p. 61.

[27] Ibid, p.70.

[28] Ibid, p. 63.

[29] Ibid, p. 119.

[30] Ibid, p. 70.

[31] Ibid, p. 80.

[32] Ibid, p. 81.

[33] Ibid, p. 83.

[34] Ibid, p. 88.

[35] Ibid, p. 89.

[36] Ibid, p. 91.

[37] Ibid, pp. 92-93.

[38] Ibid, p. 61.

[39] Ibid, p. 72.

[40] Ibid, p.74.

[41] Wolf, Dan, *Do You Want to be Free?,* Telemachus Press, 2013.

[42] Ye'or, Bat, *The Decline of Eastern Christianity under Islam: From Jihad to Dhimmitude*, p.78, Farleigh Dickinson University Press, 2002.

[43] Ibid.

[44] Ibid, p. 79.

[45] Ibid, p. 64.

[46] Ibid.

[47] Ibid, p. 130.

[48] *Chronique de Michel le Syrien.* 4 vols. Edited and translated from Syriac by Jean-Baptiste Chabot. Paris: Ernest Leroux, 1899-1905. 2:412, as cited in Bat, Ye'or, *The Decline of Eastern Christianity under Islam: from Jihad to Dhimmitude,* p. 57, Farleigh Dickinson University Press, 2002.

[49] Wolf, Dan, *Collectivism and Charity,* pp.36-57 and 116-8, Living Rightly Publications, 2016.

[50] Ye'or, Bat, *The Decline of Eastern Christianity under Islam: From Jihad to Dhimmitude*, p.123, Farleigh Dickinson University Press, 2002.

[51] Ibid, p. 66.

[52] Ibid, p. 67.

[53] Ibid, pp. 79-80.

[54] Budge, Sir E. A. Wallace, *The Monks of Kublai Khan Emperor of China*, 1928, Assyrian International News Agency, http://www.aina.org/books/mokk/mokk.pdf.

This is a translation of the original Syriac text. This quote comes from the Introduction to this work.

[55] Ibid.

[56] Ibid.

[57] Ibid.

[58] Ibid.

[59] Ibid.

[60] Ibid.

[61] Ye'or, Bat, *The Decline of Eastern Christianity under Islam, From Jihad to Dhimmitude*, pp. 346-7, Fairleigh Dickinson University Press, 2002. An extract from the chronicle of Bar Hebraeus is reproduced.

[62] Ibid, pp. 356-9. An extract from the chronicle of Bar Hebraeus is reproduced.

[63] Ibid, pp. 350-6. An extract from the chronicle of Bar Hebraeus is reproduced.

[64] The Editors of the Encyclopaedia Britannica, 2002, Mamluk Islamic Dynasty, In *Encyclopaedia Britannica Online*, retrieved from: http://www.britannica.com/topic/Mamluk. Accessed 01/2016.

[65] By Gabagool (Own work) [CC BY 3.0 (http://creativecommons.org/licenses/by/3.0)], via Wikimedia Commons. Retrieved from https://upload.wikimedia.org/wikipedia/commons/b/b3/Mamluks1279.png. Accessed 01/2017.

[66] *The Editors of the Encyclopaedia Britannica, 2002, Mamluk Islamic Dynasty, In Encyclopaedia Britannica Online, retrieved from: http://www.britannica.com/topic/Mamluk. Accessed 01/2016.*

[67] Justinian43 at en.wikipedia [GFDL (http://www.gnu.org/copyleft/fdl.html) or CC BY-SA 3.0 (http://creativecommons.org/licenses/by-sa/3.0)], via Wikimedia Commons, accessed February, 2016.

[68] Yapp, Malcom Edward and Shaw, Stanford Jay, 2016, Ottoman Empire, In *Encyclopaedia Britannica Online*, retrieved from: http://www.britannica.com/place/Ottoman-Empire, accessed January, Accessed 01/2016.

[69] Ye'or, Bat, *The Decline of Eastern Christianity under Islam, From Jihad to Dhimmitude*, pp. 113, Fairleigh Dickinson University Press, 2002.

[70] Ibid, p. 115.

[71] Yapp, Malcom Edward and Shaw, Stanford Jay, 2016, *Ottoman Empire*, In Encyclopaedia Britannica Online, retrieved from: http://www.britannica.com/place/Ottoman-Empire, accessed January, Accessed 1/2016.

[72] Ibid.

[73] Ibid.

[74] Ibid.

[75] Ibid.

[76] Ye'or, Bat, *The Decline of Eastern Christianity under Islam, From Jihad to Dhimmitude*, p. 120, Fairleigh Dickinson University Press, 2002.

[77] Ibid, p. 132.

[78] Ibid, p. 147.

[79] Ibid.

[80] Ibid.

[81] Ibid, p. 187.

[82] Ibid, p. 195.

[83] Yapp, Malcom Edward and Shaw, Stanford Jay, 2016, Ottoman Empire, In *Encyclopaedia Britannica Online,* retrieved from: http://www.britannica.com/place/Ottoman-Empire, Accessed 1/2016.

[84] Blunt, Joseph (1830), *The American Annual Register for the Years 1827-8-9,* Vol. 29, pp. 268-270, New York: E. & G.W. Blunt. [On-line], URL: http://www.archive.org/stream/p1americanannual29blunuoft.

[85] Ibid, pp. 270-1.

[86] Ibid, pp. 273-4.

[87] Ibid, p. 274.

[88] Wolf, Dan, *Do You Want To Be Free?*, Telemachus Press, 2013. http://www.livingrightly.net.

[89] Wolf, Dan, *Collectivism and Charity*, Living Rightly Publications, 2016.

CHAPTER 7:

[1] The Pew Research Center, *How Muslims See Themselves and Islam's Role,* July, 2005.

[2] The Pew Forum on Religion & Public Life, *The World's Muslims: Religion, Politics, and Society*, April, 2013.

[3] Pew Research Center, *Muslim Publics Divided on Hamas and Hezbollah: Most Embrace a Role for Islam in Politics,* December, 2010.

[4] Pew Research Center, *How Muslims See Themselves and Islam's Role,* July 14, 2005. Other Pew Research Center surveys used in this article include *Most Embrace a Role for Islam in Politics: Muslim Publics Divided on Hamas and Hezbollah* (December 2, 2010) and *The World's Muslims: Religion, Politics, and Society* (April 30, 2013).

5 Also see *Islam and Form of Governance* at http://www.livingrightly.net/Blog/tabid/87/id/29/Islam-and-Form-of-Governance.aspx for more information.

6 Pew Research Center, *The World's Muslims: Religion, Politics, and Society*, p.32, April 30, 2013.

7 See http://www.memri.org/clip/en/0/0/0/0/0/0/4263.htm. Accessed 10/2016.

8 Pew Research Center, *How Muslims See Themselves and Islam's Role,* July 14, 2005. Other Pew Research Center surveys used in this article include *Most Embrace a Role for Islam in Politics: Muslim Publics Divided on Hamas and Hezbollah* (December 2, 2010) and *The World's Muslims: Religion, Politics, and Society* (April 30, 2013).

9 See https://www.youtube.com/watch?v=vkWVdAfXbXI. Accessed 10/2016.

10 Qutb, Sayyid, *Milestones*, p. 89, SIME ePublishing, 2005.

CHAPTER 8:

1 Flynn, Lt. Gen. Michael T., *The Field of Fight*, p. 39, St. Martin's Press, 2016.

2 Qutb, Sayyid, *Milestones,* p. 41, SIME ePublishing, 2005.

3 Ibid, p. 40.

4 Ibid, p. 47.

5 Websites include those such as Bill Warner at https://www.politicalislam.com/.

6 Darwish, Nonie, *Cruel and Usual Punishment*, Thomas Nelson, 2008 is one source.

7 Wall Street 24/7, http://247wallst.com/special-report/2014/11/20/countries-with-the-most-slaves/. Global Slavery Index, http://www.globalslaveryindex.org/. Both accessed 09/2016.

8 Council on Foreign Relations, http://www.cfr.org/global/global-conflict-tracker/p32137#!/. Wikipedia, https://en.wikipedia.org/wiki/List_of_ongoing_armed_conflicts. Both accessed 09/2016.

9 Refugee Reprocessing Center, http://www.wrapsnet.org/#intro. Accessed 09/2016.

10 http://www.clarionproject.org/news/american-muslims-stone-christians-dearborn-michigan#. Accessed 11/2016.

11 Wolf, Dan, *Do You Want To Be Free*, Telemachus Press, 2013.

12 http://www.centerforsecuritypolicy.org/2013/05/25/an-explanatory-memorandum-from-the-archives-of-the-muslim-brotherhood-in-america/. Accessed 11/2016.

13 http://virginiafreecitizen.com/virginia-free-citizen-watch/. Accessed 09/2016.

14 Aquinas, St. Thomas, *Reasons for the Faith Against Muslim Objections,* p. 736,2010, In St. Francis Magazine, Retrieved from

http://www.stfrancismagazine.info/ja/images/stories/7_SFM%20August%202010. pdf. Accessed 01/2013.

[15] Rodriguez, Sebastian Vilar, *All European Life Died in Auschwitz,* http://www.jdl-uk.org/2012/08/all-european-life-died-in-auschwitz.html. Accessed 12/2016.

[16] Flynn, Lt. Gen. Michael T., *The Field of Fight*, pp. 141-3, St. Martin's Press, 2016.

[17] http://statisticstimes.com/economy/countries-by-projected-gdp-capita.php. Accessed 12/2016.

[18] Flynn, Lt. Gen. Michael T., *The Field of Fight*, p. 152, St. Martin's Press, 2016.

[19] Ibid, p. 161.

[20] Wolf, Dan, *Collectivism and Charity*, pp. 172-186, Living Rightly Publications, 2016. The War on Poverty is used as an illustrative example of the meager stewardship of economic resources exhibited by centralizing control.

[21] Ibid, pp. 142-152.

[22] Ibid, pp. 152-8. A similar approach is offered by the Heritage Foundation at http://www.heritage.org/issues/education/parental-choice-in-education.